Casting the Other

It has become fashionable in recent years to speak of issues of diversity and its management. Yet diversity is not so easily reducible and inequality in the workplace is visible and demonstrable. This is not simply a matter of gender difference, as there are many ways in which difference is constructed and acted upon. Discrimination against groups such as women, immigrants and older people is commonplace. *Casting the Other* seeks to examine the ways in which difference in organizations is both produced and maintained.

By emphasizing 'difference' as something to be managed, many organizations institute 'the problem of difference'. This happens within the framework of apparent consensus as to purpose, direction and ideology. Postmodernism may have contributed to this problem via an implicit acceptance of plurality which, in practice, might be seen to undermine notions of collectivity and dissipate political praxis. While organizations pay lip-service to ideas of equality, their practices often remain unchanged and unchallenged. Programmes aimed at promoting equality exacerbate the situation by consolidating positions around diversity.

Casting the Other shows clearly the paradoxical way in which many well-intended programmes of organizational change actually work against what they seek to achieve by establishing the very practices which they hope to address. This book provides examples of the way in which power is used in the maintenance of inequality at different levels of the organization from the strategic to the local. This results in questions about how research could contribute to this process and offers a challenge to conventional approaches to diversity and its management.

Barbara Czarniawska holds the Skandia Chair of Management Studies at the School of Economics and Commercial Law, Göteborg University, Sweden, and is a Titular Professor at the European Institute for Advanced Studies in Management, Brussels.

Heather Höpfl is Professor of Organizational Psychology and Head of the School of Operations Analysis and HRM at Newcastle Business School, University of Northumbria.

Management, organizations and society

Edited by Professor Barbara Czarniawska
Göteborg University, Sweden
and
Professor Martha Feldman
University of Michigan, USA

Management, organizations and society presents innovative work grounded in new realities, addressing issues crucial to an understanding of the contemporary world. This is the world of organized societies, where boundaries between formal and informal, public and private, local and global organizations have been displaced or have vanished, along with other nineteenth-century dichotomies and oppositions. Management, apart from becoming a specialized profession for a growing number of people, is an everyday activity for most members of modern societies.

Similarly, at the level of enquiry, culture and technology, and literature and economics, can no longer be conceived as isolated intellectual fields; conventional canons and established mainstreams are contested. **Management, organizations and society** will address these contemporary dynamics of transformation in a manner that transcends disciplinary boundaries, with work which will appeal to researchers, students and practitioners alike.

Casting the Other

The production and maintenance of inequalities in work organizations

Edited by Barbara Czarniawska and Heather Höpfl

London and New York

First published 2002 by Routledge
11 New Fetter Lane, London EC4P 4EE

Simultaneously published in the USA and Canada
by Routledge
29 West 35th Street, New York, NY 10001

Routledge is an imprint of the Taylor & Francis Group

Selection and editorial material © 2002 Barbara Czarniawska and
Heather Höpfl; individual chapters © the contributors

Typeset in Times by RefineCatch Limited, Bungay, Suffolk
Printed and bound in Great Britain by
Biddles Ltd, Guildford and King's Lynn

British Library Cataloguing in Publication Data
A catalogue record for this book is available from the British Library

Library of Congress Cataloging in Publication Data
A catalogue record for this book has been requested

ISBN 0–415–27501–6 (hbk)
ISBN 0–415–27502–4 (pbk)

Contents

Illustrations

Figures

Tables

Contributors

Helene Jonson Ahl is a doctoral candidate at Jönköping International Business School writing a thesis on the discourse of women's entrepreneurship. She holds an MBA from the Anderson Graduate School of Management at the University of California, Los Angeles. Her previous works include papers on women's entrepreneurship, work on pricing practices among entrepreneurs and the role of pricing in building an identity as an entrepreneur.

Barbara Czarniawska holds a Skandia Chair of Management Studies at Gothenburg Research Institute, School of Economics and Commercial Law, Göteborg University, Sweden. She is also a Titular Professor at the European Institute for Advanced Studies in Management, Brussels. Her research focuses on control processes in complex organizations, most recently in the field of big city management. In terms of methodological approach, she combines institutional theory with the narrative approach. She is a member of the Swedish Royal Academy of Sciences and the Swedish Royal Engineering Academy.

Leena Eräsaari is a Lecturer in Social Policy at the University of Tampere. Her research interests concentrate on the institutions of the public sector and quite often from the viewpoint of gender. The tools she is using in getting to know present-day public organizations are a mixture of (auto) biographies and symbolic interactionism as well as other symbolisms. The motto in her work is 'One picture can tell more than thousand words', and this is why her chapter in this collection contains also visual images.

Ulla Eriksson-Zetterquist, PhD, works as a researcher and teacher at the Department of Business Administration and Gothenburg Research Institute, both at the School of Economics and Commercial Law, Göteborg University. She is interested in construction of gender in companies, the topic of many of her writings, and the consequences of e-commerce.

Karin Fernler is an Assistant Professor at the Department of Public Management at the Economic Research Institute at the Stockholm School of Economics. She is also associated to the Stockholm Center for

Organizational Research (SCORE). Her research focuses on decision processes in public organizations. Presently she works on a study on the establishment of new medical practices within the publicly funded Swedish health care.

Valérie Fournier is Senior Lecturer in Organization Studies at Keele University. Her current research interests centre around critical perspectives on management and organizations, and in particular on (gendered) subjectivity at work. She has written about the making and disciplinary effects of the professions, 'new career' discourse in organizations, and identity work in family businesses. Her recent writing includes work on the experience and construction of gender in organization, and more recently she has developed an interest in alternative forms of organizations.

Marja Gastelaars is a sociologist. She has taken her PhD in the social studies of science and technology, on a historical reconstruction of the interconnectedness of the development of Dutch sociology and the social state. She also has written – from an actor-network perspective – on such cultural transformations as consumerism, health policies, considerations of privacy, as are associated with such apparently solid 'things' as the water-closet and the cigarette. At present she is a senior lecturer and researcher in the field of organization and management studies at the Utrecht School of Governance. The past few years she has been publishing on the cultural embeddedness of so-called human service organizations and co-ordinating an 'On Location' research group of the so-called 'Management of Meaning' programme associated with the CERES school of research in the Netherlands.

Heather Höpfl is Professor of Organizational Psychology and Head of the School of Operations Analysis and HRM at Newcastle Business School, University of Northumbria, UK. Her career has been varied and interesting. On completing her first degree she went to work in Operations Research for an engineering company in Bristol. She then became a teacher, a tour manager for a touring theatre company and a researcher working on a research project with ICL and Logica. She publishes widely. Her recent papers deal with existential aspects of organization and experiment with style.

Päivi Korvajärvi, PhD, is Research Fellow at the Work Research Centre at the University of Tampere, Finland. She has also worked as Research Associate at the Five College Women's Studies Research Center at Mount Holyoke College, USA. Päivi Korvajärvi has an extensive experience of doing ethnographic case studies both in public and private sector work organizations. Her research interests include social and emotional competencies and the relationships between gendering practices and transformations at white-collar workplaces in Finland. Currently, she is involved in research around information society and its impact on women's work in the service sector, especially in call and contact centres.

Deborah R. Litvin is Assistant Professor of Management at the School of Business, University of New Haven, West Haven, Connecticut, USA. Her research interests include the discourse(s) and practices of diversity management, leadership, organizational strategy and change.

Anshuman Prasad, PhD, teaches strategic management and organizational analysis at the School of Business, University of New Haven, Connecticut, USA. His research is primarily concerned with understanding organizational processes from a critical, symbolic, and noninstrumental perspective. Within this broad framework, his publications and conference presentations have dealt with such themes as strategic action in the global petroleum sector, postcolonialism, organizational ideology, workplace resistance and empowerment, management of technological change, critical pedagogy, and epistemological issues in management research. Before joining academia, he was an executive in State Bank of India for nine years.

Pushkala Prasad, PhD, is the Zankel Chair Professor of Management for Liberal Arts Students at Skidmore College in Saratoga Springs, New York. She has also held faculty positions in Clarkson University, the University of Calgary and Lund University in Sweden. Her research interests include workplace resistance, the computerization of work, workplace diversity, post-positivist research, discourse analyses and organizational legitimacy.

Hildegard Theobald, holds a diploma in Psychology and a doctoral degree in Political Science. She is research fellow at the Social Science Research Center in Berlin (WZB). Her main research has been concerned with questions of international comparisons of welfare states, labour market and (working) organizations in a gender perspective.

Acknowledgements

The editors would gratefully like to acknowledge a number of people who made the publication of this book possible. First, Professor James G. March, whose careful reading of the outline of the book provided a fresh perspective and gave a more specific emphasis to its direction. We would also like to thank Professor Martha Feldman for her comments and Catrona King at Routledge for her help throughout the production. Special thanks go to Dr Andrena Telford, Senior Lecturer in Management Development at Newcastle Business School for reading and advising on the papers from non-native English speakers. Thanks also to Lindsay McCulloch and Lise-Lotte Olausson for their help in various administrative and organizational matters. We are grateful to Esa Sulkanen for kind permission to use the photograph on p. 147 and to Jenny Eräsaari for the drawing that appears on p. 159. Finally, we would like to express our appreciation to the organizers of the 2000 EGOS Conference in Helsinki who provided the space for the development of the ideas.

Barbara Czarniawska and Heather Höpfl
Göteborg, Sweden and Newcastle, UK

Casting the Other
Introduction

Barbara Czarniawska and Heather Höpfl

By emphasizing 'difference' as something to be managed, many organizations institute 'the problem of difference'. This happens within the framework of apparent consensus as to the purposes, direction and ideology of the organization. Postmodernism may actually have contributed to this problem via the implicit acceptance of plurality which, in practice, may be seen to undermine notions of collectivity and dissipate political praxis. While organizations pay lip-service to ideas of equality, their day-to-day practices may be unchanged and unchallenged. Discrimination of various groups such as women, immigrants and older people continues and its dynamics remain unclear, not least because of the difficulties of studying it in the field. Additionally, various kinds of programmes aimed at removing inequality, such as gender equality or managing diversity programmes, may actually promote it by making differences visible and stabilizing them. Management, under such circumstances, comes to refer to the management of appearances which substitute for (other) more radical acts.

Does it mean, then, that this book aims to provide a conservative, or at least anti-reformist, argument against positive action? On the surface, the book seems to be subscribing to what Albert O. Hirschman called 'the perversity thesis', and the contributors to be drawing upon that 'group of social analysts [that] found itself irresistibly attracted to deriding those who aspire to change the world for the better' (Hirschman 1991: 26).[1] We do not feel comfortable with such a classification We tend to see, like Hirschman and the representatives of the Scottish Enlightment, the 'perverse effects' as one kind of unintended consequence accompanying all human endeavours. It must be remembered, though, that most such endeavours also have intended consequences, and that not all unintended consequences are undesirable (Hirschman reminds his readers of Robert Merton's early appeal to that effect).

We also follow Hirschman in a belief that, in debates between 'conservatives' and 'progressives', 'progressives have remained mired in earnestness. Most of them have been long on moral indignation and short on irony' (1992: 165). Attempting to redress this asymmetry might help 'to move public discourse beyond extreme, intransigent postures of either kind, with the hope that in the process our debates will become more "democracy friendly"' (ibid.: 168). In short, closing one's eyes to the defects of a favoured reform damages it as much as a blind attack against it.

Positive action brings mixed blessings, but so do all collective actions. The gain is *attention*, for which the price is *reification*. Sometimes attention is worth its price, sometimes not, and no amount of positive research is going to establish, once and for all, which times are which. Contingency will have its play, and political and moral choices their space. We, the editors and contributors to this book, experienced personally both the benefits and the costs, some as women, some as foreigners, some as both. The existence of benefits must not prevent us from scrutinizing the costs.

With this in mind, it is pertinent to scrutinize the *production* of ordinary, everyday assumptions that contribute to the *maintenance* of the inequalities. Consequently, this collection of papers is concerned with the way in which such assumptions construct the Other, with the problems of alterity, of difference, and of deferral. All chapters address, in one sense or other, various ways in which the Other is cast.

So, for example, there are dramaturgical interpretations which deal with the notion of being cast in a role, and with the implications for required performances. Other interpretations take on the notion of being cast, as in being pressed into a mould, or conformed to a pattern. At the same time, a cast not only imposes a form but it is also concerned with immobilization. Thus to put into a cast, as for example in the case of a broken arm, is to ensure that the damaged part heals successfully by preventing movement.

There is also a sense in which it is possible to conceive of casting a shadow, both in terms of the shadow which is cast, and also in terms of the ability to mimic and caricature the original through the production of replicas. Finally, it is possible to see the action of casting as to do with the act of throwing forward, with defining a trajectory, a point of arrival, with forecasting and prediction.

But what do all these definitions have in common with everyday life in organizations? The condition of postmodernity has led to a situation in which relativities have rendered the construction of the Other problematic. It seems that everything is reduced to competing definitions without reference to the ways in which such definitions come into vogue, and, in turn, become fashionable assumptions which shape the construction of otherness. So, for example, the concern with diversity, and more particularly with the management of diversity, might be argued to be a means by which difference is subsumed within the prevailing orthodoxy. Difference, then, becomes a property of something, and is rendered abstract by this process. The management of diversity is a tautology which subordinates difference by reducing it to taxonomic structures and giving it a place within a system of categories.

When Durkheim and Mauss wrote in 1903 about 'primitive classifications', they wrote with the youthful arrogance of early modernity that was triumphantly leaving behind 'the primitive' together with vestiges of the old century.

One century later, we are quite certain that 'we have never been modern' (Latour 1993), and scholars as different as Michel Foucault (1974), Mary Douglas (1986) and Karin Knorr Cetina (1994) have convincingly demonstrated the undiminished force of collective classifications.

This topic is focused upon in the first chapter in our collection. Marja Gastelaars discusses the role of statistical aggregates in casting people into stable roles that they might or might not want to espouse. She describes three paradigms in social statistics and data-collection: the demographic version of social planning, the discourse of normalcy and deviance supplied by statistically confirmed generalizations, and the current discourse of individual negotiation and of cultural fragmentation, in which people use statistics to constantly categorize themselves and others, and equally constantly refuse such categorizations. It is the second of these paradigms or discourses that is particularly relevant to positive action, but the third may be most relevant for the times we live in. In times of growing fragmentation and fluidity of identities, the social aggregates attempt to maintain their stabilizing function, offering safety that comes from 'knowing one's place in life'. As this safety, however, is no longer supported by the massive block of the social state, the attraction of social classification becomes somewhat doubtful. At any rate, Marja Gastelaars suggests, we should make the classificatory process transparent.

If early modernity provided us with statistics, late modernity has its own numbers that are identity-giving. Karin Fernler recounts a fascinating history of a Swedish centre for people with anorexia. Social statistics, and accounts of social fundings, all contribute to t e anorexia to women, and vice versa, to make anorexia an attribute of femininity. This association is a by-product of care and concern shown towards people with eating disorders, an unintend-ended consequence that nevertheless might prove momentous. In the process, 'the women' become more and more stabilized into a homogenous object, cast in a shape that does not allow variability.

If the association between women and eating disorders might seem problematic, the association between women and entrepreneurship is commonly assumed to be only benevolent. Women entrepreneurs, and the institution of female entrepreneurship, seem to be given prominence, in Europe as well as in Asia, Africa, Australia and the Americas. But both the social category and the social institution are in need of an essence, of the special attribute that will differentiate women entrepreneurs and female entrepreneurship from the other types of entrepreneurship. There is, alas, but one other type of entre-preneurship – the male one – and therefore the search for the core of female entrepreneurship becomes, in Anglo-Saxon research, a process of comparison, and of distinguishing women from male entrepreneurs that long ago became the norm. Helene Jonson Ahl shows in her contribution how this construction of a new institution unwittingly yet unavoidably portrays women entrepreneurs as deviants from what is a male norm. Policies built on such an assumption portray women entrepreneurs as weak, different and in need of special assistance. Paradoxically, the programmes most conspicuously aimed at disposing of the stereotype of women as 'the weaker sex' might be instrumental in strengthening it.

By now, the reader might have reached a conclusion that women are indeed the weaker sex: classified and categorized, associated with issues and objects, they carry the consequences of various types of social casting without protest. Valérie Fournier's study of Italian women entrepreneurs shows the opposite. It depicts women cunningly playing the 'game of disconnection', accepting the cast when it suits them, and protesting it vehemently when it does not. In this way, the heavy cast of social categories becomes a repository of roles, bits and pieces of which can be used for construction of fleeting identities. Valérie Fournier reveals also, for the first but not the last time in this book, that researchers are among many well-intentioned people who do the casting and the classifying.

But is the metaphor of casting appropriate at all in the context of gender, as we are using it here? Are not gender-appropriate behaviours, if not inborn, at least learned at the early stages of socialization, in childhood and early adolescence? Ulla Eriksson-Zetterquist's study of a trainee programme at an international company shows that newly recruited candidates for managerial positions need to learn appropriate gender behaviour in a given company. In this sense, learning gender at work can be seen as yet another chapter in what the anthropologists call enculturation – a mimetic process of learning one's own culture, but also of acculturation, a meeting of different subcultures, for example, student culture and working culture. The study reveals yet another paradox of organizational casting: keen as they are to change the participation of women in management, no company can afford socializing practices that will go against that which is a norm in a given society. Thus attempted changes end up reinforcing the patterns that already exist.

But how widely are these kinds of roles, stereotypes and appropriate behaviours cast? Does an international company inculcate international gender roles or, as in Ulla Eriksson Zetterquist's study, Swedish ones? Hildegard Theobald contrasts patterns of gender discrimination and women's coping strategies in Sweden and Germany. The two countries were chosen as examples of two different welfare state regimes: Germany as a conservative welfare state with a more traditional gender order, and Sweden as a social democratic regime with a specific focus on gender equality. Theobald has chosen to look at how the same kind of role – the female middle manager – is shaped against different stage sets. In Sweden, the legislation and the social setting encourage and permit collective action, which enhances solidarity, which in turn increases the possibility of a successful social action. In Germany, collective action is discouraged, which diminishes solidarity, strengthens the preference for individual action, and decreases the chances of successful change. Casting can be a circular process.

One of the problems in fighting negative gender discrimination is the fact that both discrimination and the action against it assume a clear-cut gender difference. This difference, claims Päivi Korvajärvi, tends to fade when an observer sets out to observe it in closeup at a workplace. In part, the explanation lies in yet another stage-set, this time that of Finnish organizations, where the issues of gender are concealed by silence. To some extent, however, it concerns the gendering process itself. What was considered to be a 'male' job may, in time, become a 'female' job, in the very same organization, and in the course of less than a decade. In addition, gendering is not the only type of casting, gender discrimination is not the only type of discrimination, and strategies of coping with gender discrimination are not the only coping strategies developed by employees. Casting and resistance to casting happen in organizations on many planes simultaneously, in an interactive mode, and with differing results for different groups of employees.

This complication is a topic taken up in another study from Finland, by Leena Eräsaari. Her chapter plays on the ambiguity of metaphors – in research and in the field. Engel was the architect who built Helsinki, and therefore it was only appropriate to call the privatized National Board of Building an 'Engel corporation'. But Engel, translated into English, means angel, and the process of privatization made the disenchanted employees of NBB recall a popular song from the 1980s, that is, the time of depression in Finnish economy, about 'the bad Black Angel'. The bad Black Angel of privatization did not treat everybody in the same way, however. The differences ran along two lines. One was the professional line: architects were treated differently (and had different options) from cleaning personnel. Within the architecture profession, moreover, male and female architects were treated differently and had different options. But even within the same gender and profession, the casting continued. As Leena Eräsaari puts it, 'the jobs did not go to those women who needed them most'. Casting reflects and relates to economic realities, inside and outside concrete organizations.

This is, in fact, the main thesis of Deborah R. Litvin's chapter. The study was conducted in the USA, where the idea of 'managing diversity', on the surface a programme to counteract casting and the resulting discrimination, originated. Deborah Litvin reveals, however, a surprising motivation behind these kinds of programmes. They are not inspired by egalitarian ideas or citizen's rights: 'Managing diversity is a *bottom-line issue*. It is a *business imperative*'. But does this motive count? Litvin explains that the 'business case for diversity' leads management to implement the programmes without being really interested in its results. Diversity management becomes but the latest business fashion, and demonstrating its adoption makes it a 'business case'.

The majority of the chapters show clearly the paradoxicality of many well intentioned programmes of organizational change, that may well stabilize the casting that they purport to overthrow. In most examples, however, it is people in power, or sometimes even the rank-and-file employees who produce or perpetuate these paradoxes. Valérie Fournier mentions the possibility of the researcher's contribution to this process, and Pushkala Prasad and

Anshuman Prasad explore this phenomenon thoroughly. One of the best intentioned moves within organization theory was recognition of organizations as cultural entities, and the resultant borrowing of methods and approaches from anthropology, ethnology and other cultural sciences. Unfortunately, as Pushkala Prasad and Anshuman Prasad point out, this transdisciplinary loan led to an inadvertent impact by the colonial tradition that shaped the beginnings of anthropology. Under the pen of organizational ethnographers, contemporary managers become exoticized, romanticized and 'primitivized', to be rescued by wiser folk.   .

Alterity cannot be captured by such devices; it is always deferred. The need to capture otherness is an attempt to make it safe, but instead it becomes a metaphysical activity, a relentless process which produces only more abstract relations. Managing diversity or writing organizational ethnographies are admirable activities as such, but they may become merely additional monitoring devices. The term 'monitoring' comes from the Latin word meaning 'to warn'. To monitor is to seek warning: the question is, what is the warning about? The danger of otherness, or the possible loss of otherness? Is diversity management a way to run a cultural museum, or a way to fence off the danger? We leave these questions to be pondered by the reader.

Notes

1 Readers unfamiliar with Hirschman's *The Rhetoric of Reaction* might wish to know that, historically, the most famous (successful) application of the perversity thesis can be found in Edmund Burke's accurate prediction of the course of the French Revolution (Hirschman 1992: 12ff.).

1 How do statistical aggregates work?

About the individual and organizational effects of general classifications

Marja Gastelaars

This contribution to the debate on positive action – and its consequences for the management of organizational diversity – starts on a societal level. I shall not focus on the everyday practice of positive action nor on its possible effects. I shall discuss its starting point, the discourses of diversity it has been associated with in the course of its existence. I shall demonstrate that 'positive action' is closely related to the massive nation-wide collection of social data, the classificatory infrastructure associated with the development of both the social state and of contemporary organizations (Bowker and Star 1999). I shall mostly be using examples from the Netherlands, complementing them with experiences from other countries, within and outside Europe. Although the Netherlands' provision of social statistics can be considered as quite specific, the general tendencies I am discussing here apply to most social states in the west.

In the first part – the first two sections – I shall argue, then, that in fact positive action takes the distribution of such physical attributes as 'gender', 'age', 'physical condition', 'race' and/or 'ethnicity' among the population as its starting point. As a consequence, it fits in with the discourse of diversity produced by the demographic version of social planning, including the statistics providing its infrastructure, although it may never have been intended to do so. It reproduces the physically defined processes of inclusion and exclusion that are produced by this type of social planning. Its concern with *positive discrimination* on an apparently physical basis invites individuals to associate with these physical attributes, and even produces a sense of belonging in the associated group.

In the second part – the third and fourth section of my contribution – I shall argue, however, that positive action as it has been developing since the 1970s derives its legitimacy in particular from the discourse of normalcy and deviance supplied by statistically confirmed generalizations. This discourse of diversity is strongly associated with the socio-political intention to redress inequalities, as a part of the development of contemporary social states. Most versions of positive action we currently recognize as such invite organizations to redress their internal classificatory infrastructures and, again, invite individuals to identify with the abstract categories they employ, or to *be* identified with them by others. In so doing, they inadvertently produce *stigmatization by statistical association*.

In the third part of my contribution I shall argue that this type of positive action does not appear to fit in any more, at least not with contemporary discourses of diversity, precisely *because* it invites individuals to identify themselves – and be identified – as members of such abstract categories or groups. Positive action particularly interferes with the current discourses of cultural fragmentation that tend to stress the importance of *individual negotiations*, in which people may continuously categorize themselves and others, as humans tend to do, but at the same time are encouraged to reject any categorization at all. Of course, positive action still may appear to be quite compatible with the IT-supported social monitoring that – paradoxically – accompanies both the alleged retreat of the social state and the virtualization of any fixed identities, like organizations. But it also appears to be losing ground both in everyday life and, as a consequence, in the realm of organizations. Not unlike the social state itself, such positive discrimination is becoming less and less popular with subjects claiming to negotiate their identities individually and to produce a course of life of their own.

The demographic infrastructure: territory, population and state

The tendency to think and act politically in terms of general statistical aggregates such as women, immigrants, older people, etc., does have firm historical roots. As Ian Hacking demonstrated in his *The Taming of Chance* (1990), society 'became statistical' in the course of the nineteenth century. In Scott's words, this strategy first of all produced a legible society from a top-down perspective (1998: 77). It usually expresses an often quite naive belief in 'hard data' or in 'scientific evidence' (ibid.: 4). However, these 'tools of modern state-craft' are not by definition related to an authoritarian state 'willing and able to use the full weight of its coercive power to bring these high-modernist designs into being' (ibid.: 5) nor with a 'prostrate civil society that lacks the capacity to resist' (ibid.). It is generally agreed that these attempts at legibility and simplification do provide the representatives of any state with some oversight, and, consequently, with a sense of control (Stone 1988: 113; Bowker and Star 1999).

In most western countries the development of the census – in the Netherlands relatively unproblematic until a massive boycott in 1971 (Van Maarseveen 1999: 127) – demonstrates some of the specific effects of this type of data-collection. Its basic aim is the physical classification of an entire population. It involves a tendency to count 'real' people, but above all to standardize them, and classify them into apparently homogeneous groups, making use of such 'unequivocal' physical categories as gender (included in the Netherlands census since 1889), date of birth or age, place of birth (also since 1889), lineage and/or ethnic and/or racial origin (in the Netherlands, religious denomination figures as an apparently similar category), marital status and – very popular in the Netherlands – marital fertility. It also investigates the distribution of these characteristics among such geographic entities as neighbourhoods, municipalities, regions, and national states. These so-called demographic categories create physically defined communities and label their constituency in physical terms, leaving no one out (Bowker and Star 1999: 300).

Of course they have lost much of their legitimacy, since they have been so fatally instrumental in such processes of 'ethnic cleansing' as have been practised in the Second World War and the USSR, and more recently in the Balkans and in some non-western countries. They are still used, however, by most nation states. Very well-known, of course, is the connection between territory, population and state that is used as a part of the inclusion and exclusion strategies concerning refugees. Categories like these are also used to redefine the rights of dispossessed but 'native' minorities as opposed to those of immigrants and/or refugees from foreign countries (Kymlicka 1998: 127ff.). As long as 'nation states' are territorially defined, it appears very difficult to avoid them. Attempts at a 'positive' redefinition of the fate of specific groups may even unintentionally reinforce their use. The coming US census, for example, proposes to employ six racial categories: 1. American Indian or Alaska Native; 2. Asian; 3. Black or African American; 4. Native Hawaiian or Other Pacific Islander; and 5. White, leaving room for all kinds of combinations, and, 6. – for those who claim not to be identified by any of these categories – Some Other Race.

Such categories are still considered to fit in also with the inner workings of the social state. In the Netherlands, for instance, the category of 'religious affiliation' has long been treated as a category individuals are 'born into' – an *ascribed* category. For instance it has been successfully applied in the postwar social planning of 'pillared' state provisions, i.e., the distribution of state-financed but religiously denominated schools, hospitals and welfare agencies. They were founded in numbers proportionate to the distribution of the membership of various religious denominations in the region they were to serve – and of course Islamic institutions now claim similar rights. Another well-known Dutch example is the population of the newly reclaimed polders, where the required entrepreneurial assets of prospective farmers were coupled with such characteristics as age, good health, region of origin (the South or the North of the Netherlands), the composition of household or family, and, again, one's religious denomination (Gastelaars 1985).

The notion of culturally homogeneous, or at least appropriately stratified, social units – and organizations – is strongly associated with this type of management of diversity. It helps us to define 'black' neighbourhoods, homogeneously populated hospital wards (for men or women only), schools with either homogeneous or differentiated populations (single sex or co-ed) and gendered organizations like Boy Scouts. Seen from this perspective, the explicit state arrangements for positive action can be interpreted as another attempt at a physical redistribution of local populations, on the basis of such attributes as gender, ethnicity and race.

An interesting aspect of the uses of these physical categories is that they often are used on the assumption that such a balanced distribution of physical categories automatically produces some kind of cultural homogeneity too. An interesting case in point is provided by Canada's 'multiculturalism policy', where, as elsewhere, a certain appreciation of the 'cultural heritage' of the various ethnic minorities has been acknowledged, together with their recognition as a politically relevant category. Moreover, the Canadian government has expressly denied such claims, asserting a cultural homogeneity to non-ethnic but physically recognizable groups such as women and people with disabilities, to less 'recognizable' entities like gays and lesbians and – unlike the Netherlands – to the adherents of specific ideological beliefs or religious denominations (Kymlicka 1998: 60ff.).

Of course, the latter claims have been triggered by the apparent legitimacy of some minorities' preference to 'come out' and create a recognizable category and associated counter culture (as opposed to 'only' being identified as such by others). And, to some extent, the conceptualization of positive action – in so far as it has been associated with the express 'promotion' of such groups as women and ethnic minorities – may even be confounded with such apparently legitimate conceptualizations of cultural homogeneity, too. However, individually, people often do object to the possibility that such 'physical' or 'visible' attributes, into which one may be 'born' but with which one may not choose to identify, develop into identities one has to put up with, and even into unavoidable life-long attributes.

Organized demography: the individual's sense of belonging

Yet such 'ascribed' categorizations, producing 'life-long' attributes, may very well contribute to an individual's sense of belonging. In particular, organizations that make use of them may eventually (re)produce the associated processes of inclusion and exclusion. Of course, we have become quite reluctant to recognize physically homogeneous organizations, unless they are expressly so designed (like religious organizations, political parties, women's clubs). Nevertheless, organizations that selectively incorporate individual lives into their 'corporate cultures' obviously try to make use of the homogenizing effects of these individual identifications. But do contemporary individuals still wish to belong?

The least that can be said is that many organizations – or their managers – act in this way. But the apparent inevitability of a notion of 'cultural homogeneity' that is associated with strategies like these is also confirmed by students of contemporary culture. For instance, in an essay on what he calls the changes in the 'we – I – balance' in the individual's orientation (1987), Norbert Elias suggested, that, however much in contemporary culture one is inclined to start from the 'I', in our utterly complex societies each individual is, in the course of her lifetime, affected by a very large number of interrelated contexts. Moreover, in any of these encounters, he argues, the balance between 'I' and 'we' still can be expected to shift – however temporarily – toward the 'we' (ibid.: 245).

Such 'opportunistic' we-identities, then, do create a sense of belonging (ibid.: 270). To Elias the contemporary social state presents an interesting case in point. It may even reinforce a sense of belonging similar to that produced by such 'natural' entities as family, friends, village, town and neighbourhood. We may even assume that this tendency also helps organizations – including the organizations of the social state – to be very real in their effects upon the individuals within them. The most extreme examples in this respect are, of course, provided by the so-called total institutions (Goffman 1961). Their physical superiority, their tendency to produce all-encompassing relationships with both their personnel and their clients, their tendency to maintain a one-sided communication, etc., are surprisingly often mimicked by many contemporary organizations. In a way, positive action may be explicitly directed against some of the more undesirable effects of such institutional regimes. As a consequence, however, positive action may interfere with this sense of belonging and inadvertently produce its reverse.

Managers in particular seldom fail to observe, that positive action by definition interferes with the organization's 'private jurisdiction', recognized by law. But, underneath its legal surface, this managerial claim may effectively be supported by the development of an encapsulated 'we' as opposed to an intruding 'them' produced by positive action. Positive action may, in short, inadvertently re-affirm existing processes of inclusion and exclusion. We should realize that, as Herzfeld argues, these we-identities may function as simulacra of familial social relations (1997: 7). Herzfeld points out that even contemporary 'individualised' human beings appear to be in need of a logic that 'helps them to convert their own deaths into a shared immortality' (ibid.: 6). He even suggests that such cultural *intimacy* provides them with 'culturally persuasive explanations of apparent deviations from the public interest' when performed by the trusted inmates of such an apparently homogeneous community (ibid.: 9). 'We know he is a liar and a cheat, but he's our President, you know!' And in a similar manner, even sexist or racist managers may be temporarily excused.

As a consequence we may have to face the fact that, to some parties *in situ*, positive action does interfere with those processes of identification that help individuals cope with the vicissitudes of life.

Statistical probability, statistical correlation and the rise of the social state

Some of the disadvantages of the statistical reproduction of such physically defined we-identities may be taken away by statistical monitoring on the basis of probability sampling. According to Hacking, sampling made it possible, for instance, 'to see that the social world might be regular and yet not subject to universal laws of nature' (Hacking 1990: 1). As social determinism was eroded 'a space was cleared for chance' but at the same time chance was 'tamed' by the laws of probability (ibid). This 'taming of chance' produced permanent, all-encompassing, and state-induced processes of statistical monitoring. According to Hacking such uses of statistics do fit in with libertarian, individualistic, atomising ideas about the individual's relationship to the state and to society (ibid). For instance, they do not obliterate individual choice or action as they usually allow for a range of variation within the population that is analysed.

A recently published history of the Netherlands Central Bureau of Statistics (Van Maarseveen 1999; Kuijlaars 1999) confirms the difference between the census and the sampling methods Hacking describes. The former – making use of a demographic infrastructure – is based on the presumption of 'stable' physical properties; the citizen's participation is compulsory and all citizens of a given physical unit are included. Moreover, when interviewed they are legally required to provide straightforward answers to the questions. In the end, it may even turn out to be fairly easy to relate specific data to specific individuals in specific locations, as the data are in fact 'strictly local' and are also presented in a recognizable form.

Social statistics on the basis of probability sampling, however, develop classifications that are assumed to be 'representative' of clearly defined but abstract populations that cannot be found in everyday life; moreover, even if the distribution of characteristics among specific physical regions or groups is measured, it is related to a 'normal distribution' defined by statistical procedure and is not to be regarded as an indication of any intrinsic qualities; the characteristics themselves often are specified in a rather abstract manner and it is precisely this 'lack of context and particularity' (Scott 1998: 346) that protects the anonymity of those that provide the data. Providing data is a voluntary act. As a consequence, the preoccupation of this type of data-collection is not 'visibility' or 'identification' of individuals but rather the more abstract 'legibility' of normalcy and deviation. Its apparently quite modest ambition is to eventually provide an empirical basis for a scientifically valid attribution of causes and effects.

These sampling procedures are often performed in order to provide social policies with a sound basis in statistical inference. In the Netherlands – as in most of Western Europe, to be sure – the development of the social state, particularly of those welfare measures that we became familiar with in the 1970s, gave rise to a true proliferation of such uses of social statistics. The failure of the Dutch census of 1971 can be explained from this perspective. It was announced as an 'x-ray (of) the population (and) as an indispensable starting point for taking measures and making provisions on behalf of problem categories in our society: the elderly, the handicapped, low-income groups, young workers, etc.' (quoted by Van Maarseveen 1999: 306) but, as censuses do, it also made use of a demographic infrastructure. However, by this time the idea of a census itself was associated with a kind of top-down 'authoritarian' state coercion considered utterly out of date and, most of all, it was felt to interfere with the entitlement to 'free choice' associated with contemporary cultural liberation So eventually the census disappeared from the Dutch governmental repertoire and sampling came to be accepted as an appropriate alternative.

In the Netherlands this 'change of method' – among many other factors – may have been instrumental in the founding of a Social and Cultural Planning office (SCP) in 1973. This institute was expected to supply the state with data on the *social* state of the population, and was considered as complementary to the purely *physical* and *demographic* activities of the National Planning Service (RPD) and the strictly *economic* data-gathering of the Central Planning Bureau (CPB). Together these three offices provided a quite elaborate classificatory infrastructure, whose degree of centralization may be considered to be uniquely Dutch, and only comparable to that of Canada. Yet similar activities are to be found in most western countries. From now on, in the Netherlands as elsewhere, such complicated attributes as health, unemployment, poverty, victimization by crime and safety (Van Maarseveen 1999: 451) or even decency in housing' (ibid.: 316) were to be statistically associated, not only with our familiar regional, physical and demographic variables, but also with new standards – *achievement* criteria, in the language of contemporary sociologists – like income level and level of education.

Many of these social policies are produced with the express intention to redress inequalities and to achieve equity, and at least to improve the equality of opportunity of some disadvantaged groups. It is the hierarchical effects of such characteristics they propose to redress. First of all, this statistical reasoning helps us to put some of the apparently unequivocal labels referring to ethnicity or race into perspective. But it also helps us specify the normalcy attributed to a population, for example, in a book on cultural differences in management: 'When we use the term Americans, we refer to those people whose forebears came to the US from northern Europe, the predominant group in American business today' indicating that many others may be excluded by means of the cultural dominance of a specific group (Hall and Hall 1990: 137). But, as independent variables referring to 'gender', 'ethnicity' and 'race' can easily be associated with such dependent variables as the probability of the development of a criminal career, of poverty and/or a need of care, or even the degree of integration or assimilation into 'our culture', they particularly help the social state identify and target certain groups or categories as being at risk or as a potential danger to society. Accordingly, positive action also is expressly designed to do something about the lack of opportunity of such a category or group.

Of course, this statistical strategy does not eliminate politics, although, as with any statistical infrastructure, it expressly derives much of its effectiveness from its 'objective' and self-evident appearance (Bowker and Star 1999: 33ff.).

On the contrary, according to Stone: 'Every number is a political claim about "where to draw the line"' (1988: 130) and consequently politics can be seen as a 'constant struggle over the criteria for classification, the boundaries of categories and the definition of ideals that guide the way people behave' (ibid.: 7; see also Bowker and Star 1999: 34). The same accounts, according to Stone, for such 'general' guiding principles as equity, security and even efficiency. They may all seem to be generally accepted, but are also subject to permanent processes of (re)negotiation, to public debate.

Again, there is Stone's suggestion that 'to count something is . . . to create a community' (ibid.: 135). 'To categorise in counting or to analogise in metaphors is to select one feature of something, assert a likeness on the basis of that feature' (ibid.: 129). And thus the inclusion and exclusion of individuals on the basis of the suggestion of such clear borderlines between specific categories, may again appear to create 'identities', recognizable to those involved. Of course the 'lack of context and specificity' of such abstract and complex demarcations as the 'multiple complexity' of a demand for help (used by Dutch institutes providing care) or 'a real minimum income during a required number of years', 'phase 4 unemployed', and 'the physical ability to perform a specific task' (all used by Dutch social security agencies) may prevent this from happening. Even these categorizations may tend to stigmatize just like the physically 'observable' categories we discussed in the preceding section.

The statistical reasoning that is used to identify the 'disadvantaged' groups – i.e. those entitled to 'care' or to 'financial support' – often includes as many characteristics – i.e. variables – as it can hold. It often starts with such independent variables as 'older/disabled/female/black/single parent', and associates them with as many other (dependent) variables as it can manage. It is in this context, then, that we should heed Hacking's warning that 'the systematic collection of data about people has affected not only the ways in which we conceive of a society but also the ways in which we describe our neighbour' (1990: 3). To those people who are inclined to forget that it is merely a statistical probability that is being pronounced, such a statistical procedure may confirm that *all* women (or blacks, or other representatives of a minority group) lack ambition, are involved in the caring professions, are responsible for the children they have, have a lower level of education, etc., and hence *as a category* are entitled to a lower position in society. To those people who tend to forget that a statistical correlation does not imply causality by itself, it may even appear that being a woman (or being black, etc.) must be considered the effective *cause* of it all. Inadvertently, these statistical procedures may produce *stigmatization by statistical association* and help confirm precisely that aspect of societal hierarchy they originally set out to redress.

Moreover, they also invite individuals to relate to the fate of their 'category' rather than to their individual opportunities. We should realize, then, that these statistically informed socio-political strategies also affect the concept of liberty, i.e. the individual's right to 'deliberation and the exercise of choice' as defined by John Stuart Mill (Stone 1988: 87), which to some contemporary observers also includes the individual's entitlement to protection against the 'emotional and psychological effects' of discrimination (ibid.: 90), even of the 'positive discrimination' that lies at the basis of positive action.

Organized selection and classification efforts: the effects of statistical associations

Whether positive action is presented as a general rule (e.g. women should be given preference) or as a proportional rule, related to the specific composition of an organization's population (with targets such as specific percentages of specific categories among its population) and/or its hierarchy (e.g. more women in the higher ranks), it interferes with the selection and classification processes organizations perform.

At present, many organizations only appear to intensify their attempts at selection of their clients and of their prospective personnel, as they are more than ever required by their own headquarters or by the state to account for their 'production'. These organizational selection processes 'at the gate' are intended to establish whether the organization has something to offer or not, although the question often turns out to be: which clients or which workers should be barred from this organization? As Mary Douglas never tires of arguing in her *Risk and Blame*, contemporary evaluations of risk do not deal with both the pros and cons of a probable outcome, but focus on the 'cons'. They focus on the 'dangers', the 'bad' risks defined as detrimental to the continuity of the organization (1992: 27).

Thus commercial organizations like banks and insurance companies often are overtly committed to 'risk selection' making use of the type of statistical associations I am discussing here. But also public services, particularly organizations that are assigned preventive tasks such as policing health or safety, have developed a profound interest in the risk factors associated with such apparently well-defined categories as poverty and social disadvantage. And, although it could be argued that 'inclusion and exclusion do not necessarily entail prejudice (negative preconceptions) or discrimination (unjust decisions)', one should realize that 'prejudice and discrimination are often built into the . . . schemes of differentiation' (Ericson and Haggerty 1997: 257). This issue is complicated further by the fact that the 'good ones', i.e. the ones accredited by selection procedures, often appear to positively evaluate these selection efforts (Rule 1974; Kuitenbrouwer 1991). In fact positive action usually intervenes in an attempt to redress these (unintended) discriminatory effects, trying to reverse the interpretation of the very same statistical generalizations. And again, positive action of this kind may inadvertently provoke a 'we-effect' among those who were *not* excluded, as they object to being labelled as politically *in*correct.

But the story becomes even more complicated when we realize that organizations always select 'at the gate'. In fact creating an organization *means* excluding everyone and everything else. Moreover, organizations also classify all the time, by definition. Organizing as an activity *implies* processes of classification. And so we are all familiar with the division of labour and with the many formal and informal classifications that are used when designating personnel to particular tasks and when judging their actual behaviour. In a similar manner, organizations also classify their clients, for instance when they are trying to provide an answer to the question, how a specific client should be treated. And indeed, contemporary organizations are very much inclined to further elaborate these classificatory efforts, producing for instance 'product market combinations' that will satisfy both the organization's desire to control its activities and the client's wish to be individually served.

Interesting from an organizational point of view – but from ours as well – is the fact that, unlike the selection efforts I discussed earlier, such organizational classifications do not necessarily involve the production of a homogeneous 'we'. On the contrary, these processes appear to define the *range of accepted diversity* within an organization. Once more, the effects upon the 'objects' of these labelling activities could be a lifelong stigma, but on the whole categorizations like these allow individuals to 'make a difference' without being excluded. As Herzfeld (1992) argued in his book on the workings of bureaucracy, the mechanical management of difference involved with these 'classificatory policies' may even create a feeling of belonging, but a 'belonging' that is not associated with a homogeneous 'we'. On the contrary, the apparent homogeneity that is produced should be phrased in a different manner: 'In spite of our numerous differences, all of us seem to fit in!' These classificatory efforts somehow guarantee the survival of organizations in the face of a massive differentiation of their constituencies.

In this context, the 'gender', 'ethnicity' or 'handicap' issue should be appreciated, not as a group identity, but as *one consideration among many others*. But as the many well-worn well-intended formulas – 'In the case of two equally qualified candidates, women are to be given precedence' – demonstrate, it is difficult to generalize about one *specific* attribute amidst a large number of complex considerations. As a consequence, organizations may actually succeed in rationalizing their 'natural' range of diversity, and reproduce the specific hierarchies of various professional groups or categories of clients they serve, not allowing the intended effects of positive action to interfere. And again, individuals may feel that they are either excluded or included *because of* this one attribute that happens to be explicitly labelled, and may even expect this to influence their future positioning as a part of the organization. And of course, this sense of discrimination may inadvertently be reinforced by the statistical monitoring that usually accompanies positive action of this kind.

The culturing of statistics: the monitoring of individual aspirations, preferences and ways of life and the virtualization of the social state

Let us start here with a technical argument. Traditional census was associated with the development of the Hollerith machine (a punch card machine similar to the devices that frustrated the recent presidential elections in the US). The calculus of probability has greatly benefited from the computer. The development we are discussing here, however, must not only be associated with the unprecedented volume and range of data contemporary IT can handle, nor with the speed with which they can be processed and analysed (Van Maarseveen 1999: 125); it should be associated most of all with the still quite unfathomable potentialities involved with their ubiquitous availability in real time. The latter, in particular, appears to reinforce the virtualization – this post-modern version of *un*accountability – of the statistical infrastructure of such apparently stable entities as organizations and the social state.

The effects of this transformation of the statistical infrastructure are quite remarkable indeed. For instance, the development of contemporary IT appears to destroy the 'lack of context and specific-ness' (Scott 1998) that used to provide the subjects involved in the processes of data-collection with some protection. The data are re-contextualized, and re-localized as well, and it even becomes possible to re-identify individuals on the basis of their contributions. Expressed in the language of the statisticians, the 'lowest level of aggregation' can be approached, and its relation to the relevant environment can be construed correspondingly, from the national state to local government, to markets and even to individual citizens. As statisticians have it, information can be detailed on a micro level, and can be provided very quickly indeed (Van Maarseveen 1999: 124). At the same time, however, this whole process may remain invisible to the individuals involved, as the process itself can be performed on any location, provided it is linked to the data-networks concerned. And, apart from that, the aggregated data may even produce an entire virtual personality, yet bearing some real individual's name.

Another remarkable effect is the 'institutional curiosity' these processes appear to have produced. IT-supported data-systems can be fed by all kinds of information on an everyday basis. Commercial mass service deliverers like supermarket chains or telecom companies – but also the governmental institutions we discussed in the previous paragraphs – have become quite insatiable in their attempts to gain an overview of current lifestyles and consumer choices. The same applies to governmental agencies, particularly those organizations that deliver prevention work. As Ericson and Haggerty (1997) demonstrate in their Canadian research, the notion of police surveillance apparently has taken on a quite different meaning. It used to denote a physical activity, with watchful people in cars moving about but it has turned into 'risk knowledge production', i.e. the collection of feed for the data-eating machines. Second hand users of this type of information are of course insurers and banks but such (de-)centralized and even semi-autonomous public sector organizations as care-providers, social security agencies and even schools are becoming ever more interested, as well.

The Netherlands' Central Bureau of Statistics, for example, has discovered 'the possibilities of linking administrative data and survey data' (Van Maarseveen 1999: 62), making use of the new kind of central data-storage provided by the Municipal Basis Administration, collecting data in all Dutch municipalities on behalf of their local governments, yet linked to a national network. This activity fits in very well, of course, with the selection efforts I discussed in the preceding paragraph, and indeed they have been intensified with the help of these IT-supported devices. Such selection efforts, however, may now very well infringe upon our entitlement to anonymity – that state of privacy that is effected 'when an individual is in public places or performing public acts but still seeks, and finds, freedom from identification' (Westin 1970: 31; Gastelaars, in press). No wonder the privacy debate started somewhere around the 1970s and has been rekindled ever since, with every new development of such electronic surveillance. The debate particularly focuses on the long term consequences for the individual of these intensified data-collecting efforts. Anonymity is not what it used to be!

Another remarkable fact associated with this kind of data-collection is that, in spite of this growing aversion to the possible discriminatory effects of such data-collection, neither consumers nor citizens appear to be particularly averse to providing the required data, particularly when it appears to serve their individual interests. In this context, individuals even tend to take for granted, if not to take into account that, moving from situation to situation, they are 'leaving innumerable electronic traces behind on their daily rounds' (De Ruijter 1998: 13, my translation). Bauman argues that on the one hand this 'storage of massive quantities of data, amplified with every use of a credit card and virtually each act of purchase, results ... in a "super-panopticon"' (Bauman 1998: 50). On the other hand we are dealing, according to him, with 'a Panopticon with a difference: the surveyed, supplying the data for storage, are prime and willing factors in the surveillance' (ibid). Whatever the eventual consequences, people seem to enjoy being visible and being properly identified by a service deliverer, when they get in touch.

But something else is changing as well. For instance, as statisticians now find, quite a number of potential respondents fail to produce the proper figures or refuse to answer the questions posed (Stone 1988: 137ff.). Some of them attribute this to the irritations caused by the call centres and tele-marketers employed by the commercial forerunners of this type of data-collection, claiming that their own government institutions behave better. US data suggest for instance that 93 per cent of the respondents think they are entitled to say no to telemarketing and that 'only' 68 per cent of them think that they can say no to scientific research (Van Maarseveen 1999: 61), and the Dutch statistician who reports this feels encouraged by the difference. In fact, however, people are encouraged to become more streetwise as to the dangers associated with this kind of data-collection and to claim individual ownership of their 'personal data' (Van den Boomen 1995). Moreover, individual consumers may decide to expose the limitations of such centralized data-collection, by faking the data they enter into the data-machines or swapping their individual chipcards, setting out to produce virtual personalities themselves.

All this points to a fundamental change I would like to label, with the term introduced by Du Gay *et al.*, the *culturing* of social statistics (Du Gay *et al.* 1997). As it turns out, this new type of data-collection does not provide us with data about who we physically are, nor does it help us calculate the probability of societal deprivation or societal success, although to be sure, these old-fashioned uses of data-collection are still far from outdated. As culture critic Dick Hebdige assures us: 'We (still) live in a world and in bodies which are deeply scored by the power relations of race and class, sexuality and gender.' Yet these new data-systems perform something quite different. According to Hebdige: 'We also live – whether or not we know it consciously – in a world of style-setters, innovators, sloanes, preppies, empty nesters (working couples with grown-up families), dinkies (dual-income-no-kids), casuals, sensibles, the constrained majority, and today's prime targets, the pre-teens and woofies (well-off-older-folks)' (Hebdige 1992: 173). Traditional classifications are overtaken by new ones that, according to Hebdige, do not indicate our 'demographic characteristics', nor our 'social stratification', but rather the ever changing distribution of *who we want to be*, the aspirations we profess. He labels the associated statistical output the *social map of desires* (ibid.: 173). Again, the commercial world certainly has taken the lead in (re-)producing these culturing efforts, but governmental agencies and public sector organizations – particularly the arrangements of the social state – have followed suit.

According to Kenneth Gergen, then, the technological achievements of the past century have intensified this apparent increase in flexibility of identification processes. According to him, individuals are undergoing 'an enormous barrage of social stimulation' as they are 'thrust into an ever widening array of relationships' and are forced to somehow permanently (re-) negotiate their identities and identifications accordingly, and usually in relation to others (1991: xi). He even suggests that 'one ceases to believe in a self independent of the relations in which he or she is imbedded' (ibid.: 17). Individuals negotiate this all-encompassing relatedness to others on the basis of an entitlement to a free and uninhibited choice.

In itself, this affirmation of 'subjectivity' is not entirely new. The development of pluralist democracy always has been associated with the development of opinion polls, the development of our consumer society with that of advertising and marketing research. The state and other organizations have always made use of such insights into the expected degree of public support for governmental interventions or into the expected volume of demand for consumer goods. At that time, however, the social scientists providing these figures assumed that they were producing quite permanent generalizations. But both 'pluralism' and 'consumerism' appear to have taken a quite flexible turn, dislocating in the process not only the mass producers of consumer goods but also our contemporary social states and our traditional political institutions.

But, however much these lifestyles are 'made legible' by such commercial – or even governmental – marketers, they also appear to be part and parcel of the everyday negotiations of individuals, as can be demonstrated by the permanent processes of naming and framing young people perform, switching on or off specific identities in specific situations, while at the same time trying to avoid the suspicion of conformity and loss of individuality that is implied by being a member of a category or a group (Antaki and Widdicombe 1998: 17). I quote from Widdicombe's conversation with two alleged punks: '(People) calling themselves punks . . . it's categorising themselves . . . (but) it's against being an individual . . . being yourself. (Yet) it just so happens that so many people . . . just seem to look like each other . . .' (Widdicombe 1998: 59–60). You may choose to call yourself a punk and even decide to look like one, but this does not keep you from being individually unique. In his more recent work Herzfeld also argues that it may be worth our while to pay some more attention to this 'semiotic bricolage' (1997: 20). Identifications are not what they used to be.

Positive action and the culturing of organizations

On an individual level this 'subjective turn' has been profoundly reinforced by the insistence on *the right to self-identification as opposed to identification by others*. It has also been reinforced by the general acknowledgement of the individual's entitlement to perform her own negotiations. And as a consequence, traditional emancipation as a member of a category or of a group – however important such issues still may be – has gradually faded into the background. Being 'victimized' or being associated with the collective emancipation of a 'disadvantaged group' has become quite a burden to an individual bent on negotiating her own course of life. As a result, positive action does not appear to fit in with the contemporary discourse of diversity. It may even be considered an infringement, not only upon the organization's jurisdiction, but particularly upon the individual's entitlement to self-determination.

Contemporary organizations, both public and private, are – at least in theory – encouraged to answer to the challenge of these all-pervading effects of culturing, as well. The relevance of 'culture' and of individual sensemaking processes does not remain limited, or so it appears, to the wishful thinking usually exhibited by managerial teaching courses and the associated admonishing texts. Although many contemporary organizations prefer not to lose cultural control, and to perform the required 'cultural change' from a top down perspective (or at least try to delegate the 'cultured-ness' of their every-day activities to specific boundary roles, such as design and marketing), in many other organizations, such culturing is becoming part and parcel of their everyday negotiations (Gastelaars 2000). Many organizations do pay attention to the many ways in which even the contemporary 'cultured' classifications mix in with their everyday organizational routines. In the end, Chia may not have overestimated the impact of his new 'upstream' organizational discourse nor have overstated his argument that 'we need to begin to think of "organizations" not as "things" . . . but rather as loosely emergent sets of organizing rules which orient interactional behavior' (1996: 150).

In their everyday negotiations, organizations appear to be moving beyond the 'indirection' that in the past was often considered best practice in the case of cultural diversity, i.e. the 'looking the other way' and 'not noticing' the effects of everyday classifications on the basis of the formal argument that 'everyone is equal' (Sennett 1991) and even beyond the 'indifference' that Bailey (1996) associates with the 'domestication of ethnic groups'. On the contrary, some more room appears to be provided for the active processes of acknowledgement of the differences that play a part in the everyday negotiations within organizations (Abma 1998). For instance, Minson quotes some particularly interesting examples of the practical ethical competence that is needed when negotiating such 'effects of diversity' as are provided by racist incidents and by instances of sexual harassment (1993: 35–9). He focuses on the power differences between the categories or groups involved, and suggests that people should be organizationally capacitated to deal effectively with such differences *in situ*, with the express aim of providing sufficient space for the victim to feel organizationally acknowledged, while at the same time avoiding the often quite detrimental effects of public – and juridical – exposure, for all parties involved. In fact, without labelling it as such, he tries to keep organizational intimacy intact, as public exposure may – apart from exceptional cases – be considered to be excessively harmful, to offending 'superiors' and to the offended 'inferiors' alike. According to these suggestions – which share a starting point in the negotiations 'in situ' – dealing with diversity should preferably not be arranged by numbers, but should become a part of the organizational negotiations themselves.

And yet we need to acknowledge that classifications are and will remain a fact of life and so will their aggregate effects. Even power differences will remain in place, and more often than not they will be permanently (re-)produced both by the 'we-identities' of physical groups and by the 'generalizations' provided by statistical association, as they are (re-)produced in the mutual classifications of individuals, and within organizations as well. We also may safely assume, then, that to some extent the social data infrastructures I discussed in the previous paragraphs – and summarized in Table 1.1 – will all remain in place. Moreover, I think that such processes of data collection may still provide us with some good causes for positive action, and that we should not refrain from using them for such purposes either.

Table 1.1 Versions of social data-collection

Demography	Probability sampling	IT-supported data-collection
Legibility of the population as a whole	Legibility of the distribution of normalcy and deviance	Monitoring of cultural diversity and change
Distribution of 'natural' and physical properties ('ascription')	Statistical distribution of socially produced attributes ('achievement')	Distribution of individual aspirations and preferences ('choice')
Respondents not voluntary (census), technically not anonymous, data explicitly contextualized	Voluntary respondents (sampling), effectively anonymous, 'lack of context and particularity' of data (Scott)	Respondents voluntary but 'virtual' collection of data, data relocatable (area codes)
Cultural homogeneity and differentiation/distribution of physical properties among a physical population or a group (segregation)	Cultural differentiation/ distribution of 'statistical associations' among a statistically defined population (stratification)	Cultural fragmentation and flux, individual negotiations and processes of identification (flux)
The right to belong/ identification as a member	Positive identification/ stigmatization by statistical association	Encouragement of individual self-determination and freedom of choice

However, we do have to provide some more room for the everyday negotiations concerning this issue 'on the floor'.

2 Gender order and disorder

The articulation of women and disorder as resources in the establishment of new medical practices

Karin Fernler

In this chapter I explore how women can be associated with eating disorders in general, and with treatment of these disorders in particular. My interest in these issues was awakened by a study aimed at understanding the establishing and organizing of specialized treatment of eating disorders in the 1990s in Stockholm. Trying to follow these processes I met large numbers of heterogeneous and variable allies: laboratory rats, political representatives, competing groups of the medical sciences, rating scales, civil servants, significance tests, patients' associations, etc. I also met women – women of flesh and blood – as, for instance, most of the political representatives involved in the field of eating disorders, who are women. Women as the taken-for-granted target group of treatment. Women as one example of the objects of knowledge that are constructed in various research projects on eating disorders.

In meeting all these women, I was intrigued by their role in these processes. Without questioning that there might be personal causes or reasons for an individual to diet excessively or binge-eat, when discussing the causes of eating disorders I had assumed that culture, or rather the gendered society, would be given a primary causal role. But though women's situation in society was frequently associated with these disorders, when it came to discussing specific causes or suitable treatment such associations tended to disappear. *How does it happen?* is the issue to be explored in this chapter.

For this purpose I will take a closer look at the variable and heterogeneous ways in which women are associated with eating disorders, and with suitable treatment of these disorders. By exploring when and how these associations are made, and by looking at the implications of various articulations of eating disorders as women's disorders I will show that the field of eating disorders is an illustration of the fact that 'women' have become a financially and politically useful, but highly mouldable, resource that can be employed to promote various interests, whatever these may be.

The difficulties of studying an asymmetrical world

This chapter is based on a small part of a larger, still not completed study that explores the organizing of clinics specializing in the treatment of eating disorders in Stockholm in the 1990s. A particular focus will be on the Centre for Anorexia, here called the Centre. This clinic started in the early 1990s as a small research group. In the summer of 1997 the County Council of Stockholm signed a regular health care agreement with the Centre. In financial terms, it made the Centre potentially the second largest clinic in Stockholm specializing in eating disorders.

The theoretical argument underlying the practice of the Centre is that eating disorders are caused by the reward system of the brain being activated by reduced food intake and increased physical activity. Psychiatric symptoms, it is argued, are an effect of these disturbed eating and activity habits, and not vice versa as it is generally assumed (Bergh and Södersten 1996a). Thus, contrary to other clinics in Stockholm specializing in eating disorders the Centre does not form part of a psychiatry department and it does not offer any psychotherapy. Instead, eating practice at the Mandometer forms an important part of the Centre's therapeutic practice for treating anorexia and other eating disorders (Wedbjer 1998).

The Mandometer is a computerized eating training device that consists of a plate that is put on a scale connected to a computer containing a number of computer programmes. The programmes provide reference standard curves for a normal rate of food consumption and a normal degree of satiation. They also register the user's real rate of food consumption and her or his experienced degree of satiation. The user can see all the curves on the screen. By eating at the Mandometer while looking at, comparing with, and adapting one's own curves to the standard curves the user should gradually 'normalize' his or her eating behaviour and be cured (PRV 1996; Wedbjer 1998).

The study of the Centre and other clinics specializing in eating disorders forms part of a larger research project on the establishment of new medical practices. Inspired by the sociology of translation, an assumption underlying this project is that the establishment of such practices is the result of these practices being supported by strong networks of heterogeneous allies, humans as well as non-humans. In order to understand the establishment of a therapeutic field or medical practice one therefore needs to map these allies, as well as explore how they have been enrolled and controlled to support this field or practice (Callon 1986; Latour 1987). To use other concepts, one needs to explore how potential associates have been linked up with, and how these associations have been articulated to support a specific field or practice (Latour 1999).

The establishment of the Centre in Stockholm was dependent on the support of a large number of heterogenous associates, largely enrolled via an extensive amount of research and development activities: research funded by well established Swedish research foundations, like the Bank of Sweden

Tercentenary Foundation and the Swedish Research Council (which have also funded this project); professional argumentation in reputable international medical journals like the *Lancet* and *Nature Medicine* (Bergh *et al.* 1996a,b; Bergh and Södersten 1996a,b); the development of a new therapeutic practice (PRV 1996); clinical studies of this practice (Bergh *et al.* 1996a); and the treatment of an increasing number of patients with anorexia and bulimia nervosa.

In this chapter, however, the focus is on women as potential associates, and in professional medical argumentation associations with women play a minor role. What will primarily be explored in this chapter therefore is the use of women in public representation (Latour 1999). Though some references will be made to other publicly available material collected in the full study, and to the forty interviews conducted with politicians, civil servants, professionals and others involved in the field of eating disorders, a main focus of the analysis will be on news articles referring to the Centre from the summer of 1993 to the summer of 1997.

Most of these articles belong to the genre of science journalism. This is a peculiar genre where imagery often replaces content, stories are being unfolded as a series of dramatic events, and the world is referred to as composed of races and competitions (Nelkin 1987/1995). It is therefore important to note that what is analysed in this chapter is the discourse as presented in these articles. Neither the journalists, editors or headline writers, nor the researchers, patients, parents or other interested parties appearing in the articles have been interviewed in the study.

As there are innumerable translations between an interview with a person and a final article presented and headlined in a paper, this is a serious limitation. For instance, this chapter sheds little light on the original source of the associations made between women and eating disorders in the various articles. These might be the journalists' aims to interest potential readers or they might have been a dominant theme in the interviews on which the articles are based. Neither on this issue, nor on the issue of who initiated these articles, does this chapter provide any answers.

One methodological basis of this chapter, as well as of the larger project on the establishment of medical practices, is the principle of symmetry (Bloor 1976; Latour 1987). According to this principle, the same causes should be sought for in determining whether a statement or practice is considered true or false, appropriate or inappropriate, efficient or inefficient. Because of this principle I do not wish to take any position on which medical practice is suitable for treating a specific medical condition, but only to study what makes such positions possible. However, pursuing this principle in practice has presented some obstacles. One obstacle is that the world is not symmetrical.

An asymmetry of particular relevance here is that, though my study indicates that the establishment of all the clinics specializing in eating disorders in Stockholm was heavily dependent on public and political support, largely raised by an extensive public representation of eating disorders in the media, there was little need to argue in public why psychiatric clinics should benefit from this increased support. Since anorexia nervosa was 'discovered' and named by the medical sciences in the 1870s, eating disorders have been defined as psychiatric conditions. In Stockholm and Sweden in the early 1990s, this situation prevailed. Thus, it was taken for granted by politicians, civil servants and by the public that these disorders should be treated by psychiatrists at psychiatric clinics.

In contrast, in the public representation of the Centre, chains of associations had to be produced that explained to the public, not only why there was a need for increased support in the field of eating disorders, but also why this support should be directed to the research and treatment of the Centre. It is this asymmetrical situation that makes the public representation of the Centre an unusually good illustrative basis for exploring the role of women. At the end of the chapter, I will also explore some chains of associations relating women to eating disorders which support the use of psychotherapy and drugs. However, due to the asymmetry of the world, a more complete study of these chains is too time-consuming a task for me to pursue.

Constructivist studies exploring how the political, the financial and the social are intertwined in the development of a therapeutic field are sometimes misinterpreted as a devaluation of the reality, seriousness or importance of these fields (see for instance the preface in Showalter 1997). I therefore want to emphasize that I do respect the fact that anorexia nervosa, bulimia nervosa and other eating disorders can be very serious illnesses. I also respect those researchers, clinicians, parents, patients and others who devote their time and energy to improving resources, and to finding ways of preventing and treating these disorders. To argue that this work necessitates securing public support and that medical research and development are always dependent on such support is not to question the seriousness, need, value, or truth of that field of research. Neither does this chapter attempt to question the fact that eating disorders primarily are women's disorders.

Eating disorders like anorexia nervosa and bulimia nervosa are well known to the public today. However, this general knowledge is a rather recent phenomenon. In order to situate the establishment of specialized treatment of eating disorders in time and place, and to clarify that women are not the only issue here, I will start with a brief history of the field of eating disorders in general and the establishment of the treatment of eating disorders in Stockholm in particular.

From no treatment to controversies about treatment

The 1970s and 1980s: an increasing focus on eating disorders

Though *anorexia nervosa* was 'discovered' and named by the medical sciences in the 1870s, it was not until 1979 that the first two books on self-starvation were published in Swedish (Palazzoli 1963/1979; Möller 1979).

In 1979, anorexia nervosa was not only almost unheard of among the Swedish public, it was also quite unnoticed within the medical professions. Specialized treatment of eating disorders was largely non-existent. A large majority of the girls and women (and the few men) affected by this condition were treated either at general psychiatric or child psychiatric wards, or if their medical condition so required in intensive care units. Treatments appear to have varied between different clinics. However, apart from common sense methods aimed at convincing the patient to eat, behaviourist reward and punishment schemes formed part of the prevailing treatment practice.

In the 1960s and 1970s, partly influenced by the feminist movement (Hepworth 1999), the focus on food and weight gain was criticized and new methods of treatment were developed and given primacy. One of the causes most frequently pointed to was a dysfunctional family pattern, particularly featuring dominant mothers. Psychotherapy, in particular family therapy, began to be seen as a 'gold standard' of treatment (Palazzoli 1963/1979; Möller 1979; Hepworth 1999).

Another important event of the late 1970s was the 'discovery' of *bulimia nervosa* (Russell 1979). Binge eating and purging had not been unknown to the medical sciences, but it had been seen as a part of anorexia, a phase preceding full recovery. However, in 1979 bulimia was defined as a separate disease entity. A year later, in 1980, it entered the third version of the DSM.[1] As most epidemiological studies indicate that bulimia is at least as common, maybe more than twice as common, as anorexia, the inclusion of this new disorder in DSM-III at least doubled the number of eating-disordered women (and men).

In the 1980s, partly due to this new, second eating disorder, there was an increased focus on these disorders in Swedish media. The number of patients approaching health care increased and a recurrent theme in the media became the lack of treatment. An illustrative example is an article published in Sweden's largest morning paper, *Dagens Nyheter*, in October 1986. In this article the story of a 25-year-old woman was told. Having been anorexic since the age of thirteen, she was presently, after two years of binge eating and purging, on sick leave. However, after treatment by the only team specializing in eating disorders in Stockholm, she had begun to improve. In the article, the reader was told that four to five per cent of all young women suffered from an eating disorder. Still, there was almost no treatment available. The chair of the patients' association, 'Anorexia-contact', was quoted as saying : 'The situation is disastrous' (*Dagens Nyheter* 1986).

Nevertheless, the 1980s passed without much happening. In 1988, the County Council of Stockholm carried out an investigation into what specialized treatment was available for patients with eating disorders. It concluded that for adults the only organized treatment was offered by a small team in the area of Södermalm. For children under the age of eighteen, the situation was judged slightly better, with most child psychiatric clinics claiming knowledge of anorexia nervosa. Still, the main conclusion drawn by the investigators was that:

> In spite of some increased efforts during the last years it still appears to be difficult for anorexics/bulimics to cbtain adequate care: the treatment of anorexia and bulimia offered by the County Council of Stockholm is characterised by lack of staff as well as lack of knowledge.
>
> (*Stockholms Läns Landsting* 1988)

However, in the early 1990s the situation began to change.

The 1990s: a increasingly important public health problem

In the early 1990s, eating disorders begin being referred to as public health problems, that is, disorders that are of such magnitude that they affect the general health of the Swedish population. In 1992, following a governmental hearing the National Institute of Public Health and the National Board of Health and Welfare are commissioned by the Swedish government to make an inquiry into the prevalence and causes of the problem, the availability and suitability of treatments, as well as the possibility of preventing eating disorders. The investigation is published in the autumn of 1993 (*Folkhälsoinstitutet och Socialstyrelsen* 1993).

In 1993, the medical community of Sweden also increased its focus on eating disorders. In April, a national guideline concerning the treatment of anorexia nervosa is published: a consensus statement by the Swedish Medical Research Council (*Medicinska Forskningsrådet* 1993). In this statement, the recommendations of the established Swedish medical sciences on how to treat anorexia are presented. The prevalence of and causes of anorexia are also discussed.

Since anorexia nervosa was given a name in the 1870s, a large number of causes, psychiatric as well as somatic, have been proposed without much success (Ward *et al.* 2000). In the early 1990s this situation is reflected in the Medical Research Council's conclusions about the causes of anorexia:

> The following possible causes of onset of the illness have been identified: heredity, physiological factors, family structure, personality and cultural and social factors.
>
> (*Medicinska Forskningsrådet* 1993: 6)

A survey carried out by the Medical Research Council of existing treatment practices indicates that the therapeutic practices dominating Swedish health care are family-therapy for children and individual counselling for adults. Control of body weight, somatic measures, diet counselling, physiotherapy and drug treatment also form some part of the treatment available. The Medical Research Council concludes that scientific evaluations of these prevailing treatment practices are almost non-existent. For instance, only one controlled study of the effects of psychotherapy has been found. This study indicates that younger patients with a short duration of illness should be treated with family therapy (*Medicinska Forskningsrådet* 1993: 14–15).

Given the lack of scientific studies, the recommendations of the Medical Research Council do not depart significantly from the prevailing practice. The importance of having a close co-operation with somatic medicine is stressed. But it is taken for granted that psychiatry is the sub-discipline of medicine that should treat serious cases of self-starvation and it is stated that some form of psychotherapeutic counselling should be included in the treatment (*Medicinska Forskningsrådet* 1993:15).

In the early 1990s, the county councils of Sweden responsible for the actual provision of health care to Swedish citizens also started dedicating funding to the treatment of eating disorders.

The 1990s: building treatment and building controversies

In 1991, the County Council of Stockholm allocates an initial one million Swedish kronor to the psychiatric clinic at Huddinge hospital for establishing a team specializing in the treatment of eating disorders (*Stockholms Läns Landsting* 1991). A year later all local health care committees are directed by the County Council Assembly to increase their resources dedicated to the treatment of these disorders. By the end of 1993, the sum spent on specialized treatment of eating disorders has increased to almost 12 million kronor and several specialized teams and clinics have been established (*Stockholms Läns Landsting* 1993).

There are some differences between these teams and clinics. Several teams are small, providing outpatient counselling and short-term psychotherapy, often with a focus on getting control of eating habits. Among the two larger clinics, the clinic EMBLA provides day-care as well as outpatient counselling. A variety of therapies is employed: short-term psychodynamic therapy, network therapy, family counselling, acupressure, movement therapy, gestalt therapy etc. Eating practice and counselling by a dietician are also available. The second clinic, located at the hospital of Löwenströmska, provides 24-hour in-patient care, day-care and outpatient care. The focus is on a structured manual-based form of cognitive behavioural therapy.

There are also some similarities between these teams and clinics. First, they all form part of psychiatry. Second, though different in character, they all provide some form of psychotherapy. Third, neither of them can accept patients under the age of 18 (later 16). Children with eating disorders are directed to the organization of child psychiatry where family therapy is the dominating treatment. Therapeutic practices focused on food and eating habits are almost non-existent.

When the psychiatric clinic at Huddinge hospital receives funding in 1991 to start its specialized team, three persons are intended to co-operate: a male psychiatrist, a female social worker with a PhD who has been involved in the field of eating disorders since the early 1980s, and a male psychologist who has done extensive research on the neuroendocrinological aspects of the food intake and physical activity of laboratory rats. Some co-operation is initiated, but within a few years, the psychiatrist has left Huddinge hospital and the other two have moved to the somatic clinics of this hospital. There they continue their research on eating disorders, developing the Mandometer and their therapeutic practice. In the summer of 1994, together with a third colleague, they apply for a patent on the Mandometer. A first group of patients is also under treatment. Gradually, the Centre, as a clinic that offers computerized eating practice and that represents an alternative to psychiatric treatment, grows into an effective unit.

In July 1993, a short notice appears in one of the largest evening papers in Sweden announcing that a well-known Swedish skier has donated funds to a research project on anorexia. In the article it is stated that this project will be led by experienced doctors and psychologists from the Centre for Anorexia at Huddinge hospital (*Expressen* 1993). To my knowledge this is the first time the name of the Centre is mentioned in the Swedish media.

At the end of 1994 and early in 1995, two of the largest papers publish articles introducing the theories and treatment of the Centre (*Aftonbladet* 1995; *Dagens Nyheter* 1994). Six months later, in the summer of 1995, another article based on an interview with parents whose daughters have been treated at the Centre appears in a third large paper (*Expressen* 1995).

In September 1995, some Swedish newspapers file reports from a press conference held by the Swedish Sports Confederation where the results of a research project conducted at the Centre have been presented (*Dagens Nyheter* 1995; *Göteborgsposten* 1995; *Svenska Dagbladet* 1995). Six months later, in March 1996, a new group of articles appear where associations between sports, eating disorders and the Centre play an important role (*Aftonbladet* 1996a–e; *Dagens Nyheter* 1996a–g; *Svenska Dagbladet* 1996a).

A year passes without much being heard about the Centre in the media, apart from some articles based on two press releases published in the autumn of 1996 (*Aftonbladet* 1996h; *Arbetet* 1996; *Dagen Nyheter* 1996h; *Göteborgs-Posten* 1996; *Helsingborgs Dagblad* 1996a–b; *Svenska Dagbladet* 1996b–c). At the end of March 1997, an article is published in a major evening paper (*Aftonbladet* 1997). Between then and the end of May a number of articles referring to the Centre appear in newspapers covering the Stockholm area (*Dagens Nyheter* 1997a–d; *Expressen* 1997a–e; *Svenska Dagbladet* 1997). In June 1997, a regular health care agreement is signed between the County Council of Stockholm and the Centre.

In all these articles, a large number of heterogeneous variables are associated with eating disorders in general, and with the Centre and its therapeutic practice in particular. This chapter focuses on one such variable: women.

The art of associating and dissociating women

Chronologically and thematically, the coverage of the Centre in the Swedish media can be separated into three periods. During the first period, from late 1994 to early 1995, the Centre is introduced to the public. In the second period, lasting from mid 1995 to early April 1996, the Centre is identified in the media as a clinic specializing in eating disorders among athletes, and its therapeutic practice is presented as an alternative to psychiatric treatment. In the third period, covering September 1996 to May 1997, the recurrent themes are: results of treatment, queues for treatment, costs of treatments, and the allocation of funds to psychiatry versus the Centre. Bureaucratic inertia and political inability to act are also focused upon. In the three periods women play various roles.

The years 1994 to 1995: introducing the Centre and its therapeutic practice

In December 1994, the largest morning paper in Sweden publishes an article based on an interview with the two main researchers and clinicians at the Centre, hereafter called the researchers. The article is headlined 'Anorexia biological. Nonsense that anorexia is only psychological, says scientist' (*Dagens Nyheter* 1994). The article starts by concluding that self-starvation, anorexia nervosa, is the third most common illness among girls between 15 and 20 years and that almost all treatment consists of psychodynamic therapy, 'according to its critics without much success'. According to the article, the researchers therefore argue that the time has come to change the methods of treatment and start looking more at the biological processes involved in eating disorders. In the article, several arguments are presented as to why this change of focus is needed.

First, according to the article, one of the researchers states that it is probably not until anorexia nervosa is seen as somatic that its status and the resources for research and 'alternative treatments' will increase. Second, it is wrong to stigmatize anorexic girls as 'psycho-cases', as these girls do not want to be classified as psychiatrically disordered. Third, the reason why '70–80 per cent of the psychiatric treatments are based on psychodynamic theories' is that it is assumed that the causes of anorexia are located in a dysfunctional childhood, particularly dysfunctional relations with the parents. Therefore, family therapy is the most common method of treatment. However, in the article it is stated that according to the researchers the anorexic family is a myth. There is nothing to differentiate these families from other families.

The biological causes of anorexia are also explained in the article. The journalist concludes that it proves to be a complex hormonal process. Anorexic patients have an elevated level of a hormone, CRF, which is related to stress and depression in the brain. This elevated level of CRF makes the level of another hormone, ACTH, increase. ACTH in turn increases the level of cortisol, which makes the brain produce more dopamine. The increased amount of dopamine acts as a drug and the anorexic senses a feeling of well-being. This is the reason why self-starving patients initially feel very well. Further, according to one of the researchers:

> Well-meant comments from the environment concerning the person's weight and beauty ideals in commercials can actually have a similar effect on the dopamine-system of the brain. These systems are very sensitive to conditioning, which explains why the anorexic can react to signals that are in fact neutral.
>
> (*Dagens Nyheter* 1994)

The reader is also told about promising results of a first experiment with nine anorexic patients. Apart from increases in body weight and normalizing of eating behaviour, the patients are free from their previous feelings of anxiety and depression. They have started taking part in social activities and according to the article, 'they have even got themselves a boyfriend'.

In a second article, published three weeks later in the 'women's section' of one of the largest evening papers, similar arguments are reproduced and combined with a special focus on women and women's situation in society (*Aftonbladet* 1995). The article opens by stating that according to the researchers:

> The time has come to kill the myth about the anorexic family. Not everything is the mother's fault. Mothers of anorexic girls are no worse than other mothers. Mothers have unnecessarily taken on the blame . . .
>
> (*Aftonbladet* 1995)

In the article, this statement is elaborated. It is explained that according to the researchers there is a tendency within psychiatry to explain anorexia as a result of the girl's development being hindered by a dominant mother, or by other problems in the family. But the talk about the unhealthy and demanding 'anorexic family' is one of many 'myths' surrounding anorexia. Naturally, problems emerge in a family when a child might be about to die, but to put mothers of anorexic patients on sick leave, as psychiatrists have done, is to go too far: 'A mother should be used as a resource' (*Aftonbladet* 1995).

Two other common 'myths' about anorexia that are also presented and contested in the article are that sexual abuse is more common among eating disordered patients and that anorexics are characterized by the (psychiatric) diagnostic criteria of suffering from a disturbed body perception. The first is not proven and the second, a disturbed body perception, is not characteristic of all anorexics. Furthermore, according to the article, the experience of one of the researchers is that:

girls are fed up with only going for psychotherapy. They also want to do something concrete. They want to be active.

What if anorexia had mainly affected men? Would they have been content with psychiatric treatment? I believe men would have demanded research and concrete methods for attacking the problem.

(Aftonbladet 1995)

It is explained that no one knows exactly what anorexia and bulimia depend on, nor why nine out of ten sufferers are women. However, at the Centre they want to do more research on the relationships between chemical and psychological factors. It is emphasized that the researchers do not contest all psychological explanations of an eating disorder. Two discoveries by psychiatrists are referred to in the article as being considered important by them. The first is Hilde Bruch's statement that anorexia nervosa is 'the woman's way to fight for an identity in a complex society', the second Arthur Crisp's conclusion that 'anorexia is the individual's way of saying no to the demands of puberty'. Having referred to these statements, the article continues by explaining: 'In short: they experience stress' *(Aftonbladet* 1995).

But why, the article asks, is anorexia the result of this 'teenage stress'? Here the body comes into it. Referring to the fact that the knowledge of the researchers is partly built on studies of the eating behaviour of rats, the article goes on to state that the connection between stress and self-starvation is related to stress hormones. A young girl experiences stress, maybe due to 'an unhappy love affair' or due to 'a problem with her family'. She goes on a diet and the complex hormonal process that leads to anorexia nervosa is set in motion.

The article ends by stating that research on anorexia is neglected, perhaps because it is a 'women's disorder' and has a low status *(Aftonbladet* 1995). According to the article, one of the researchers has a solution to this:

I believe the status would be raised if one started talking about the fact that anorexia also has to do with the stomach and the brain – because then there is a defect in the apparatus . . .

(Aftonbladet 1995)

From the woman's fight for her identity to laboratory rats and the hormonal processes of the body

These two articles of 1994 and 1995 introduced the theoretical arguments and therapeutic practice of the Centre to the Swedish public. How were women associated with eating disorders (or rather anorexia nervosa) in these articles? Moreover, what were the implications of articulating anorexia as a women's disorder?

The first association, anorexia being the third most common illness among young women, was dependent on a statistical aggregate. Due to the intimate relationship between positive action and the collection of social data (Gaste-laars, this volume), such statistical associations could almost be expected. But, as indicated by the second article, the predominance of women in eating disorders is already so well known that, in this case, statistical figures are not necessary to identify these disorders as a women's disorder. Rather, as the location of this second article indicates, eating disorders have a 'natural' space in the 'women's section' of papers.

The predominance of women in eating disorders might appear a simple factual claim. Facts, however, do not state themselves. Further, descriptions of a disorder as a women's disorder can have various implications. What were the implications in the articles explored above? First, identifying anorexia nervosa as a women's disorder both implied that and explained why this illness had a low status in society and why the medical sciences and society had neglected this disorder. Second, the association of eating disorders with women explained why resources for research and the development of treatments for anorexia nervosa were insufficient.

To argue that illnesses that mainly affect women have been neglected by the medical sciences is not a very radical statement. On the contrary, the reason an association with women can support claims about lack of resources is the widespread acceptance of such utterances. But why should lack of resources imply support of the Centre rather than psychiatric clinics? In the two articles above, several arguments were presented. Two of them related to women.

The first argument explained the predominance of psychotherapy within the field as a consequence of anorexia being a women's disorder: men would never have settled for lack of concrete methods to attack the problem. A second argument portrayed the representatives of the Centre as spokes-persons and protectors of women. Unlike psychiatry, which located the cause of anorexia in dominant mothers, the researchers at the Centre saw mothers as a resource. And contrary to psychiatric treatment that stigmatized anorexic girls as 'psycho-cases', at the Centre they adapted to the wishes of these girls. These girls disapproved of being described as suffering from a psychiatric disorder; they were fed up with psychotherapy; and they wanted to be active and do something concrete.

Common knowledge includes the knowledge that psychotherapy consists of a lot of talking and that psychiatric disorders are stigmatizing. That mothers of anorexic girls have been blamed for their daughters' illness is not unknown to the public either. Who could disapprove of a clinic that wants to use a mother as a resource and that wants to support anorexic girls in their wish to take an active part in their treatment and avoid psychiatric stigmatization?

The answer is: a lot of people. Public representation can never ignore what is already common knowledge. It must start with the beliefs and opinions held by the woman and man on the street (Latour 1999). Stigmatizing or not, the assumption that eating disorders are psychiatric conditions is well established, not only within the medical sciences, but also among the public.

Furthermore, many laypersons would probably agree that eating disorders are in some way or other related to the demands of puberty or even to the young 'woman's way to fight for an identity'. How could this psychological identity-struggle, which seems to imply that eating disorders should be treated with psychotherapy, be translated into a support of the causal theories of the Centre and its computerized eating-practice?

In the articles explored above the solution was to translate this struggle into an issue of stress: 'teenage stress'. Then, since a problem with the psychological explanations was their lack of understanding of bodily processes, from stress further translations were made to stress hormones, to hormonal processes of the body and to research on laboratory rats. Having been provided with an explanation of how such hormonal processes could result in a little ordinary dieting ending up in anorexia nervosa, it began to be understandable to the reader why the appropriate way to treat anorexic girls was to 'explain the physiological processes of the body to them, at the same time as they concretely practice their eating behaviour'.

Starting thus by defining anorexia nervosa as a women's disorder that had therefore been badly treated as far as research and treatment goes, then by casting the representatives of the Centre as spokespersons for and protectors of anorexic women and their mothers, the argument ended in dissociating women from this disorder through a chain of translations that transformed women's situation in society into an issue of hormonal processes of the body. The implication was that those interested in improving women's situation should support the use of eating practice at the Mandometer.

In August 1995, the Public Health Committee of the County Council of Stockholm grants the Centre 2.5 million Swedish kronor. The funding is to be used for clinical development of the therapeutic practice of the Centre on another thirty patients (*Stockholms Läns Landsting* 1995). There are no indications in the protocol of this decision that associations between women and eating disorders have had any influence on this decision. Rather, judging from interviews with the politicians and civil servants involved, the use of public health money was a pragmatic solution to a practical organizational problem: how to fund clinical development of a treatment for eating disorders at a clinic that did not form part of the organization of psychiatry?

Nevertheless, these interviews make it clear that the political interest in solving this issue was driven by an awareness of eating disorders being an important and neglected problem in need of increased political and financial support. Associating eating disorders with women was one important resource in creating this political awareness.

By August 1995, another association between women, eating disorders and the Centre has also begun appearing in the media: the Centre as a clinic specializing in athletic anorexia. This association is not referred to in the protocols of the decision of Public Health Committee. Nevertheless, in the year to come it will be a recurrent theme in the Swedish media. Here too women play an important role.

July 1995–April 1996: a treatment, the greatest problem of 'girls''
sports

In July 1995, a Swedish evening paper publishes an article entitled 'Girls die waiting for treatment. Desperate parents beg politicians to wake up' (*Expressen* 1995). The article tells of twenty-five to thirty young female athletes at risk of dying while waiting to get treatment for their 'athletic anorexia' at the Centre. According to the article this clinic 'deals with athletic anorexics'. Thirteen patients have been successfully treated at this clinic, but now the project runs the risk of being closed down. In the article, the chair of the parents' association funded in support of the Centre is quoted explaining why: 'There are no funds for the clinical treatment of girls with athletic anorexia' (*Expressen* 1995).

The parents' association has appealed to the politicians of the County Council of Stockholm, and to the Swedish minister of social affairs, without success. Now the parents go public:

> Our desperate appeal is: do something, but do it quickly. The situation is acute. More girls risk dying while waiting for treatment.
>
> (*Expressen* 1995)

In September 1995, a few large newspapers publish articles that once more associate the Centre with athletic anorexia (*Dagens Nyheter* 1995; *Göteborgs-Posten* 1995; *Svenska Dagbladet* 1995). The articles refer to a press conference held by the Swedish Sports Confederation and the researchers at the Centre. At the conference the results of a research project conducted at the Centre on prevalence, causes, characteristics and treatment of athletic anorexia has been presented. The results indicate that female athletes run a fifteen-times greater risk of getting an eating disorder. As anorexia nervosa is the third most common illness among young girls and as 60 per cent of those suffering from anorexia also get bulimia, the result is that every sixth female athlete will get an eating disorder (*Dagens Nyheter* 1995; *Svenska Dagbladet* 1995).

Counteracting this negative news, the results of the research at the Centre indicate that a distinction should be made between *anorexia nervosa* and *athletic anorexia*. Athletes with anorexia are not characterized by two of the diagnostic criteria of anorexia nervosa: weight phobia and disturbed body perception (*Dagens Nyheter* 1995; *Svenska Dagbladet* 1995). In addition, there is no proof of psychological disturbance being the cause of (athletic) anorexia. Rather, the research at the Centre indicates that the cause is that 'dieting and intensive physical activity might speed up the hormonal systems of the body that attend to reward and attention' (*Dagens Nyheter* 1995; *Svenska Dagbladet* 1995). Apart from differences in diagnostic criteria and cause, according to these articles, athletes suffering from eating disorders also appear easier to cure. So far, twelve girls suffering from anorexia or bulimia have been successfully treated at the Centre. Half of them are elite athletes and they are all back on the track (*Dagens Nyheter* 1995).

The press conference in September 1995 marks the end of a research project at the Centre funded by the Sports Confederation. Six months later, in the second half of March 1996, a new series of articles referring to the Centre is published in the Swedish media (*Aftonbladet* 1996a–e; *Dagens Nyheter* 1996a–g; *Svenska Dagbladet* 1996a). Most of these articles are published on the sports pages; a few appear in the women's section or the general news sections of the papers. Many of the articles are based on interviews with female ex-anorexics and their parents. One article, published on the most prestigious debate page in Sweden, is even written by the parents of five former anorexic girls (*Dagens Nyheter* 1996d). In these articles, there are two recurrent themes.

The first theme is a critique of psychiatric therapies (psychotherapy) as a treatment for eating disorders, as illustrated by headlines such as 'You can't talk yourself out of anorexia' (*Dagens Nyheter* 1996e) or 'Psycho-care a death trap for anorexics' (*Dagens Nyheter* 1996d). Much of this critique is presented by individual ex-anorexics who have been unsuccessfully treated within psychiatry before coming to the Centre, or by their parents.

The critique of psychiatric treatment is further supported by some references to scientific studies and arguments. For instance, a reference is made to a study published by the Swedish Medical Association in a book called 'Women-Un-Health'. The study indicates that only 50 per cent of anorexics will be cured within ten years, 15–20 per cent will never be cured and 5 per cent will eventually die from their illness (*Dagens Nyheter* 1996d). In some articles the lack of evaluation of the effects of psychotherapy is also pointed out (*Dagens Nyheter* 1996d,g).

Running parallel to and intertwined with the critique of psychiatric treatment is a second theme in the articles of March 1996. Most of these articles are published on the sports pages. Some even constitute a series of articles on 'athletic anorexia' (*Dagens Nyheter* 1996a–g). Though a distinction between athletic anorexia and 'common' anorexia is seldom explicitly made, many articles state that they are about eating disorders among female athletes, and the Centre is explicitly or implicitly described as specializing in treating these kinds of eating disorders. In contrast to earlier articles presenting similar descriptions of the Centre and its therapeutic practice, some of the articles of March 1996 describe the sports movement as being too unaware and incapable of handling the problem of eating disorders. In a few articles a comparison between doping and eating disorders is also introduced (*Aftonbladet* 1996d; *Svenska Dagbladet* 1996b). I shall return to this comparison later.

What associations were made between women and eating disorders in articles referring to the Centre from July 1995 to early April 1996? As in earlier articles of 1994 and early 1995, associations were made with women as statistical aggregates. Apart from anorexia being the third most common illness among young girls, such statistical associations included references to eating disorders being fifteen times as common among female athletes as among women in general or to eating disorders affecting every sixth female athlete. Second, it was implied that the prevalence of eating disorders among women was related to the gendered character of the sports movement or society in general. These descriptions included references to lack of female coaches and the role of 'thoughtless' remarks made by male coaches, as well as references to the influence of the fashion and marketing industry. Third, all ex-anorexics appearing in the media were female and there were frequent references to the relational label 'daughter'. Such personalized associations between eating disorders and individual women had two characteristics: the young women and their parents were sometimes depicted as spokespersons of eating disordered women in general and, as most of these young women were described as having been seriously ill, they illustrated and emphasized the seriousness of these disorders as indicated by other references to statistical figures on lack of recovery and premature death.

Two scenarios arguing for increased funding of the Centre as an obligatory point of passage (Callon 1986; Helgesson 1999) for those wanting to improve women's situation in society were also constructed in these articles. A first dramatic but specific scenario was presented in the article in July 1995 where increased funding to the Centre was identified as an obligatory point of passage to save the lives of twenty-five to thirty girls who were at risk of dying from their athletic anorexia.

A less dramatic but more general scenario was constructed in an article of early April 1996 where an appeal to the Swedish Sports Confederation was launched. This is the scenario in my rendition:

> Anorexia is the most serious problem in girls' sports. Doping is the greatest problem of (male) sports. The resources dedicated by the sports movement to fight doping are much larger than the resources dedicated to fighting eating disorders. In order to remedy this unequal state the Sports Confederation ought to increase its funding of the Centre, a clinic specializing in the treatment of eating disorders among athletes.

The Swedish Sports Confederation, however, refused to accept the scenario attempting to increase its funding of the Centre. In the same article as this scenario was presented, the Chair of the Confederation contested the chains of association producing it. More specifically, he contested that doping and eating disorders could be compared. According to him, such a comparison was 'like comparing apples with pears. The issues are different. Doping we must attend to as it is against the rules of sport' (*Aftonbladet* 1996). He also denied that the sports movement had any responsibility for the treatment of eating disorders. In his view, the discussion was not about the responsibility of the sports movement for the prevalence of eating disorders among (female) athletes.

The issue of anorexia is special, as it is unclear within the health care machinery how it should be treated. It is a conflict of interests between different groups of specialists – one does not know where the illness belongs. We cannot go in and take the responsibility that, for instance, belongs to the county councils.

(Aftonbladet 1996)

The development of a therapeutic practice is, however, a continuous process (Latour 1987). Most of the articles published in late 1995 and early 1996 had been published on the sports pages and the former anorexics appearing had been dedicated athletes. Consequently, the focus of these articles was on eating disorders within the sports movement. In contrast, the articles of 1994 and early 1995 that introduced the theoretical arguments and therapeutic practice of the Centre to the Swedish public concerned anorexia nervosa in general. From later articles it is also clear that research had been done and treatment administered to patients that did not form part of the sports movement. In late 1996, the therapeutic practice of the Centre continues to be seen in the Swedish media as a treatment of eating disorders in general.

September 1996–May 1997: women lost

In September and November 1996, some newspapers publish short articles based on two press releases written by the researchers at the Centre. The first press release relates that the results of a study of eight women with anorexia nervosa, who have been successfully treated at the Centre, have been presented in the *Lancet*, an internationally reputable medical journal (*Arbetet* 1996; *Helsingborgs Dagblad* 1996a; *Svenska Dagbladet* 1996b). In the second press release, the prescription to anorexics of anti-depressant drugs (SSRIs or selective serotonine reuptake inhibitors) is criticized, as these drugs might result in a loss of weight (*Aftonbladet* 1996f; *Dagens Nyheter* 1996h; *GöteborgsPosten* 1996; *Helsingborgs Dagblad* 1996b; *Svenska Dagbladet* 1996c). In the articles referring to these press releases there are almost no associations with women.

At the end of March 1997 an article headlined 'The doctor who can cure all anorexics', is published in one of the largest evening papers in Sweden. The article starts by concluding that 50 per cent of patients with anorexia nervosa will never recover and 15 per cent will die, but now the Centre provides new hope. Out of thirty patients treated, thirty have been cured. In the article, one of the researchers is quoted, explaining how these results have been achieved:

We start from known facts about anorexia only. We know that anorexia is caused by dieting and/or increased physical activity. Therefore we reduce the level of activity and increase the food-intake of the person who is ill. The basis of our treatment is to fight the visible symptoms . . . We have seen that a psychiatric approach to the illness fortifies rather than fights the illness. Our treatment is more concrete and has been proved to bring results . . .

(*Aftonbladet* 1997)

In the next few months a number of articles referring to the Centre appear in newspapers covering the Stockholm area (*Dagens Nyheter* 1997a–d; *Expressen* 1997a–e; *Svenska Dagbladet* 1997). Apart from references to the successful results at the Centre compared to the unsuccessful results of psychiatric treatment, other themes presented in these articles are: the situation of the 150–180 severely ill anorexic patients at risk of dying while waiting in line for treatment at the Centre (*Dagens Nyheter* 1997d; *Expressen* 1997a); the small sum of two million Swedish kronor allocated by the County Council of Stockholm to the Centre, compared to the large sum of 30 million kronor allocated by the Council to psychiatric clinics specializing in the treatment of eating disorders (*Expressen* 1997a); and the low cost of treatment at the Centre compared to the heavy costs of psychiatric treatment. In one article an associate professor in economics, whose daughter has been successfully treated at the Centre, even presents a calculation showing that Swedish society would save 16 billion kronor if all Swedish anorexics were treated at the Centre (*Expressen* 1997d).

Another recurrent theme in these articles is a critique of (majority) politicians and civil servants of the County Council of Stockholm for letting bureaucratic inertia and incompetence risk the lives of young girls. Here politicians from the opposition take an active part in the debate. In April, one article refers to a letter written by a representative of the County Council Assembly to the social-democratic politicians in charge, asking why there is no health care agreement with the Centre (*Svenska Dagbladet* 1997). In early May, two members of the liberal party express their support of increased funding of the Centre on the Stockholm debate page of another paper (*Dagens Nyheter* 1997a). They start their letter by stating:

Anorexia is a common, but life-threatening, illness among women of today. In spite of this, there are long queues for care and treatment. This especially applies to young girls.

(*Dagens Nyheter* 1997a)

On May 28, an article announces: 'Now the politicians get moving' (*Expressen* 1997c). Two days later the headline of another article states: 'Treatment for anorexics gets increased support' (*Dagens Nyheter* 1997d). In June 1997, a formal health care agreement is signed between the Centre and the County Council of Stockholm. In financial terms, this agreement potentially makes the Centre the second largest clinic specializing in eating disorders in Stockholm.

Looking at how women were associated with eating disorders in the articles published in the spring of 1997, there were references, as in previous articles, to women as statistical aggregates (the third most common illness among young girls). A few individual anorexic girls, daughters and their parents also appeared in the articles expressing their support of the treatment offered at the Centre. In a few articles, associations were also made between women, body-ideals and eating disorders. For instance, one article referred to a seminar where the editor of a teenage magazine, a media researcher and a researcher from the Centre had discussed the body-focused society and its effects on young women (*Dagens Nyheter* 1997c).

The focus of this article, however, was on the terrifying prognosis of eating disorders presented by the researcher at the seminar, and on the hope provided by the therapeutic practice of the Centre. This focus reflected that of other articles published in early 1997. Their focus was on results of treatment, queues to treatment, and costs of treatment. Bureaucratic inertia and inability to act were other issues discussed. Compared to previous articles associations with women played a minor role.

In speculating why women played this comparatively minor role, one reason might be that in the spring of 1997 a number of patients had been successfully treated at the Centre. Thus, there were now concrete results of treatment to refer to. But another difference is that, in contrast to previous articles identifying the Centre as a research project in need of funding for research and development, or as a clinic specializing in athletic anorexia in need of special funding for this particular kind of eating disorder, in the spring of 1997 the discussion concerned the regular funding of treatment from the regular budget of health care.

In this discussion a description of eating disorders as a women's disorder might have been of less importance. It might even have caused some complications. For the question might have been asked: who in the field of eating disorders represents the legitimate spokesperson of women? Asking that question one might have found that associations with women have also been used in support of psychiatric treatment too.

Women as mouldable associates

'Women' as an associate of psychotherapy

A recurrent theme in the media articles referring to the Centre from 1994 to 1997 is a critique of psychotherapy as a treatment of anorexia nervosa. Part of this critique is based on the experience of former anorexics and their parents, but it is also pointed out that scientific studies supporting psychotherapeutic treatment are missing. As previously mentioned, this critique finds support in the consensus statement on anorexia nervosa made by the Medical Research Council in 1993 (*Medicinska Forskningsrådet* 1993).

The Medical Research Council does not discuss why psychotherapy, in spite of this lack of scientific support, dominates Swedish health care.

However, in the media coverage of the Centre, some possible explanations are proposed. One is that the dominance of this therapeutic practice is due to anorexia nervosa being a women's disorder. But women have also been associated with support for psychotherapy in the treatment of eating disorders. In order to explore this relationship I will return to the 1970s when psychotherapy was established in Sweden as a 'gold standard' of treatment.

In 1979, the two first books on eating disorders are published in Sweden. One of these books, *Self-starvation*, is a short and easily accessible book (Möller 1979). It is written by a journalist, and it addresses parents, teachers and other non-professionals. Apart from a study of the then available professional literature, the book is based on interviews with former anorexics, their parents and the experts of those days. In the book, associations with women play an important role.

First of all, the anorexic portrayed in *Self-starvation* is clearly a woman. On the back of the book, it is stated that self-starvation 'primarily affects teenage girls or young women'. Second, in the introductory chapter anorexia is related to women's situation in society. Thus, whereas self-starvation has historically been a rare illness, according to the book, most experts now agree that the prevalence has increased heavily. This increasing number of cases can, it is argued in the book, be read as an indication of the conflicting demands on young women of our time. Therefore, the saint of the late twentieth century ought to be called Sancta Anorexia: an emaciated girl who is prepared to offer her life for the sake of the slender body ideal. However, Sancta Anorexia is more than that:

> Sancta Anorexia is also a rebel of freedom, who refuses to grow up, given the conditions offered to her. She does not accept her role as a sex object. Her rebellion against the contempt for women is expressed through her refusal to let her body become a female body.
>
> (Möller 1979: 12)

'Conflicting demands on young women', 'a refusal to become a sex object', 'rebellion against the contempt for women' – what is provided here is a radical feminist articulation of anorexia as the result of a gendered society. What then does this radical interpretation imply in relation to causes and treatment of these disorders?

Self-starvation is an introductory book aimed at providing laypersons with a basic understanding of this disorder. Therefore, no one expert, possible cause or specific treatment is focused upon in this book. Rather a recurrent message is that there is great disagreement among the experts of the time. But in spite of emphasizing this disagreement, some clear conclusions are drawn in the book. In particular, after the conclusion that self-starvation has been cured with very different therapeutic practices, a question is posed whether it matters what therapeutic practice is used. The answer provided in the book is a clear 'yes':

Average weight or over-weight, regular periods, a crushed self-esteem, remaining feelings of shame and psychological problems have been the result for many women of male psychiatrists' despotic ways of confronting their illness. A treatment that is solely focused on body weight and on the physiological effects of self-starvation might be directly harmful for the patient and aggravate her psychological status.

(Möller 1979: 81)

Apart from a strict focus on body weight and physiology, the despotic ways of male psychiatrists to which the author refers seem to be an expression of an unwillingness by (male) doctors to listen to and understand anorexic women. This unwillingness is vividly illustrated in the book by a number of quotations from interviews with formerly anorexic women. For instance, a 30-year-old woman who was treated in the 1960s is quoted as saying:

But no one asked how I felt, what was wrong. They only treated the visible symptoms, said that I was too thin and that they wanted me to regain weight. When I was let out I certainly had put on some weight, but I still did not understand what was happening to me.

(Möller 1979: 81–2)

In the late 1990s, the researchers at the Centre could provide such an understanding. According to them, the reward system of the brain had been activated. However, in the late 1970s the author of *Self-starvation* went directly from quoting the former anorexic women to translating their wishes into a demand for psychotherapy:

In the last decade, understanding of the experience of the illness appears to have increased considerably. Today some kind of psychotherapy or family therapy is used at most institutions. Of course, there are no foolproof methods that always cure the patient. . . . But in the hands of skilled and wise persons, different forms of therapy can produce excellent results.

(Möller 1979: 82)

Some patients and parents who have experienced family therapy are interviewed in the book. Not all of them have a favourable experience of this practice, but many appear to be positive. One mother is even quoted demanding that all mothers of anorexic children should be entitled to psychological counselling.

There might be a number of reasons why the opinions of the anorexics and their mothers of the late 1970s appear to differ so much from the opinions of the anorexics and their mothers of the late 1990s, who favoured concrete eating practice before psychotherapy. My intention here is only to demonstrate that chains of associations between women and eating disorders have been produced in support of psychotherapy too. Fragments of such chains can be found in many media articles on eating disorders of the late 1990s.

In the chain produced in 1979, women were first associated with anorexia nervosa by stating that the anorexic was a woman. Second, a radical feminist articulation of self-starvation as an expression of women's condition in society was produced and the anorexic girl was described as in rebellion against the condition of women. Third, this societal problem was translated into the despotic ways of male psychiatrists in confronting anorexic women. Fourth, acting as spokesperson for anorexic women and their mothers, the author translated their experiences and wishes into a demand for psychotherapy. Thus it was implied that psychotherapy was an obligatory point of passage for those wanting to listen to women's voices and improve women's situation in society.

But 'women' is a mouldable creature. I will provide a short example of how women have been used in support of drug treatment, too.

'Women' as an associate of drugs

Contrary to its activities in relation to many other illnesses, the pharmaceutical industry has played a very minor role in increasing society's focus on eating disorders, the main reason being the lack of efficient drugs. Drugs, however, need not be formally approved by the authorities in order for individual doctors to prescribe them. Over the years a very large variety of drugs have also been tried in the treatment of both anorexia and bulimia.

In a press release in the autumn of 1996, one of the researchers at the Centre criticized the use of a specific drug in the treatment of anorexia: selective serotonine re-uptake inhibitors or SSRIs. The argument was that these drugs reduce the appetite and body-weight of anorexic patients. So far no drug has been approved by Swedish authorities for the treatment of anorexia nervosa. Thus, what this critique was concerned with was the clinical use of these drugs. However, in March 1998 the SSRI fluoxetine, better known under its American brand name Prozac, was approved by the Swedish Medical Products Agency as a treatment for bulimia nervosa (*Läkemedelsverket* 1998).

The relationship between anorexia nervosa and bulimia nervosa is anything but clear. In psychiatric diagnostic manuals they are defined as two distinct disorders, but it appears that many bulimics have previously suffered from anorexia, and a large number of anorexics later develop bulimia. Whatever the relationship, they both belong to the diagnostic group of eating disorders. It is therefore of interest to ask whether 'women' who have been associated with eating disorders are in support of fluoxetine, too?

A difficulty in answering this question is that the approval of fluoxetine as a treatment of bulimia has hardly been noticed in the Swedish news media. Professional medical articles belong to a completely different genre. In these articles, neither women's situation in society, nor preferences or personal experiences of individual patients are of any importance. What matters in these articles are other 'allies', for instance statistical significance.

Still, in five articles summarizing most of the studies on which the approval of the Medical Products Agency was based, a common introductory statement was that bulimia nervosa is the most common illness among young women (Fichter *et al.* 1991; Foss *et al.* 1990; Fluoxetine Bulimia Nervosa Collaborative Study Group 1992; Wood 1993; Goldstein *et al.* 1995). Furthermore, only in a few exceptional cases the preferences of patients were actually invoked. Yet in one of the articles, when discussing the pros and cons of treating bulimic patients with fluoxetine, Fichter *et al.* concluded that one advantage with fluoxetine is that this substance

> lowers the patient's 'set-point' for body weight and thus helps the bulimic patient to achieve more easily what he or she is striving for: a slim figure corresponding with the ideals of Western societies concerning physical appearance.
>
> (Fichter *et al.* 1991: 4)

In spite of the politically correct reference to 'he or she', thereby ungendering the gendered character of this statement, by associating eating disorders with women and by taking the position as spokespersons of these women, here too a scenario is created where those who want to adhere to women's wishes are invited to promote the use of fluoxetine as a treatment for eating disorders.

Who speaks for 'women'?

The focus of this chapter has been on women as associates in support of increased attention to eating disorders in general, and specific therapeutic practices in particular. The possibility of using associations with women as allies is of course located in a specific time and space. The late nineteenth century medical definition of anorexia nervosa as an (extreme) expression of the natural irrationality of female nature is an illustrative example of how such associations for a long period had the very opposite effect, making a preoccupation with food and weight appear a strange activity that affected a small number of emotionally unstable, unusually irrational human beings (Hepworth 1999).

The medical sciences of today have not abolished their attempts at finding the cause of eating disorders in the biology or psychology of the individual woman, but due to the general strengthening of women's position in society, it is likely that these contemporary attempts have a different effect compared to similar attempts in the late nineteenth century. Furthermore, since the 1970s the hegemony of the medical sciences over eating disorders has been challenged by feminist scholars articulating these disorders, not as a reflection of dysfunction in the individual woman, but as a reflection of women's situation in gendered western society (Ohrbach 1978, 1986; Chernin 1986;

Bordo 1993). These feminist interpretations of eating disorders have two implications. First, rather than being a pathology that affects a small and distinct group of abnormal individuals, the dimensional character of feminist theories portrays eating disorders as a concern of all women. Second, feminist theories imply that rather than being the responsibility of the medical sciences only, eating disorders are a political issue that is also the responsibility of society.

Radical definitions by small groups of academic scholars often stay in the corridors of the universities. However, in Sweden (and many other western countries), the feminist articulation of these disorders appears to have gained a rather widespread and general acceptance. 'Media-diagnosis' such as 'anorexia light' to describe the pre-occupation of large numbers of women with food and weight, and statements in public investigations that eating disorders should be understood in relation to a gendered society are indications that women today have become an important ally in placing eating disorders on the public and political agenda, thereby improving resources for research and treatment. In fact, a positive account describing the field of eating disorders as an illustration of the value of defining illnesses as women's illnesses could easily be produced along the following line of argument:

> Before the 1970s there was little focus on eating disorders as most doctors were men and women's disorders had a low status within the medical sciences and society. Then the women's liberation movement began to challenge the male gaze of medicine with its focus on the individual woman, articulating instead the cultural and political dimensions of eating disorders, and demanding more room and respect for women's needs and experiences. In the 1990s, because of this articulation and of a general strengthening of women's position in society, resources for research and treatment of eating disorders have finally started to improve.

But rather than painting such a rosy picture in this chapter I have presented a slightly more ambiguous story. Though women can be valuable associates in attempts to increase the focus on and resources for eating disorders, women are also a highly mouldable resource that can be used in support of various kinds of research and treatment. Associations with women can as easily be made as unmade. When made they can be articulated in a variety of ways. They can be presented as a simple fact that warrants no further analysis. They can be articulated to serve as an ally in demands for increased funding. They can also be articulated in more radical ways, identifying eating disorders as *women's* disorders that need to be understood in relationship to the gendered character of society. However, it is not difficult to displace the interest away from women's situation in society to the biology, physiology or psychology of women.

The examples of different articulations, as presented above, have provided some illustrations of the dynamics of the phenomenon. At least two forces are at play. One is the opportunity to act as spokesperson for the wishes of eating disordered women that presents itself to the advocates of different therapeutic practices – psychotherapy, computerized eating-training and drugs. The other force is the number of opportunities to produce chains of association that make the support of various research and therapeutic practices an obligatory point of passage for those wanting to fight the gendered society.

Both these opportunities depend on the simplicity with which the feminist political articulation of eating disorders can be combined with the pathologization built into the labelling of eating disorders as *disorders* (Bordo 1993). While the feminist analysis contests the casting of the disordered as the other and thus assists in interesting journalists, politicians and the public in these states of un-health, the pathologization built into this label reproduces and keeps up a distinction between the healthy and the sick. As a result, the ultimate say on the causes and treatment of the disordered remains with the representatives of the medical sciences. As the standard medical model has difficulty recognizing culture as a productive force in the development of ill-health, in this medical understanding references to (the gendered) society tend to be reduced to the background, whereas the 'real' causes are sought in the psychology or biology of the individual woman (Bordo 1993).

When discussing the effects of 'the medical model' it is important to realize that it is not only representatives of the medical sciences that might have an interest in maintaining a distinction between sickness and health. For instance, though it can be argued that the dimensional character of the feminist articulation has been important in interesting the public in this field of ill-health, many 'ordered' women would probably protest if no distinction were made between their continuous attempts at controlling their body weight, and the 'disordered' eating behaviour of eating 'disordered' women. Further, the distinction between sickness and health also has its strong financial and political allies.

Political representatives interviewed in this study frequently described eating disorders as women's disorders that concerned all women (and men) in society. But some political representatives who were, or had previously been, in charge of balancing the health care budget also emphasized the importance of making a distinction between sickness and health. Such an emphasis could be interpreted as saying that there is a great difference between being completely obsessed with food and weight and being a bit careful about what one eats and drinks, but it could also be understood as an indication that in order for our health care system to function we need to make a distinction between the healthy and the sick.

Thus, it appears difficult to question whether the ultimate say on causes and treatment of eating disorders should be left with the health care system and the medical sciences. I did not intend to question this situation, either. After all it is the medical sciences and the health care system that are responsible for treating the women whose preoccupation with food and weight has gone much too far. However, what I do want to point out is that, as a consequence of this situation, the feminist articulation of eating disorders loses much of its political power. In spite of the dimensional character of this articulation, the casting of the disordered woman as the other remains.

Furthermore, the question arises whether another consequence of this is not a major effect of the relative success of the feminist articulation of eating disorders has been to identify women as a valuable and highly mouldable resource for advocacy of various therapeutic practices, without demanding much change either in focus or action?

The theme of this book is the casting of the other and as the editors note in their introductory chapter such casting is an integral part of all social life. By exploring the ambiguities of associating women with eating disorders I might myself, for instance, be responsible for one such casting: a casting of advocates of different therapeutic practices as being less interested in improving women's situation in society than in furthering their own interests.

A relevant question to ask at the end of this chapter therefore is how a more radical or at least more consequential articulation of eating disorders as a women's disorder should be produced? I am not particularly interested in trying to answer that question. What I have wanted to explore are only the dynamics that make associations with women a valuable but mouldable resource in support of various causal theories and therapeutic practices. What theories or practices are in the end most favourable for women, whether diagnosed as disordered or not, is an entirely different issue that I find very difficult to answer.

How does one, for instance, judge the attempts of the medical sciences to explain the prevalence of women among those diagnosed with an eating disorder by exploring whether the female hormonal system in general, and the hormonal system of eating disordered women in particular, is more sensitive to dieting than the male one (*Folkhälsoinstitutet och Socialstyrelsen* 1993)? Should it be seen as an attempt to displace the focus away from political dimensions, like the statistics on dieting in the western world? Or should it be greeted with joy as a small contribution to improving the medical knowledge of the workings of the female body? No doubt this knowledge needs to be improved. But what are the consequences of such a focus? Can it be used as an associate to emphasize the construction of the female slender body-ideal? Or will it result in an up-dated version of the nineteenth century articulation of eating disorders as a reflection of the irrationality of female nature? Who knows?

A particular focus of this chapter has, however, been on the Centre. I would therefore like to point out that a feminist articulation of the theoretical arguments and therapeutic practice of the Centre as emancipatory for women and consistent with a feminist/cultural paradigm of eating disorders could easily have been produced. Here, for once, is a causal theory anchored in the medical sciences that rather than pathologizing the character of the individual woman, emphasizes the learned addictive dimension of these disorders, making it possible to explain the predominance of women as a consequence of the statistics on dieting in the western world. Thereby gender can be given a primary and productive, rather than causal and contributory, role in the development of these disorders (Bordo 1993). Here also is a therapeutic practice that, rather than configuring the eating disordered women as suffering from bizarre distortions that must be cured in psychotherapy, present her as a sensible person who can listen to arguments and who wants to take responsibility for herself and be an active participant in her treatment (Fernler and Helgesson, 2001).

On the other hand, what feminist/cultural theories have also pointed out is that women and men are cast by society into rather predefined social roles. Women of today confront two such highly contradictory roles demands to be an autonomous, self-assertive and self-centred individualized woman, and demands to be an adaptable and self-sacrificing traditional woman. One of the few cultural images that manage to combine these highly contradictory roles is the slender female body ideal (Bordo 1993). If some young women confronting these contradictory demands can find no better way to solve this unresolvable conflict than by taking control of their bodies through excessive dieting and exercise, should not society provide psychotherapeutic assistance to help these women to find a more productive way of handling these roles?

I will therefore refrain from joining the club of spokespersons either of women in general, or of women diagnosed with an eating disorder. The reader must judge for herself what – if any – is the true feminist causal explanation and treatment of these disorders. It might also be that the alternative to a casting of the other as disordered (or as the victim of neuroendocrinological processes) is a casting of the other as woman.

Notes

1 The American Psychiatric Association's Diagnostic and Statistical Manual for Mental Disorders.

Press and other documents analysed in this chapter

Aftonbladet:

January 18, 1995. 'Skyll inte på mamma! Forskare: Det är inte mammans fel att dottern blir anorektiker.'
March 14, 1996a. 'Ny larmrapport om idrottstjejers anorexi.'
March 18, 1996b. 'Jag sprang mitt bästa lopp när jag vägde minst.'
March 25, 1996c. 'Vem får henne att börja äta? Anorexicentrum upptäckte vi av en slump.'
April 3, 1996d . 'Idrotten sviker anorektikerna. Anorexin minst lika viktig som dopingen.'
April 3, 1996e. 'Så vill Andersson bekämpa anorexin bland idrottare.'
November 23, 1996f. 'Anorexi-flickor smalare av lyckopiller.'

50   Karin Fernler

March 22, 1997. 'Läkaren som kan bota alla anorektiker.'

Arbetet:

September 9, 1996. 'Lyckad vård ändrar bilden av anorexia. Sjukdomen går att bota.'

Dagens Nyheter:

October 22, 1986. 'Anorexisjuka får ingen vård. 'Situationen är katastrofal'.
December 27, 1994. ' "Anorexi biologiskt". Nonsens att självsvält enbart är psykiskt, hävdar forskare.'
September 9, 1995. 'Elitidrottare drabbas ofta av anorexi.'
March 14, 1996a. '75 patienter i kö – hälften från idrottsvärlden.'
March 14, 1996b. 'Nära att dö i idrottsanorexi. I dag är Rebecca, 15, frisk och levnadsglad. "Jag börjar om löpandet på nya villkor".'
March 15, 1996c. "Hon vårdades som ett psykfall". Mamman till Rebecca, 15, angriper ansvarige läkaren. Får stöd av andra föräldrar.'
March 16, 1996d. 'Psykvård dödsfälla för anorektiker. Fem föräldrar skriver om sina anorexisjuka döttrar som kom ur psykiatrins grepp och återvände till livet.'
March 26, 1996e. ' "Går inte att prata sig ur anorexi". Jenny är kritisk till psykiatrisk behandling. Nu får och ger hon stöd i ny patientförening.'
March 26, 1996f. 'Praktisk träning att äta.'
March 26, 1996g. 'Psykoterapi dominerar.'
November 29, 1996h. 'Läsarnas DN: Bantningsmedel till anorektiker.'
June 6, 1997a. 'Stockholm Debatt: ' "Oacceptabla köer till anorexivården". Desperata föräldrar lämnas i sticket.'
May 29, 1997b. 'Cici började banta som elvaåring.'
May 29, 1997c. 'Anorexi vanlig sjukdom. Kroppsfixering. Var hundrade tonårs-flicka lider av självsvält.'
May 30, 1997d. 'Anorexivård får ökat stöd.'

Expressen:

June 2, 1993. 'Torgny Mogren ger pengar till anorexi-sjuka.'
July 8, 1995. 'Tjejerna dör i vårdkön. Föräldrar vädjar desperat: "Vakna politiker' "
April 25, 1997a. 'Anorexi-sjuka får inte bästa vården.'
April 25, 1997b. 'Landstinget vägrar betala för Lina.'
April 28, 1997c. 'Nu blir det fart på politikerna.'
April 28, 1997d. 'Striden om Anorexicentrum. Docentens kamp för sin sjuka dotter.'
April 30, 1997e. 'Nu får Lina hjälp.'

Fichter, M. M., K. Leibl, W. Rief, Evelyn Brunner, Susanne Schmidt-Auberger, and R.R. Engel (1991) Fluoxetine versus placebo: A double-blind study with bulimic patients undergoing intensive psychotherapy. *Pharmacopsychotherapy* 24 (1991): 1–7.
Fluoxetine Bulimia Nervosa Collaborative Study Group (1992) Fluoxetine in the

Treatment of Bulimia Nervosa. A Multicenter, Placebo-Controlled, Double-blind Trial. *Archiven of General Psychiatry* 49 (February): 139–47.

Foss, I., O. Trygstad, and S. Jettestad (1990) *Fluoxetine Treatment in Bulimia Nervosa: A Prospective Randomized Double-Blind Study.* Paper presented at the Fourth International Conference on Eating Disorders, New York, April.

Goldstein, David J., Michael G. Wilson, Vicki L. Thompson, Janet H. Potvin, Alvin H. Rampey Jr, and The Fluoxetine bulimia nervosa research group (1995) Long-term fluoxetine treatment of bulimia nervosa. *British Journal of Psychiatry* 166: 660–6.

Göteborgsposten:

September 9, 1995. 'Ny behandling räddade Emelie.'
November 23, 1996. 'Cipramil förvirrar anorexia.'

Helsingborgs Dagblad:

September 9, 1996a. 'Så blev de botade från anorexia. "Psykiska problem en effekt av svälten".'
November 23, 1996b. 'Anorektiska flickor sämre av fel medicin.'

Läkemedelsverket (1998) Läkemedelsmonografi Fontex (fluoxetin) – Ny indikation: Bulimia nervosa.
Möller, L. (1979) *Självsvält.* Helsingborg: Wahlström & Widstrand.

Stockholms Läns Landsting:

April 22, 1988. Vård av bulimia och anorexia nervosa inom Stockholms läns landsting. *HSN* 322/49524.
May 21, 1991. Utfördelning av centralt anslagna medel för anorexiateam. *HSN* 9104–0427.
November 23, 1993. Motion 1992:67 av Bosse Ringholm m fl (s) om en samordnande enhet för forskning och behandling av anorexi-/bulimi. *LS* 9211–1340.
August 28, 1995. Förslag till disposition av medel ur folkhälsoanslaget för utvecklings projekt avseende viss behandling av anorexi-bulimi. *HSN* 9507–0665.

Svenska Dagbladet:

September 9, 1995. 'Datorstödd träning skall bota anorexi.'
March 16, 1996a. 'Anorexi är idrottens dolda baksida.'
September 9, 1996b. 'Lyckade försök mot anorexi. Åtta flickor fördubblade matintaget.'
November 23, 1996c. 'Anorektiker fick fel medicin.'
April 22, 1997. 'Anorexiplatser står tomma.'

Wood, A. (1993) Pharmacotherapy of bulimia nervosa – experience with fluoxetine. *International Clinical Psychopharmacology* 8 (1993): 295–8.

3   The construction of the female entrepreneur as the Other

Helene Jonson Ahl

The last decade has seen an increased interest in entrepreneurship from the media, politicians and academics/academia. In the light of recession, unemployment, downsizing and cuts in the public sector, entrepreneurship is acknowledged as the engine of economic growth (Kirchhoff 1994). Research in entrepreneurship confirms the role of small and newly founded companies as job creators (Birch 1979; Case 1992; Davidsson *et al.* 1994).

The Swedish government has responded by designing programmes aimed at stimulating entrepreneurship in the Swedish economy. Special efforts have been made to stimulate women's entrepreneurship. Women have access to special counselling, special loans and additional start-up benefits. The counsellors are women, by design, and the loans are available only to women entrepreneurs. Women are eligible for one year of start-up support as compared to half a year for men. The European Union social fund looks positively at applications for projects specifically aimed at supporting women entrepreneurs.

Women's entrepreneurship has also received increased attention from the research community. Entrepreneurship has been an established research area with its own research journals for about twenty years. The main focus has been on mapping the qualities of the successful entrepreneur, and on factors correlated with business performance. Since the late 1980s, with the increased number of women entrepreneurs, particularly in the US, many papers have been published on women's entrepreneurship. Here a main focus is on how women entrepreneurs differ from men. So, both from practitioners and from academics, attention is focused on women entrepreneurs, a category which was basically invisible twenty years ago. The increased impact of and attention to women's entrepreneurship should be a positive development from an equality perspective. However, the efforts made to strengthen the position of the female entrepreneur may, despite good intentions, produce a contrary result. This chapter argues that:

- The 'entrepreneur' is a male gendered construction in research as well as in practice.
- Women entrepreneurs are constituted as 'the other' and portrayed

as something weaker and in need of special assistance in research as well as in practice. As the entrepreneur used to be 'the other' of the executive, the female entrepreneur is now constituted as 'the other' of the entrepreneur.

- The institution 'female entrepreneurship' is under construction. It puts a label on women entrepreneurs that they did not have twenty years ago, and which is not to their benefit. It has instead become yet another arena for the ongoing reproduction of women's secondary position in society.

The arguments are organized in the following way: first, 'the academic story' which briefly discusses mainstream research on female entrepreneurs, its underlying assumptions and arguments and the way it constructs the female entrepreneur; second, 'the public story', which discusses the increased public interest in female entrepreneurship: the different arguments put forth, the programmes instituted and the resulting construction of the female entrepreneur. Third, I discuss 'the Other's Other'; the coincidence of the glorification of small business at the expense of large corporations, and the female entrepreneur taking on the role of 'Other' which the (male) entrepreneur used to have in relation to the executive.

The academic story

Entrepreneurship research as an academic sub-specialty is a young but rapidly growing field. Research specifically on women's entrepreneurship is even younger, but by the late 1980s and early 1990s, women's entrepreneurship was definitely on the research agenda.[1]

Most of the articles published in English language journals in this field are from the USA. Only around a fifth are from non-English speaking countries. The US studies are (at least explicitly) motivated by the exceptional rise in female entrepreneurship in the United States. Whereas women owned about 5 per cent of businesses in 1970, their share in 1997 was 37 per cent and they are expected to reach 40 per cent by the year 2005. Brush (1997) writes that women today are represented in all types of businesses, even those that were previously an all-male domain like construction and manufacturing. The main concern for the researchers is, however, that women's businesses as yet score lower average figures on performance measured as profitability and growth. The 'problem', or the thing to be explained, in several of the studies is why women entrepreneurs, in spite of their burgeoning numbers, perform less in terms of company size, profit or growth than men do.

Several studies look for signs of overt sex-based discrimination to explain this. The most commonly researched theme is discrimination by moneylenders. Some look for systemic discrimination as, for example, the likelihood of women having less relevant education and less relevant management, industry and entrepreneurial experience. These hypotheses may be traced to liberal feminist thinking – if women were not discriminated against they would perform as men do. Other studies assume that perhaps women have different desires. Such studies typically look for differences between male and female entrepreneurs in values, behaviour and motivation. Motivation and values are measured by standard attitude measurements, as for example the Rokeach value survey.

There is an implicit formula governing much of this research. The dependent variable is company performance measured as sales, growth or profit. The independent variables are usually personal background characteristics of the entrepreneur, such as education, experience, motivation, values systems or management style. The idea is to find differences between men and women – how they are, how they are treated or how they behave – that may explain the differences in performance. Very few differences are found, however. Those that have been found are small, and the within-sex variation is much larger, making between-sex differences less meaningful. In their research review of studies done prior to 1992, Fischer *et al.* (1993) conclude that the hypothesis that women, because of overt or systemic discrimination, or because of lack of motivation or having different values from men, should be less successful as entrepreneurs, receives little or no support. Starr and Yudkin (1996), in a later review, write: 'the research literature to date has found that along many psychological and demographic characteristics, women entrepreneurs are more similar to than different from male entrepreneurs'. My own review of studies from 1982 to 2001 in leading entrepreneurship research journals such as *Entrepreneurship Theory and Practice, Journal of Business Venturing* and *Journal of Small Business Management* confirms their findings; the results of the reviewed studies are as full of null findings and mixed results as found in previous reviews (Ahl 2001).

All in all, a few differences between male and female entrepreneurs have been found, but the similarities are many, many more, and gender ranked well below other factors in its ability to predict performance (Carter *et al.* 1992; Kolvereid *et al.* 1993; Rosa *et al.* 1994). What is consistently shown, however, is that women's businesses are smaller than men's are, they are less profitable and they do not grow as rapidly. The apparent conclusion is either that there are no differences between male and female entrepreneurs explaining performance, or that the 'real' explanatory variables in terms of gender differences have not been found yet. The difference in performance between men's and women's businesses thus remains a riddle to be solved. And research within this tradition continues to search for *the* difference.

When reading these articles from a feminist constructionist perspective, many questions come to the surface. I have organized them below, under three headlines: 'ontological and epistemological assumptions', 'assumptions of causality' and 'the construction of the Other'.

Ontological and epistemological assumptions

Most of the research reported above takes a realist worldview. The world is 'out there' to be discovered and explored. From a realist assumption follow assumptions of 'essence'. Men and women are supposed to have essences to be examined. There is something real that makes you a man or a woman, above and apart from (or as a result of) the reproductive differences. There is further a belief that there is something innate in people that makes them start and grow a company, and this something presumably differs by sex.

One of the basic tenets of constructionist theory is that reality is socially constructed through a process of externalizing your subjective experience as an objective fact and then internalizing the same thing as 'reality'. Previous generations' objectivations that are just 'out there' to be internalized seem particularly objective, factual and unchangeable (Berger and Luckmann 1966). They have become institutionalized. Following from this, there are no special innate masculine or feminine essences. Whatever we call masculine or feminine is something of our own making. Things like courage, caring, listening skills, leadership ability, achievement orientation, family orientation, self-confidence, competitiveness, service-mindedness, persistence, self-efficacy and so on are socially constructed and will differ from one person to another, in one context to another, and from one point in time to another, irrespective of whether you were born with a male or a female body. From this point of view, the innate, stable characteristics that the female entrepreneurship research looks for are very elusive targets.

The research methods may likewise be questioned. The way the reviewed studies find out about reality is typically through mail questionnaires and cross-section studies. Attitude measurements are used to assess value systems and motivation, usually on a Likert scale or similar. Strategy is assessed in similar tests. Networking behaviour is measured by counting the number of contacts on various levels. Discrimination is usually measured by asking respondents questions by mail. The answers are then coded and run through statistical tests. Most typically means and frequencies are reported and compared. Sometimes multivariate techniques are used. In this way a snapshot, *a contextual* picture is taken where the degree to which the different variables correlate with each other is measured. From a constructionist perspective, this way of finding out about the world does not make much sense. If reality is socially constructed, it will be different in different social contexts. The basis for your reality construction is not (only) the particular body you were born with but also how reality was presented to you in your particular family, town, race, culture, school, etc., that is, by the particular institutions in your environment. It is further based on how this particular environment taught you to interpret and make sense of things happening in the world. Cross-section snapshot pictures where one divides the universe into only two groups, based only on bodies, and where one primarily measures means will most likely give a very shallow understanding.

Assumptions of causality

Not only does the research assume that men and women have different innate characteristics like attitudes, values and motivation, these characteristics are also assumed to *explain* behaviour, entrepreneurial strategy and, as a consequence, entrepreneurial performance.

Wicker conducted a review of forty-six empirical studies of attitudinal-behavioural consistency. The result was a big disappointment for scholars advocating causal relationships between attitudes and behaviour: 'Taken as a whole these studies suggest that it is considerably more likely that attitudes will be unrelated or only slightly related to overt behaviours than that attitudes will be closely related to action' (Wicker 1969: 76). Foxall's review of the literature from 1970 to 1979 presented a more optimistic account. The big difference was that factors other than attitudes/values were taken into account, such as

> *personal factors* which include other attitudes, competing motives, verbal, intellectual and social abilities, and *situational* factors such as the actual or assumed presence of certain people, normative prescription of proper behavior, alternative available behaviors ... inspecificity of attitude objects, unforeseen extraneous events and the expected and/or actual consequences of various acts.
>
> (Foxall 1984: 79)

With all these factors added, a picture emerges that is highly situation-specific, and where simple attitudinal-behavioural consistency is very weak. This makes any model attaching importance to the mediating role of pre-behavioural mental processes quite irrelevant. It is the situation and the context that matters.

Behavioural decision researchers Payne, Bettman and Johnson (1992) question not only causality relationships, but also the very existence of stable inner attitudes and values. They write that preferences and beliefs about an object or event of any complexity are constructed, not merely revealed, in the generation of a response to a judgement or choice task. That is, when answering questions on a Likert scale, the attitudes are constructed in the very act of answering the question. It may even be argued that measures of behavioural intention reflect *past* behaviour, and thus serve as a justification for actions taken in the past, more so than as a prediction for the future.

Mary Douglas writes: 'In our experience we only find succession and frequency, no laws or necessity. It is we ourselves who attribute causality' (1987: 11). March and Olsen (1989) present a similar line of reasoning and argue against the 'logic of consequentiality' altogether. According to them we do not act according to some pre-defined values, motivations or rational decisions. We act according to norms and rules, explicit or internalized. We do what we find suitable in the situation and what accords with our personal self-identity conception. They call this the logic of appropriateness. The logic of consequentiality is invoked after the fact, as a way to justify and legitimize action. The logic of consequentiality should be seen as exactly this, and not as something having explanatory value for future behaviour.

Summing up, the reviewed research on female entrepreneurship is looking to find something that most likely does not exist to explain something that anyway cannot be explained by that non-existing entity it is looking for. Which presumably explains the meagre results. It is not, however, an innocent, but unfortunately as yet unproductive, undertaking. It does accomplish things.

The construction of the Other

My conclusion is that the research on women entrepreneurs, in its assumptions, choice of problems, measures and independent as well as dependent variables, constructs the female entrepreneur as 'the Other'. Measures defined by men and applied to men are used to assess women, who almost by definition come out on the weak side. There are at least three ways that this effect is accomplished in the texts.

The first is the choice of dependent variable. The dependent variable is usually performance, measured as size, profit, sales growth or employment growth. Women are found to start smaller businesses, grow their businesses more slowly than men, and to be less profitable, which is not surprising since they favour retail and service businesses which are labour intensive and have a local and highly competitive market. The relevance of the performance measure, as defined, is not questioned, however. Nor are alternative ways of assessing performance discussed. One might, for example, consider long-term duration, liquidation rates or perhaps tax frauds, which should be equally important from a societal perspective.

But size, growth and profit prevail as the standard, and why women's businesses do not perform as men's in these regards and what policies to recommend in order to amend this seem to be the questions that worry policymakers and motivate researchers. This shows how a taken-for-granted performance norm is imposed on women, rendering them inadequate. The result is doubly oppressive, since the majority of men's businesses actually come out on the same 'weak' side as women's in terms of size, growth and profit, but this point is seldom made in the research texts. Davidsson (1989: 209) writes that 'most existing small firms are not characterized by being very entrepreneurial, neither do they grow to any considerable extent'. This is true for male as well as female entrepreneurs. The very few firms that do grow quickly happen to be mostly male owned and will therefore cause the means in measures such as size, growth rate, etc. for male businesses on the whole to be bigger than for females. So, provided that lack of growth is a problem, it is a problem for the majority of all firms, irrespective of the sex of the owner, but the research texts construct it as a female problem. The rhetorical effect is very peculiar. Somehow all men get to be free riders on their few growth-oriented fellow businessmen in these texts, while the women are marked out as the non-growers. Why some men grow their businesses is not explained by how 'men' are, but, surprisingly, it seems perfectly all right to try to explain it by how women are *not*.

The choice of independent variables might also illustrate how a male norm is applied, rendering the female secondary. Entrepreneurship research has produced a picture of the entrepreneur as a person with a high need for achievement, a high need for independence and a certain configuration of his value system. This research has been conducted on men, and the measurements are developed on men.

McClelland's work on need for achievement, for example, which has been very influential in the entrepreneurship literature, focused explicitly on men (McClelland 1961). Stevenson (1990) reports on an early study which explicitly excluded the female survey responses since they might contaminate the results. The resulting construction of the entrepreneur is the stereotypical independent self-made man. This is not an image which fits women (nor indeed many men) very well. The research models 'make little attempt to "discover" the world of the woman as business owner, but impose on her an already structured perception of the world of the business owner based on male centered notions' (Stevenson 1990: 442). Women's experience is not written into the research models; they are only used as research objects. Since male centred notions and standards may not represent the experiences of women entrepreneurs the latter are by implication rendered insufficient.

A third way of demonstrating the secondary position of women is the conclusion, which several authors draw from their results, that women entrepreneurs are different from ordinary women. If women entrepreneurs are similar to male entrepreneurs, the reasoning goes, then they must not be 'ordinary women'. The lack of differences found, some studies speculate, may be explained by the 'self-selection' of the female entrepreneurs studied. They have been found to be achievement oriented, to strive for independence, etc., factors that previously have been attributed to male entrepreneurs. Female entrepreneurs may have been found to be similar to male entrepreneurs because women with relatively 'male' values are those who are attracted to entrepreneurship, or alternatively, they have had to adapt to the (male) values and behaviours in the business world in order to succeed. In a study by Aldrich *et al.* (1989), the authors write that 'the women in the American sample were members of a very male-dominated group, and the women in the Italian sample were taking courses at a male-dominated institution. Thus, we cannot necessarily infer from our results that the gap between the "male" and "female" worlds is closing.' (ibid.: 354). This may be so, but implicit in the text is the assumption that men and women are, or at least should be, different. And if the women are not (different from men, the standard), then there is something unusual about them.

Throughout the studies I reviewed, women entrepreneurs were thought of as 'something else', that is, something else compared to male entrepreneurs. Most of the research on entrepreneurs up until the mid-1980s was done on samples of entrepreneurs that were all or almost all male. Knowledge about entrepreneurs was thus derived from research on men. With the advent of the increase of women entrepreneurs, the tests were repeated, using the same variables for comparison. The construct 'entrepreneur' was taken for granted and perceived as something neutral. The effect was that female entrepreneurs became the exceptions to be explained. They were 'the Other' (de Beauvoir 1949, 1986). The basis for explanation and comparison was a male gendered construction, but thought of as neutral. The notion of 'female' entrepreneurship itself suggested not only that it was related to the unspoken norm of (male) entrepreneurship, but also that it constituted 'something different, something weaker or some unused resource which, at best, may be regarded as a complement to the norm' (Ericsson and Nilsson 1997).

Attempts have been made to construct women's entrepreneurship as a positive alternative. Brush (1992: 16), building on Gilligan (1982), writes that 'women perceive their businesses as "cooperative networks of relationships" rather than separate economic units'. Buttner (2001) advocates a relational frame for the study of women's businesses and finds the women she has studied to be participative and encouraging business leaders. The Good Woman is being portrayed, with many traits similar to the Good Mother. The attempts are a response to the mail norm which does not adequately describe many women's experiences, but by assigning all the good (nurturing, relational, democratic, ethical, etc.) traits to women it leaves the male/female dichotomy intact and does not seriously challenge the male norm. An alternative stereotype to the independent self-made man is created, which is just a different sort of straitjacket, for women as well as for men. The attempts at redeeming women's role as Other are bound to fail, as they are a direct response to the male norm. Without The One there would be no need to construct the Better Other. The One is in the background, firmly established in the position as primary.

The paradox of gender-and-entrepreneurship research is that it looks for 'female entrepreneurship' but does not find it, since such a thing does not exist per se, but is modelled after male entrepreneurship. But in the process of looking, (posing research problems, choosing variables, publishing papers, arranging conferences, etc.) something is *created* that is labelled female entrepreneurship. This something is found to be something different and less than male entrepreneurship. While perhaps aiming at the contrary, the reviewed research about female entrepreneurs contributes to the recreation of women's secondary position in society.

So, while women break established gender barriers and start businesses in record numbers, the academic study of them is framed in such a way as to put them safely in place in a secondary position. There is a parallel public discourse about female entrepreneurs to which I now turn.

The public story

The increased research interest in women's entrepreneurship, motivated by the phenomenal rise of women's enterprises, is very much a US story. From 5 per cent in the early 1970s to approaching 40 per cent today is indeed a remarkable change. Also in Europe, there is, however, increased interest in women's entrepreneurship as evidenced by many public policy initiatives. This is indeed the case for Sweden, but here it cannot be motivated by the rise in the number of female entrepreneurs. In 1980, 25 per cent of businesses in Sweden were women-owned, and historically the number was even higher, but they received very little public attention (Sundin and Holmquist 1989). Twenty years later, the number is about the same but the number of actors who engage in women's entrepreneurship is substantial and the volume of discussion has exploded. Why is this? Two parallel developments in Sweden may have contributed. One is the increased public and government attention to equality questions. The other is the economic crisis of the 1990s, which made the entrepreneur the centre of attraction.

Among the many reasons put forth for paying attention to women's entrepreneurship, I see two main lines of argumentation, which are used separately or together. They are either instrumental, and see women as an unused economic resource, or they build on arguments of equality. Similar arguments are put forward for more women business leaders (see Alvesson and Due Billing (1999) for a discussion). The *instrumental* arguments are as follows:

- **The 'women as an unused resource' argument**
  Economic growth is needed for the nation's welfare. Small companies are taking over the role of large corporations as creators of new jobs. Entrepreneurship and small business creation should therefore be stimulated. Women start businesses as well as men, but their share is not yet half. Women are thus an unused resource in small business and new job creation. Female entrepreneurship should therefore be encouraged.

  Swedish public policy has extended this argument to include women's entrepreneurship as a resource in rural development, or the prevention of rural decline. Many rural areas in Sweden are quickly depopulated, and it is primarily the women who leave. Supporting female entrepreneurship in rural areas may thus accomplish two things. The women get an opportunity to support themselves, and the area gets to keep the women.
- **The 'counter women's unemployment' argument**
  The state needs to cut back public spending to improve its financial balance in order to be eligible for the EMU. Privatizations are seen as a means to accomplish this. Decentralized and less bureaucratic management will improve satisfaction, quality and efficiency, say the advocates. Public health care, day-care, schools, cleaning services, libraries, etc. are suitable candidates. Privatizing these will, however, result in many

unemployed women. Women should therefore be encouraged to continue their operations under private management, or start other businesses.

The *equality arguments* are the following:

- **The 'counter discrimination' argument**
  Women-owned businesses do not represent half of the nation's businesses. If equality ruled, there should be as many women-owned businesses as men-owned. It must be that women who want to start their own businesses are being systematically discriminated against, by, for example, money lenders or by the existence of old boys' networks. Women's businesses must therefore be supported to offset structural discrimination.
- **The 'support the disadvantaged' argument**
  Women who want to start their own business are disadvantaged because of structural/cultural forces in society, resulting in a lower level of self-esteem and less 'business guts'. Women business starters should therefore be encouraged with extra support particularly addressed to the special needs of women.

The programmes offered are numerous, and many actors, public as well as private, are involved. Nutek (Swedish National Board for Industrial and Technical Development) is a central player, but many activities are carried out outside of their control or initiative. Giving a complete picture is beyond the scope of this chapter, but I mention some examples below.

There are 144 resource centres for women in Sweden. They offer advisory services and a variety of programmes designed to help women start businesses, particularly in the rural areas. These were introduced by Nutek and ran for five years. Interestingly, at the same time as Sweden entered a business boom, the public financing of the resource centres was discontinued, giving weight to the instrumental arguments above. Equality arguments should be less sensitive to business cycles.

Nutek commissions research about women entrepreneurs, to increase knowledge about them and make them more visible. Nutek runs a programme designed to encourage female innovators.[2] It also makes available female business advisors for female clients in some of the northern regions in Sweden. The idea is that women would feel more comfortable talking to other women. At *Almi Företagspartner* (also publicly owned), women business owners have access to special loans, not available for men. Unemployed Swedish men who start a business are eligible for six months of unemployment support during the start-up phase. If you are a woman starting a business, however, you are entitled to a full year. These measures draw on both the instrumental and on the equality arguments, particularly the 'support the disadvantaged' argument.

Since Sweden joined the European Union and was able to apply for project financing within the EU's different structure funds – Target 3, Target 4, Adapt, Employment, Equal Opportunity, etc. – there has been a proliferation of programmes supporting women entrepreneurs. Equality between men and women is one of the 'corner stones' of the EU, and chances for project approval improve if a programme addresses these issues.[3]

A public discourse about women's entrepreneurship, which was largely absent twenty years ago, is thus present in today's Sweden. What does this discourse accomplish? How does it portray women? How do actors draw on it?

The measures that are intended to help, in fact define the helpless. Some of the programmes, as for example giving women one year of start-up support instead of six months, produce a picture of women being in greater need of assistance, that is, having less ability than men to successfully get a business going. So do the special loans. It is assumed that women's business ideas will not attract financing on the competitive market as easily as men's. Built into the discourse on enhancing women's entrepreneurship is therefore a construction of women entrepreneurs as the Other, as someone in need of assistance. The 'support the disadvantaged' argument does by the same move produce the disadvantaged.

Nilsson (1997) was commissioned to evaluate the above-mentioned programme with female business advisors to women entrepreneurs in Northern Sweden. She found that both women and men, particularly those in the regular, non-gender specific business advisory services, tended to discount the advice given in this programme. It was as if an advisory system without men involved counted for less. Nilsson shows how the advisory services, contrary to design, recreated patterns of women as being something else, something different and something weaker than men. The established gender regime is thus recreated instead of changed, and equality is not accomplished.

Private actors draw upon the discourse on women's entrepreneurship. A very interesting example of how an organization has co-opted the discourse, and used it for its own purposes, is a study by Beyer (1996), commissioned by *Företagarnas Riksorganisation* (the Swedish small business owners organization) entitled *The Female Entrepreneur Profile*. Beyer surveyed a number of women entrepreneurs to map their business characteristics and personal demographics and to find out what their needs were. The not-so-surprising result was that nothing would help women entrepreneurs more than lower taxes. Lower taxes are what this organization, which is basically a lobby organization, has always worked for. Using 'female' in the title was a new angle, and they were able to attract some fifteen members of parliament to a breakfast meeting when they presented the study.

Other examples of actors successfully drawing on the discourse on female entrepreneurship are the many consultants who run EU-programmes for entrepreneurs. A colleague of mine and I were commissioned to evaluate one of these programmes (Ahl and Samuelsson 2000). It was designed to test the 'empowerment model' in networks of female small business owners, but the consultants settled for the formulation 'primarily female'. Why primarily female? Why not only female? An interpretation of the consultants' answer to this question is that they designed it for women, primarily since this was their preferred target group but also since chances then were greater for project approval. However, they did not want to close the door for willing applicants who happened to be of the other sex. The formulation 'primarily female' did thus provide necessary resources both in terms of money from the EU and in terms of participants willing to take the programme. Targeting only women was not legitimate *enough* though. By including men, additional resources were added in terms of perceived legitimacy by some of the sponsors, and of course also in terms of potential participants. Having some men present in the programme also seemed to add legitimacy in and of itself. This is an instance where the discourse on female entrepreneurship is turned into a resource, while simultaneously affirming women's secondary position in relation to men.

What conclusions to draw? The first is that a new public discourse, on female entrepreneurship, is in process, and that it produces a picture of women entrepreneurs as secondary, as the other of the (male) entrepreneur. The second is that this discourse on women entrepreneurs is a useful resource to be drawn upon to obtain resources, while leaving the primary position of the (male) entrepreneur unchallenged. The third conclusion is that the discourse and the programmes and activities are creating a new institution of female entrepreneurship. This institution may not be to the benefit of women entrepreneurs. Contrary to intentions, it recreates the established gender regime. Women entrepreneurs are made visible but kept in place. The academic and the public discourse thus go hand in hand.

The Other's Other

The increased interest in women's entrepreneurship coincides with the economic development of the last two decades, which made the entrepreneur the centre of attraction. Before that, entrepreneurs, entrepreneurship and small business were positioned as marginal, in economic theory as well as in daily discourse. It was the big corporations and the executives that enjoyed the centre position.

Edith Penrose wrote in *The Theory of the Growth of the Firm* in 1959 that large firms have so many competitive advantages over small, or new, firms that, theoretically, there should be no room in the economy for entry or growth of new firms. However,

> [w]e have seen that even under the most favorable external conditions imaginable the rate of growth of an individual firm is limited and that no firm can take advantage of all possible profitable opportunities for expansion. It follows from this that the fact that large firms have a competitive advantage over small firms in every type of production is not

sufficient to ensure that they will actually be in a position to act on their advantage. If, therefore, the opportunities for expansion in the economy increase at a faster rate than the large firms can take advantage of them and if the large firms cannot prevent the entry of small firms, there will be scope for continued growth in size and number of favorably endowed small firms, some of whom will themselves enter the 'large' category in time. I propose to call these opportunities for small firms the interstices in the economy. The opportunities of small firms are thus composed of those interstices left open by the large firms which the small firms see and believe they can take advantage of.

(Penrose 1995: 222)

If successful, however, the small firms will either grow into large firms, or get absorbed by large firms. The entrepreneurial firm is here positioned as marginal, as a passing phenomenon. The entrepreneur himself (it was a he also in Penrose's text) was some twenty or thirty years ago seen as a loner, a genius perhaps, but an outsider. Being a business owner had a low moral status. It was the equivalent of choosing to publicly display a greedy, self-interested, egotistic character. The entrepreneur was also assumed to be vulnerable to tax-fraud and the exploitation of others – not exactly a socially desirable position to be in. The desirable position was to join a large corporation, or, even better, work for the public sector. The heroes of the times were the executives, not the entrepreneurs. The 1980s saw the height of the glorification of the executives with Iacocca's autobiography in the US, with Jan Carlsson's in Sweden and many others.

Then the real estate industry and the banks crashed, Saddam Hussein invaded Kuwait, the yuppies sold their Porsches and the world no longer looked the same. Big business lost its glory, and small business took it over. From being a loner and a suspect, the entrepreneur entered the scene as the saviour. The executives – both private and public – were the ones taken to court for fraud and embezzlement.

Today, entrepreneurship is regarded as the engine of the economy. There are entrepreneurship divisions in the big universities, there are universities specializing in entrepreneurship, and there are public programmes devoted to stimulating entrepreneurship. Entrepreneurship magazines abound. The present Swedish government created a new 'näringslivsdepartement' (Ministry of Trade and Industry) with not one but two ministers, one with special responsibility for small businesses. Starting a business today has become something brave and honourable, whereas working for the public sector, with the current cutbacks, is seen as a dead-end journey.

There was a certain gendering to the construction of the entrepreneur thirty years ago. As the entrepreneurial firm was 'the Other' of the large corporation, the entrepreneur was 'the Other' of the executive. He was still a man, but he was different. He was a loner, marginal, with certain weaknesses. Today the notion of the entrepreneur has changed, and it has, as described in the previous sections, a different 'Other', namely the female entrepreneur.

Puxty (1993) points out that Saussure's language theory may shed some light on how this works. Words and sentences must be understood not separately, but within a *system* of words according to Saussure. The language is this total system. Each word in the system has a meaning only because we all agree that it has one. Saussure calls the concept that the word refers to the *signified*. The word itself is called the *signifier*. We make sense of the system of arbitrary signifiers through their difference from other signifiers, so language is only meaningful through difference. This goes for the signifieds as well. Puxty writes: 'each signified has its own conceptual space. Each signified inches out others when a space is required for it. Equally, in the absence of a signified, the conceptual space of signifieds closes in to fill the gap. However, signifieds are not "things represented by the words"' (1993: 123). And further: 'The concepts are purely differential and defined not by their positive content but negatively by their relations with the other terms of the system' (Saussure, quoted in Puxty 1993: 123).

A signifier/signified needs another one, which it is not, to give it meaning. It used to be that the entrepreneur was the other of the executive. Now the entrepreneur is centre stage and a gap is created for another other. This conceptual space is here inched out by the female entrepreneur. Add Derrida's (1978) concept of *différence* to the analysis, where what is made other is always made secondary, is suppressed, is not only different but deferent, and the effects discussed earlier seem both clear and inevitable. The female entrepreneur was invisible, is now made visible but is constructed as *different* from the male entrepreneur. Looking for gender differences is the explicit *raison d'être* for most of the academic research discussed earlier, and gender differences motivate the design of the public programmes. Observing difference is bound to result in the designation of deference. The entrepreneur used to be the deferent party. The female entrepreneur now fills this role. She is made the Other's Other.

Invisible or marginalized? Which is preferable?

I argue in this chapter that the recent interest in female entrepreneurship as seen in research and public policy might be counterproductive. Research on female entrepreneurs does, by its insistence on looking for differences between men and women, its assumptions of essences, and its choice of research questions and variables, cast women as 'the Other' of (male) entrepreneurs and contributes to the recreation of women's secondary position in society. Public policy for women entrepreneurs paints a picture of women as something weaker, something different and something in need of special assistance. Programmes for women entrepreneurs tend to sidetrack women. The established gender regime is thus recreated, instead of changed.

The discourse on female entrepreneurship is co-opted by private actors, and used as a resource for obtaining attention, legitimacy, funding or other resources, while reaffirming women's secondary place. The great irony of the talk about women as a resource in entrepreneurship is that the talk itself has become a resource.

The recent discourse about women's entrepreneurship coincides with a change in the conceptualization of the entrepreneur from a marginal figure to the hero of our times. The construction of the female entrepreneur has filled the space for 'the Other' in the discourse that male entrepreneurs used to have in relation to the executive. The result is the marginalization of female entrepreneurship.

To end this chapter on a more positive note, I should add that the research on women entrepreneurs has produced at least two very important results. First, it has made the fact that there are indeed entrepreneurs who are women visible. Second, it has laid bare the male norm for entrepreneurship and shown its limitations. It has been found to fit women poorly, and with just a small stretch of thought it is apparent that it fits most men poorly as well. Women's experiences need to be written into the research models to better describe the experiences of entrepreneurship and small business ownership (Stevenson 1990). The public/private dichotomy, which is only possible as long as women are assumed to do the unpaid domestic work, needs to be abandoned for this to be achieved. Put simply, men too should be asked questions about the problems of balancing work and family. Entrepreneurship research needs to be re-thought, and the new research models applied equally to men and women entrepreneurs. As Hirdman (1992) puts it, segregation is the basis for hierarchy. Without segregation, there can be no hierarchy. The only way of avoiding the continued marginalization of women in entrepreneurship research is to avoid the one-sided focus on sex-based differences.

Entrepreneurship scholars have struggled with 'entrepreneur' and found it a cumbersome, imprecise and hard to define construct of little analytical value. Using alternative concepts fitting the particular research questions such as 'small business owner/managers, solo-entrepreneurs, fast-growth firms', etc., is advocated (Hornaday 1990). While fully agreeing, I would also apply the same line of reasoning to the constructs 'woman' and 'man'. Instead of looking for differences between the sexes, as if an essential 'woman' and 'man' existed, attention should be given to local and situational circumstances. Research with less universal aspirations might actually be more rewarding and produce more useful knowledge.

As far as public policy goes, this chapter might serve as a warning to the designers of programmes targeted specifically at women. While the instrumental arguments for such programmes, here labelled 'women as an unused resource' or 'counter women's unemployment' seem to carry most weight in instituting programmes for women entrepreneurs, the designs of the programmes are based on equality arguments, particularly the 'support the disadvantaged' argument, which by the same act produces the disadvantaged and puts women safely in place in a secondary position. The programmes may or may not help individual women – this paper is not an effectiveness evaluation – but even if the programmes ought to be changed there will be resistance. The discourse behind the programmes fuels a support industry comprised of public and private institutions as well as private small business consultants, largely supported by EU money. There are thus vested interests in keeping the discourse on disadvantaged women going.

This leaves politicians working for equality in a 'Catch-22' situation. One might conclude that one-sex-only programmes, for men *or* women (mainstream support, which is the bulk of the money, goes primarily to men's businesses) are not desirable, but it may also be that using public money to support entrepreneurship is not desirable either. Stimulating entrepreneurship is, in a way, a contradiction in terms. Such a libertarian move might, however, result in women's entrepreneurship falling into oblivion again. A counter-move might be to name support given to men's businesses as exactly that – support to men's businesses. This reveals the false gender neutrality of 'entrepreneurship', unmasking it as a male construction. Supporting men as men is not reasonable within today's equality discourse, and the male entrepreneur's primary position as The One is thereby challenged.

Acknowledgements

I want to thank the editors for insightful and thought-provoking comments which have greatly improved this article, and I thank Marta Calás for turning my attention to Edith Penrose and the topic of the Other's Other.

Notes

1 See Brush 1992, Fischer *et al.* 1993 Starr and Yudkin 1996, for useful overviews.
2 See www.nutek.se for more information, also in English.
3 Note that even if there are many programmes and much talk on supporting female entrepreneurship, the amount of money earmarked for women is but a fraction of the total amount spent supporting Swedish businesses and Swedish entrepreneurs. If the majority of the money goes to men is an empirical question, but given the politics and industry structure of Sweden, I think it is a very safe guess.

4 Keeping the veil of otherness
Practising disconnection

Valérie Fournier

Ideas of difference and otherness have been central to feminist and post-colonialist debates and have attracted much attention in contemporary social policy and theory (Hetherington and Lee 2000). In a western world concerned to embrace diversity and multi-culturalism, it has become *de rigueur* to stand for all-embracing inclusion and recognition (Charles Taylor 1992). Under such inclusionary embrace, otherness seems to dissolve into a play of differences to be celebrated or remedied. Thus in the discourse of recognition, otherness is imagined either as an unfortunate position (a 'less' or lack) from which the Other no doubt wants to be saved, or as a resource (a 'more') to be preserved, cultivated, and added to the range of skills, cultural artefacts and experiences that make up the economic and social wealth of organizations or nations (as in the discourse of diversity popularized in the management literature, or of multi-culturalism 'our' western nations are keen to embrace). For example, women's otherness within the context of work organizations has been imagined as a 'lack' (of confidence, or assertiveness) for which help is at hand in the forms of various special training or support facilities; or as an additional set of skills ('soft skills') that will make a valuable addition to organizations' resources. In all cases, otherness calls for examination. It is assumed that if we could only break it open, strip the veil of otherness, differences could be understood, nurtured, or remedied, and the 'Other' could join 'us', maybe even be grateful for the privilege.

When these politics of recognition are couched in terms of liberal democratic principles of equality and justice, there seems to be little ground to argue against attempts to reach out to the other, to invite it/her/him in. However, this urge to recognize and include difference also has disturbing effects. Politics of recognition rely on a process of translation through which otherness is flattened out into a system of differences that can be accommodated, managed as various degrees of the same. The aim of this chapter is to explore some of these effects and to suggest a way of thinking about otherness that puts a stop to its dissolving into a play of difference and sameness. Thus I want to establish some disjunction between difference and otherness, and suggest that we could think about otherness as a 'not' rather than a 'more' or 'less'. Whilst difference invites comparison, connection, and evaluation, otherness is defined by the disconnection of the 'not' (Mark Taylor 1993), its resilience to be caught by a name, its under-determinacy (Serres 1991). And if under-determinacy is one of the conditions of 'otherness', versatility is another. For the 'Other' can only remain a 'not' by continuously shifting grounds, by withdrawing from the categories of difference within which it is framed, and moving 'somewhere else'. Otherness is a contextual matter. Unlike difference, it cannot be held to a position on a common grid of deviation and sameness. Rather it slips away under attempts to grab it as something, to name it. To remain a 'not' requires movement and versatility.

The discussion of otherness in this chapter is inspired by an ethnographic study of women farmers in Italy conducted in spring 1999. The experience of these women, and their position of multiple otherness, throws into relief the constructed and contextual nature of otherness, its versatility and under-determinacy. These women were others in many different ways: for example as 'peasants' in a country where most aspire to become part of the urban bourgeoisie, as women in a male dominated farming community, as 'farmers in their own right' rather than 'farmers' wives', as advocates of 'sustainable agriculture' against extensive commodity farming. And to a large extent, it is this otherness that attracted me to them. However, the women farmers' engagement with their otherness was ambivalent. Thus whilst they would at times deploy the above lines of division to position themselves as other (e.g. as woman, as farmer), in other contexts, they refused to settle in these positions. For example, they were at times eager to speak about how their 'womanhood' placed them on the margins of the farming community, but they would at other times shrug off that name as an irrelevance, a position they were not to be held to. Instead they became the 'peasant' Other of the urban majority, or the 'educated' Other of the farming community, or the 'entrepreneurial' Other of the 'apathetic farmers', and so on. Their otherness was not up for grabs, be it as 'peasant' or as 'woman'; it resisted naming by continuously shifting grounds.

The experience and practice of otherness of these women suggest first that 'otherness' is not (always) a passive state of victimhood to which the Other is condemned by a dominant majority (of say male farmers or an urban aspiring society in this case). As will be illustrated later, the women farmers at times actively participated in constructing their otherness through discursive and material practices of disconnection. Second, their otherness was in some contexts to remain just other, something not to be comprehended by categories of difference we may want to throw at them in our urge to include. Third, otherness can only remain other, indifferent, by being on the move, reconstituting itself in different ways, recoiling from one category and hiding behind another. Fourth, otherness is not only multiple and contextual but also unpredictable; its versatility is not limited to the divisions that have been imagined in modern social science (Munro 1997) but can be crafted out of local material in myriad ways.

In what follows, I start by discussing how the women farmers practised, constructed and experienced their multiple otherness. The first section locates these women within the various positions of otherness they are seen to occupy; the second section illustrates how they actively cultivate their 'otherness' through practices of disconnection; in the third section it is argued that although the participants could and did invoke many lines of otherness, they did not settle in any but rather used these positions flexibly. Their otherness was not to be 'framed', captured under a name but remained 'other' through its versatility, its ability to transform itself and move somewhere else. In the final section of this chapter, I discuss the implications of this study for the way in which we conceptualize the 'Other' in social sciences. In particular, the stories of these women suggest that the liberal urge in social science and social policy to grant recognition by translating the Other into a series of differences to be remedied or celebrated may not always be welcome or warranted. In order to stop 'otherness' being flattened out into degrees of sameness and difference, or 'more' or 'less', I propose to establish a distinction between 'otherness' and 'difference', and argue that 'otherness' may be best conceptualized as a 'not' to remain veiled, rather than as a 'difference from' to be invited, managed, or celebrated.

Otherness in the field

The ethnographic study of women farmers in Italy reported here was motivated by a search for otherness of some sort, a search for alternative ways of organizing to those found in large public and private sector organizations and commonly encountered in organization studies. Farming offered an interesting ground for exploring alternative modes of organizing as it is a sector that has been neglected by organization studies, and remains an oddity within western capitalist production systems. Thus even in countries such as the UK where agriculture has undergone extensive structural change and integration, it remains dominated by relatively small family units (Pile 1990; Whatmore 1991; Sachs 1996). This concentration of activities around a large number of small family units is even more marked in Italy, and Southern European countries generally (Ventura 1994; Fanfan 1998).[1]

The focus of the study on women farmers serves to articulate another line of 'otherness', this time around gender. Agriculture tends to be represented as a world dominated by patriarchal relationships, often reproduced through the 'family farm' (Whatmore 1991; Sachs 1996). If men own most of the land and control most of the farms globally,[2] women's work – often in their role as 'farmer's wife' or 'farmer's daughter' – plays an essential role in the survival of farms (Sachs 1996). Women are often represented as the silent Other or 'silent heroes' (Inhetveen 1998) in rural sociology, their contribution effaced by the official categories used in national surveys or work and employment (Lagrave 1987; Whatmore 1991). The women farmers in the study occupy a more ambivalent position than that suggested by the image of the 'silent Other'. They are part of a growing number of female farm owners in Italy;

indeed this 'feminization' is a distinctive feature of Italian agriculture (Ventura 1994; Tazza 1997; Schirinzi 1998).[3]

The coupling of 'woman' and 'farmer' has been used in some feminist theory (e.g. ecofeminism or environmental feminism; Merchant 1980; Agarwal 1992) to construct yet another line of 'otherness', this time defined around a re-articulation of agriculture away from commodity production and towards sustainable development. Thus it has been suggested that women play a leading role in the development of alternative forms of agriculture that draw upon bioregionalism (e.g. organic farming, the production of local/ typical products), and a broader conceptualization of agriculture to include not just 'production' but also the direct transformation and sale of farm products, education, agrotourism, and the preservation of local heritage (Ventura 1994; Whatmore 1994; Wells 1998).

This alignment between women's participation and alternative forms of agriculture is also reproduced in social policy, for example through EU and Italian government's funding for women in agriculture, and by trade union policies (Whatmore 1994). In particular, the association between women and sustainable development is central to the way in which the *Coordinamento per l'Impreditoria Femminile* presents itself and the activities of its members. The *Coordinamento per l'Impreditoria Femminile* (henceforth *Coordinamento*) is the women's branch of the major farmers' union in Italy (the *Confederazione Nazionale Coltivatori Diretti*, or *Coldiretti* for short). The study reported here was sponsored by the *Coordinamento*, to which all participants belonged. The fieldwork consisted essentially of participant observation conducted in the spring of 1999 in twelve women's farms selected by the *Coordinamento* to represent different regions of Italy (Lazio, Umbria, Basilicata and Piemonte). Each visit lasted a week to ten days, a period during which I participated in farm and domestic work, was involved in the hosts' social and family lives, and taken to innumerable trade union meetings. In addition to these twelve farms, eight others were visited for shorter periods, typically of a day or half a day, as hosts were keen to introduce 'the researcher from England' to other women farmers they knew, or had been asked to 'send her round'. Details about the participants' biography and farms are given in the appendix to this chapter; however, it is worth making a few general points here. Most were sole owners of their farms (only four were co-owners with their husbands, and two sisters jointly owned a farm) and all worked on the farm full time, often with occasional help from family members and seasonal workers, and more rarely a few full time workers. The farms in the study were of similar size to the average Italian farm (about 7.5 hectares) and were involved in a wide range of activities, from dairy to cereals, sugar beets, fruits and vegetables, olives and agrotourism. Whilst the majority (sixteen) had inherited the farm from their parents (or parents in law in two cases), the ways in which and extent to which they 'chose' to become farmers were highly diverse. Five had been brought up on the farm and had always expected to take it over. Seven came from farming families but on getting married had moved away from their parents' farms, either to have children or to work somewhere else. After a few years, they 'returned' to farming, often by setting up their own small farm. Finally, for eight of the participants, becoming a farmer marked a major life transition which for some was a planned move out of urban lives and careers towards a 'more peaceful and healthy' life, and for others had been unexpected. Thus four had been studying at university and preparing for different careers when their father died unexpectedly, a point at which they decided to abandon their studies and take over the family farm.

In this short preface to the study, I have outlined various lines of division commonly deployed in rural sociology and agricultural policy (and as we'll see women farmers themselves, occasionally) that serve to position women farmers as the sometimes celebrated, sometimes disparaged Other: as 'farmers', they are the Other of an Italian (western) society that since the Second World War at least has tended to privilege employment in modern organizations; as 'women' they are the Other of a patriarchal farming community; as 'women farmers', they are often represented as embodying 'other' forms of agriculture. The following two sections explore how the participants positioned themselves along these divides. The discussion is articulated around two main themes: first, the active construction of otherness through various practices of disconnection, and second, its contextual and versatile nature.

Cultivating otherness, practising disconnections

The participants did at times claim for themselves the various positions of 'Other' in which they are located by modern society and social science. Below I explore with a few examples how they invoked these divisions, but also enrolled space and their body to practise disconnection.

The women in the study never failed to invoke and lament the images of backwardness and the low status attached to farming in Italian society. They often used the term *contadino* (a term which in contemporary usage has the same disparaging connotation as the English 'peasant') to establish the divide that kept them apart from the urban aspiring majority.[4] Thus a common topic of conversation was the neglect the Italian government had always shown for agriculture, and the contempt Italian society at large displayed for farmers ('peasants') and their activities. They either heroically positioned themselves as the last bastion holding the fort of Italian agriculture, or more modestly, as doing Italy's 'dirty work' by feeding its people. One way in which they conjured up their 'otherness' as 'peasants' was by invoking the 'mass exodus' from rural areas and agriculture, to the more secure income, higher social status, and 'modern lifestyle' offered in towns and cities (a trend which has recently become a central concern in the Italian government's agricultural policy, INIPA 1999). Many of them took some pride in holding on to rural life against the tide. The desertion of rural areas was maybe most evident and most commonly invoked in Basilicata, in the south of Italy. Mina, who ran a fruit farm in the coastal area of Basilicata, never missed an opportunity to stress that 'she' was 'still' living in the country, whilst pointing out the many farmhouses in the area that lay abandoned as their owners had moved to modern houses in the nearby town. The feel of desertion was even more striking in the hills of Basilicata, where Roberta had a very small farm she kept with the help of her sister and elderly mother:

> The road from the coastal plain to the hills of Basilicata was dotted with small hamlets and farmhouses, all abandoned and in a serious state of dilapidation. Roberta's farm is located in a small hamlet of about ten farms, the first one since driving the 30 kilometres or so from the coast, that had not been entirely deserted. According to Roberta, her mother and her sister, agriculture has always been the main economic activity in the area, but it is one which is becoming impossible and that many young people are fleeing because of the lack of adequate facilities, the lack of employment opportunities, and the sheer difficulty of living off agriculture in the area. Any viable form of agriculture or related development (such as agrotourism) is made impossible by the lack of water (water pipes have not reached the mountainous areas of Basilicata, a 'disgrace' which never fails to trigger a stream of insults directed at politicians when mentioned, and which I am urged to reveal to the world), and the poor road system.
>
> (Fieldnotes, Roberta)

If their spatial isolation was at times a cause for lament, it was at others a resource to be deployed in cutting themselves off from the urban world. For example, Francesca made much of the 'remoteness' of her farmhouse to perform her disconnection from the urban life she had left over ten years ago. Her farm was indeed isolated, it lay in the Umbrian hills, a twenty-minute drive away from the nearest town, and two kilometres from her nearest neighbours, an elderly farming couple. Francesca was keen to present herself as a social recluse, enjoying the 'peace and quiet' of living on her own with her 16-year-old daughter (her husband left her four years previously), wilfully severing connections from town. She talked repeatedly about how the remoteness of the farm helps 'keep people away', 'people won't come to visit because the farm is so difficult to get to'.

This divide between 'peasant' and 'urban' worlds was also commonly invoked in the participants' accounts of becoming farmers. For example, Angela, Cecilia and Albina who had got back to farming after a few years at home to raise children, set their 'occupational choice' against those available in towns such as 'getting an office job', thus reminding us that they had repudiated what would have been the preferred option for the majority (for a combination of reasons such as wanting to work in the open air, missing farming, wanting to be their own boss). Even those who had always been farmers, and according to their own accounts never considered doing anything else, enrolled some division between rural and urban ethics to explain their 'choice':

> Silvia says that she has never thought of doing anything else than working on the farm. On several occasions, she evokes the sense of duty and responsibility toward the family 'prevalent in rural areas', which she contrasts to the 'selfish individualism' of the cities. She explains that she could never have conceived of not taking on the family farm, as this would have been a betrayal of the sacrifice her family had made.
>
> (Fieldnotes, Silvia)

Another way in which some of the women used the peasant / urban divide to position themselves as the 'misunderstood Other' was to invoke the incredulity of their city friends. For example, the eight women who had abandoned careers or studies in cities for new lives in farming all described how the move had elicited nothing but incredulity and contempt from their 'city' friends. Whilst in some cases this incredulity had led to exasperation and the cutting of contacts with people from the city, in others it was actively cultivated, and in the case of Silvia and a few others, cultivated on their body. Silvia went out most evenings to meet her (mainly non-farming) friends in town, for a drink or a meal. However, 'going out' for Silvia involved more than driving the few kilometres that separated the farm from the town; it involved over an hour of body work, of washing, dressing and applying make up. From looking like a 'peasant' in the cow shed (there she was dressed in scruffy jeans, wellington boots, a long baggy shirt, a head scarf 'to keep her hair from smelling', and gloves 'to protect her nails'), she emerged as a highly sexually charged woman: high heel shoes, tight short skirts, revealing tops, heavy make-up, painted nails and her long black hair loose on her back. Whilst the change in appearance between working on the farm and going out for a drink is maybe unremarkable (if it was not for its magnitude in this case) what is of interest is the obvious pleasure Silvia took in the transformation, in using her exaggerated femininity to cultivate the incredulity of her friends. Indeed, looking at Silvia while she was 'out', it was difficult to imagine that she was a farmer. On a couple of occasions, Silvia told me 'tell them I'm really working on the farm, they never want to believe me' at which point Silvia and her friends engaged in what seemed to be a ritual 'no you're not', 'yes I am'. The interesting things about these exchanges was the way in which they served to both call up Silvia's otherness as farmer, and mark it as something that could not be comprehended, that remained beyond the grasp of her friends. Thus she never talked about her life on the farm during these evenings out; her 'farmness' was only there as a mark of absence, something that was conjured up by its incongruity next to Silvia's sexualized body, but that was to remain just Other.

In all these accounts, being a farmer is presented in terms of opting out of urban lives for those who had had one, or refusing to be tempted by its privilege, looser morality, higher status and 'easier lifestyles', a choice that is actively constructed as being 'beyond the grasp' of the urban majority. In some cases, they had actively sought to cut themselves off from the modern world of employment to which Italian society allegedly aspired. They were not waiting to be invited to join the privileges or add to the diversity of the modern organizational world, nor to be understood. In fact at times they seemed to rejoice in the fact that the urban majority could not understand them.

However, if many clearly enacted some separation between themselves and the 'urban aspiring majority' by invoking a mass exodus, the comfort of the city, or the incredulity of their friends, they also performed themselves as the 'Other' of the farming community. These disconnections from 'farmers' were imagined by enrolling various lines of division. For example, the participants' education or femininity marked them out as Other. Many had had difficulty being recognized as 'a farmer' and echoed Lidia's feeling of exasperation: 'You have to be half covered in shit to them to be a farmer'. 'Them' in this case referred to the tax inspectors who visited farms occasionally to check that those registered as *coltivatori diretti* (farmers) were really involved in farmwork rather than merely owing land. This evaluation was important as it affected the tax rate to be paid on the land. However, the inspectors' evaluations were condemned by many women as the criteria used reproduced the image of the 'farmer' as someone who 'just works in the field, speaks only in dialect, and is dirty' (Natalia), an image that many repeatedly conjured up, and distanced themselves from. For example, Lidia had just been refused the status of *coltivatori diretti* because on the inspector's impromptu visit, he allegedly said she did not look like a farmer (according to Lidia because she was too clean and was wearing a mini-skirt).

If some invoked their femininity or education (or at least the fact they spoke Italian rather than dialect) as markers of otherness, another common motif was to portray themselves as going against the wave of modernization and commodification that had allegedly transformed (and 'ruined') Italian agriculture since the Second World War. Farmers were presented as betrayers who had sold out the main assets and resources of Italian agriculture to join the bandwagon of modernization. Many suggested that farmers themselves had contributed to the demeaning of rural traditions and values by aspiring to an urban lifestyle:

> Although all Italians have peasant origins, they all try to deny them, they all want to go and work in offices and factories. They're all *nouveaux riches* with no culture, no traditions.
>
> (Francesca)

The participants were not only critical of the 'urban' lifestyle that farmers had sought to imitate but more importantly of the fact that they had embraced (and in many cases benefited from) the modernization and commodification of agriculture. For example, many argued that by privileging mass production since the Second World War, Italian agriculture had destroyed local products, knowledge and the environment. They continuously bemoaned the standardization and poor quality of farming products. However, their attachment to local traditions was not to be romanticized into some nostalgic attachment to the past or to nature. Rather it was also made to signify their entrepreneurialism. All participants were keen to be recognized as 'entrepreneurs'[5] and indeed were well versed in the language of markets and competition, a language they commonly deployed to invoke the threat from other Southern European countries and South America where similar products could be produced more cheaply and the hotter climate allowed for earlier production (which attracted a premium price on the market). Their effort to develop 'new' products and services drawing upon local heritage (making products at home and selling them directly to shops or on the farm, arranging school visits to the farm, organic farming, agrotourism) was set against the 'apathy' of the farming community and was (at least partly) a measure of their own innovation and responsiveness to the market. What many referred to as their 'entrepreneurial skills' was again something which defined them as Other as they invoked the 'apathy' of farmers, and the prevalent 'mentality' of expecting state and European subsidies to 'carry on doing the same thing'.

Finally, the participants were also keen to distance themselves from another position which seemed too close for comfort, that of the 'farmer's wife'. For example, Silvia as a member of the local *Coldiretti* council and Association of milk producers, attended regular farmers' meetings. She talked about how much she resented being the only woman at these meetings, but later acknowledged that there were a few other women. However, 'they' attended as 'farmers' wives' rather than as 'farmers in their own right'. For Silvia and many others, this image of the 'farmer's wife' was articulated around notions of 'having it easy', 'not dirtying their hands', and 'only attending meeting as an excuse to get out of the house', all markers of their own difference.

In this section, I have discussed how the participants constructed their otherness by invoking various lines of division available in their particular context. By talking about their 'construction of otherness', I do not want to suggest that the participants made up these divisions or their positions of 'the Other'. Some rural areas, especially in the south, were indeed becoming deserted; Lidia and others were indeed refused the status of *coltivatori diretti* that would have enabled them to pay lower tax; and at some of the farmers' meetings I attended with some of the participants, many of the (mostly men) farmers did argue (with banging fists) for their rights to subsidies to 'carry on doing the same things'. The participants did not construct their otherness out of nothing, nor were they its only producers. However the concern here is with their deployment of these divisions, and the practices of disconnections they engaged in to construct their otherness. Whilst I have so far discussed the various divisions along which they positioned themselves as Other, in the next section I explore the contextual and temporal nature of these divisions.

The contextual and shifting nature of otherness

Whilst the participants could and did invoke many lines of otherness, they did not settle in any, but used these various divisions flexibly. Indeed they would sometimes escape the 'otherness' within which they were framed, through for example by questions or forms of address. by moving somewhere else, becoming 'not . . . that Other' but something else, refusing to have their otherness named. Thus they may be 'farmers/peasants', but they were not just 'field workers', they were also entrepreneurs running a business. However, if asked about the managerial or administrative aspect of their work, they would remind me of their 'love of nature and working in the fields'. When I echoed back their 'attachment to working on the land or with nature' that some had expressed so fondly, they maybe pointed to the hard work they had to put in, the financial pressures under which they were operating. When addressed as women, they would sometimes (and with a degree of irritation) talk about the irrelevance of the category. Below I illustrate the contingent and versatile use of division by discussing their flickering gender positioning.

Participants were adept at playing the 'now I'm a woman, now I'm not' game described by Riley (1988). They moved in and out of gender according to context. At times, gender could certainly acquire prominence. For example, many engaged in various forms of playful 'man bashing', some of which was no doubt for my own benefit. Maybe more fundamentally, most invoked 'being woman' to articulate the type of farming they wanted to be attached to. Thus most did at some point talked about the value they placed on producing 'healthy' food, on preserving typical products and regional food, and contrasted their commitment to a form of agriculture that respected 'local heritage', to the 'low cost, low quality' commodity production that had been developed by 'male farmers'. For many, it was mainly in their roles as 'mothers' that they had come to embrace sustainable agriculture. They wanted their children to be brought up in a peaceful and healthy environment, they wanted to 'know' what they fed their children. Indeed, many of the women who abandoned city lives and careers to start their own farm explained that they had done so partly for their children. And most of them were proud to stress that much of the food consumed at home came from the farm, the kitchen garden, the farmyard.

This alignment between being 'woman' and some commitment to a form of agriculture that respects the environment and the quality of food was maybe most forcibly articulated by Carla and Joanna, two sisters in their mid-thirties who left their careers in Turin (as a translator and a personal assistant in large companies) to start an organic farm and agrotourism. Their husbands had moved in with them to the new farmhouse, and initially had helped out and been involved in decisions. However, the husbands 'always wanted to take over', 'to do things their own ways', and 'did not understand what [Carla and Joanna] wanted to do', 'they could not stand down'. After a while the two sisters decided to leave out their husbands from the farm, and for Joanna, this also marked the end of her marriage. Joanna and Carla were both categorical about not wanting any more men's involvement in the farm:

> All the people who come and help are women, we don't want to have anything to do with men. We don't need them, we can do all the tasks ourselves and they always want to take over, they have different ideas, they don't understand what we want to do.
>
> (Joanna)

For them, both organic farming and agrotourism draw upon women's concerns, skills and experiences:

> Men go for big machines but in organic agriculture you don't need big machines. You need to have patience, to work with nature, and that's something women are better at.
>
> (Carla)

However, if most did on some occasions draw upon their 'womanhood' to talk about their commitment to sustainable agriculture, they also enrolled other social divisions to provide the foundations for their separation from 'commodity farming'. Thus for Marisa, a 26-year-old, the divide between mainstream 'commodity farming' and sustainable farming did not only or always draw upon gender differences, but also generation differences. The old generation of farmers (including her parents) had been under pressure to cut cost, modernize, mechanize and standardize products, and unlike the 'younger generation' of farmers, did not understand the idea of sustainable development.

Furthermore, being addressed as 'woman' was in some contexts not only misplaced and irrelevant, but an irritation, and a position they were keen to escape. In particular, many of the participants seemed reluctant to be pinned down as 'woman' when such a position had any connotation of 'victimhood'. Constructing rural women as victims, having to overcome some 'learned sense of inferiority', is a common trope in the literature on women in farming (Grace and Lennie 1998). However, as in Grace and Lennie's study, this is a label that the participants in this study actively rejected. For example, when I asked Elena what it had meant to her to be a 'woman' in farming, Elena quickly (and defensively) retorted that 'she could do everything on the farm'. The participants actively resisted the association of 'victimhood' and feebleness that the 'woman' label carried. They may be women but they were not passive victims waiting to be assisted, and even less 'farmers' wives'; they were 'as strong as a man'; they had had to be 'tough', and many were proud to recount the battles they had won through sheer determination.

Otherness and difference

There is a tendency in social science and policy to represent women farmers as either passive victims (indoctrinated in some learned sense of inferiority, their contribution effaced), or as the new heroines of some (eco)feminist utopian saga in which they come to embody intimate relations with, and knowledge of, nature (Merchant 1980; Shiva 1988; Plant 1989). In either case, women farmers' otherness is translated into something that can be made transparent, that can be valued or remedied, that can be pinned down. The experience and practices of the women farmers in this study suggest that this may be unwarranted. Whilst they at times did claim these images for themselves to construct their otherness (for example, they did talk about how being women barred them from recognition as 'farmers', or did draw upon their womanhood to articulate their commitment to sustainable development), they used them flexibly; they were not to be held to these positions.

In this last section, I want to use the stories of these women to say something about the way in which we think about otherness. In order to do so, I want to return to the themes of under-determinacy, disconnection, versatility and unpredictability outlined in the introduction to provide a critique of the liberal embrace of the 'Other' in politics of recognition (Charles Taylor 1992). The treatment of farm women in rural policy and sociology, and in particular the attempt to celebrate and harness 'women difference' for the contribution it can make to the regeneration of sustainable agricultural development, is representative of a broader trend in social policy and social science to embrace diversity, to respect and nurture differences.

Under the influence of postmodernism, there has been an increasing tendency in social science to recognize a proliferation of differences (Hetherington and Lee 2000). The Other is no longer to be excluded but rather celebrated for the contribution its/his/her difference can make. The explosion of 'otherness' into a play of differences has served to challenge the privileging of certain norms against which the 'Other' is established as a lack (Hetherington 1999). At least in its ideal formulation, the emphasis on differences rather than difference unsettles the privileging of particular norms. For example for postmodern feminists, gender can no longer be taken as a privileged marker of difference, nor can it be articulated in terms of a common standard or norm; rather gender differences may be experienced in different ways as gender cuts across other social divisions (Nicholson 1990; Williams 1996; Hekman 1999). Since we all differ from each other in many ways (gender, ethnicity, age, sexual orientation, etc.), our differences cannot be articulated in terms of a singular privileged norm, from which the 'Other' deviates:

> the politics of recognition has been about refusing to accept a self/other model as a way to think about difference, a model that is generally seen as hierarchical and discriminatory in character.
>
> (Hetherington 1999: 13)

Furthermore, if we are all constituted through multiple relations of difference, difference can no longer be a mark of exclusion but becomes a universal condition; our differences do no longer mark us as 'Other' and excluded, but as part of a world of differences. Thus the recognition of a proliferation of differences tends to be accompanied by politics of enfranchisement and inclusion (Charles Taylor 1992), if not celebration. The postmodern world of 'differences' becomes an all-embracing place where we are all included and respected for our differences. This urge to reach out to the Other and bring him/her/it in has not only been a dominant concern within contemporary social theory (Hetherington and Law 2000; Hetherington and Lee 2000), but has also become a central motif in governmental and organizational policies promoting diversity or multiculturalism (Charles Taylor 1992). Under such policy, what was considered 'Other' is to be invited in, its difference understood, respected and valued for its contribution to the nation's cultural wealth or the economic development.

Whilst I am broadly sympathetic with the aim to extend recognition to the unacknowledged Other, as has no doubt become apparent in the brief exposition above, I also have some problems with some of the potential effects of such approach. The colonizing effects of politics of inclusion have been well documented.[6] Under such embrace, otherness is appropriated by the urge to give it a name, to give it recognition, to give it a presence that makes it count as something; the Other is denied claim to its/her/his otherness, and maybe to its loss (Höpfl 2000a). The other is included by being translated into measures of the same; from a 'not' it becomes a series of differences that can be fitted in, accommodated, recognized, made to count by those 'inside'. For example, in organizations embracing 'diversity policy' the 'Other' is no longer to be outcast but its/his/her difference becomes an asset to be cultivated (Wajcman 1998; Cassell 2000). Thus women may be encouraged to bring in their now valuable 'soft skills' by joining the ranks of management (Itzin and Newman 1995). Similarly, women are invited to take a more active role in farming in order to bring in 'their valuable skills, values and experiences' to the development of sustainable forms of agriculture. We can of course question the extent to which these newly discovered skills and experiences are actually being rewarded (Fletcher 1999; Cassell 2000), or note that women's 'soft skills' are just being used as an adjunct of managerial control to 'soften' the blows of hard organizational restructuring (Tancred-Sheriff 1989). Whilst these are no doubt valid concerns, it is not the point I wish to pursue here. Rather my concern is that politics of inclusion only recognize difference to the extent that it can be translated into degrees of the same (e.g. some degree of softness/hardness) that can be made to add value, to count.

Of course the translation underlying such inclusionary policies may be welcome by some, some of the time. Some women may well want to use 'their soft skills' to gain access and recognition in organizations (Itzin and Newman 1995). But there is also something disturbing about having all otherness flattened into a play of differences that can be included as various degrees of the same. This conception of difference as a calculable measure of the same has been central to the project of modernity (Foucault 1970, 1977) and its urge to 'normalize' by differentiating, to establish standards and norms against which difference could be identified, and hierarchized, in other words the urge to differentiate in order to better homogenize and discipline:

> The individual and the body of society are divided and differentiated only so that they can be standardised and disciplined into conformity.
>
> (Dale 1997: 183)

In this respect, the 'post-modern' celebration of differences and diversity is no more than a continuity of the project of modernity and its obsession with differentiation and normalization; it merely brings in more differences to be turned into more of the same.[7] What started with the intention to disrupt norms by recognizing a proliferation of differences ends up just producing more normalization, for the celebration of differences share the modernist conceptualization of difference as something that has to be made present by being translated, compared, made to count. Yet this conceptualization of difference in terms of comparison and calculation is not universal but may be particular to Euro-American societies (Strathern 1996). Strathern contrasts this western conception of (gender) difference to the one she found in Melanesia. She argues that the western conception of difference relies on comparison and measurement. Thus it makes sense to talk about degrees of masculinity and femininity, about women being more/less . . . than men, to translate gender differences on scales of for example softness and hardness. And for such relation of calculation and comparability to exist, there needs to be a common measure of difference and sameness, a 'common norm' which as many feminists have argued emerges as masculine (Strathern 1996). In contrast, gender difference in Melanesia is defined by separation, thus maleness is what has been separated from femaleness, it is the 'not female' and vice versa. Such conception of difference puts a stop to comparison; male and female are not comparable but separated by a 'not'.

Strathern's notion of separation (as opposed to comparison) is useful to articulate the idea of 'otherness' I would like to put forward, and resonates with other conceptualizations that seek to put a stop between what I call here 'otherness' and 'difference', to leave otherness as just a 'not' (Mark Taylor 1993). For example, Hetherington and Lee (2000) propose the figure of the 'blank' (after Serres 1991), 'a ghostly agent of otherness that is indifferent to heterogeneity and its ready made system of difference' (Hetherington and Lee 2000: 175). The blank is an under-determined figure that is defined through disjunction; it remains absent from, indifferent to, the categories of differences we may want to cast upon it to understand or recognize it.

What these various ideas of 'separation', the 'blank', the 'underdetermined', the 'not', suggest is that there is another way of thinking about difference than in terms of relation, degrees, continuity and translation, a way of thinking about difference that is not limited by the constraints of similarity (Foucault 1972). Difference can also be established by cracks, discontinuity and disjunctures, by separation rather than comparison. And it is to refer to this idea of difference that I use the term 'otherness'. Otherness is 'a not' rather than a 'more or less', it works through break and disconnection rather than translation and calculation. It is a difference which does not/cannot respond to our recognition, or accept our invitation to join. It is a difference that is not to be called into a named presence but remains absent.

The idea of otherness as a 'not', resilient to naming and recognition, certainly resonates with the practices of the women farmers we met earlier. Their otherness was not to be captured under a name (e.g. 'woman', 'peasant'), it simply was 'Other', an absence that had a presence somewhere else. For example, womanhood may occasionally mark them as Other, but it was not to be translated into victimhood (a 'less' to be remedied), or some romantic vision drawing upon their association with nature (a 'more' to be celebrated). Their otherness remained beyond our grasp, it kept slipping away from attempts to identify it. They were at times woman, at others indifferent to (if not irritated by) the name; at times the 'peasant Other' of the urban majority, as other times the 'Other' of apathetic peasants.

Conceiving of otherness in terms of under-determinacy, as a 'not' rather than a 'difference from', suggests that it is not a passive state of victimhood, but rather requires active participation on the part of the 'Other'. This active construction of otherness was illustrated in the case of the women farmers by two related practices: disconnection, and versatility – the ability to move somewhere else. As we saw, the participants actively cultivated their otherness through practices of disconnection in which social divisions, body and space got enrolled in the making of disjunctions, separations. But remaining 'Other' does not only require disconnecting but also movement and versatility. For otherness to remain 'somewhere else', to resist being 'framed', it has to be continuously moving, moving fast, moving elsewhere. Thus movement and versatility, or motility (Munro 1997), are the very conditions of its possibility. With the notion of motility, Munro is referring to the ability to withdraw or stand apart from categories of difference, however this ability to 'stand apart' requires movement to keep out of the proliferating differences that are granted recognition. To borrow an image from Riley's (1988: 113) discussion of feminism, otherness has 'speed, versatility, foxiness'. This image of 'speed, versatility, foxiness' captures well women farmers' practice and deployment of otherness. They were adept at frustrating my (admittedly misplaced) attempts to frame them, pin them down as 'something', by withdrawing from the categories of difference I attempted to throw at them. For example, they could skilfully move in and out of gender; they did not live their lives 'soaked in gender' (Riley 1988). As such, their experiences constitute a living example of the temporal, contextual and shifting nature of the category of 'woman' emphasized by post-structuralist feminists (e.g. Riley 1988; Butler 1990; Jagose 1994).

And there is no reason to assume that the category of 'woman' provides a privileged ground of otherness, or that other forms of otherness offer any more solid foundations. If otherness is that which remains un-named, unsettled, then it won't do to decide in advance what categories it hides behind, to come with our ready nets to catch it, to privilege and perpetuate the 'grand' or 'key divisions' of social science (Munro 1997). Lines of exclusion and inclusion, them and us, commonality and difference, otherness and identity are not immutable but contingent, temporal and liable to shift (Cohen 1985; Charles and Davies 1997; Parker 1997). Otherness is not always constituted by those social categories such as class, gender and ethnicity usually recognized in social sciences, but is unpredictable. Indeed, the story of the women farmers suggests that otherness may not always be where we expect to find it; it may hide behind a myriad of sometimes conflicting local and shifting lines of division. The women farmers had at their disposal interweaving and shifting lines of divisions that they could deploy contextually to perform their 'otherness' (as 'peasant' as 'entrepreneur, as 'woman'), or not.

Having emphasized the various practices of disconnection through which women farmers constructed their multiple and shifting otherness, I would like to end this chapter with a qualifying point. By foregrounding the multiple nature of otherness, I do not want to suggest that these various lines of division are cumulative, that they can be piled up in the hope of gradually capturing more of the women's 'identity', of calling them into more presence. By talking about the many lines of divisions that shatter social categories such as 'woman', I want to resist the move to piece it back together by accumulating differences, adding forms of presence to make it more inclusive. In particular, I want to distance myself from what Butler (1990: 143) refers to ironically as the politics of the 'exasperated etc.' The emphasis on differences rather than difference in feminist theory has sometimes led to piling up categories of difference in the hope of including 'more', understanding 'more', calling 'more' into presence. Thus 'woman' becomes divided into 'woman' and 'black', and 'working class', and 'old', and 'lesbian', etc. The problematic nature of this cumulative 'politics of the etc' is well illustrated with the case of Silvia discussed earlier. Silvia rarely was 'a woman' and a 'farmer', or rather the two did not always add up to produce consistent results. In the evening she was an attractive woman whose status as 'farmer' was to remain an absence, making her femininity more conspicuous, more striking. When she worked on the farm, being woman meant something different if anything at all. Thus as she cleaned the cow's muck, being woman seemed of little relevance, all traces of the previous evening femininity effaced by baggy and scruffy clothing. At meal times (taken at the dinner table with her parents and paternal grandparents), she was a daughter in a patriarchal family, she and her mother serving her father who always sat at the head of the table. At trade union meetings, her 'woman-ness' stood out and became (to her) a marker of her entrepreneurialism (against the 'apathy' of 'men farmers') or commitment to sustainable agriculture. Thus multiple otherness is not cumulative but provides lines of movement, it makes for motility (Munro 1997), the ability to shrug off particular divisions and categories and move somewhere else. Furthermore, multiple otherness is not open to translation into a 'play of differences', some feast of multiculturalism in which the celebration of all differences ends up in the horror of indifference (Dallmayr 1997). Indeed, otherness may well at times lack the amusement of play. As was illustrated with the case of the women farmers, being woman does have material consequences (such as the tax rate to be paid on land) but it does not matter all the time, nor in similar ways, for all of them. The meaning and significance of otherness, the ways and extent to which it matters, is not transcendental but contextual. The multiple lines of division around which otherness is constituted do not provide for its translation into a play of nameable and 'valuable' differences to be recognized, remedied or celebrated. Rather these multiple and contextual lines of division provide for lines of movement, for the ability to withdraw from categories of difference that would translate otherness into more presence, for the ability to remain a veiled 'not'.

Notes

1   Although in Italy, as everywhere else in Europe, the number of farms has considerably decreased since the Second World War, it has done so much more slowly. From 1961 to 1990, the number of farms went from 4.2 million to 3 million (in Germany there are 1 million, in France 1.2 million and in the UK 300,000). Ninety per cent of Italian farms in 1994 were run by the owners and 80 per cent employed family members (Ventura 1994). The predominance of family farms in Italian agriculture is also reflected in the small size of farms; whilst the average farm size has increased in the last decades it remains relatively low (3 hectares in 1961 compared to 7.5 hectares in 1990, ISTAT 1992).
2   Sachs (1996) quotes estimates according to which women own 1 per cent of the land worldwide.
3   Women form 34 per cent of the Italian agricultural workforce (Schirinzi 1998), and Italian women farmers also account for 32.6 per cent of the female workforce employed in agriculture in the EU (followed by women from Spain 13.6 per cent, Greece 11.6 per cent, and Austria 9.7 per cent) (Schirinzi 1998). Maybe the most fundamental feature of women's presence in Italian agriculture is their increasing and relatively high representation among farm owners; between 1982 and 1990, the proportion of Italian farms owned and managed by women increased from 22 per cent to 26 per cent (Tazza 1997); and farms owned by Italian women constitute 40.9 per cent of the total number of farms owned by women in the EU (Schirinzi 1998). Although in the Italian and other national contexts the ownership of farms by women has tended to be seen as little more than a tax evading device allowing their spouse to take employment, this has been questioned (Ventura 1984; Whatmore 1991) and was not representative of the participants in the present study who did not just own the land but also ran the farm mainly on their own.
4   The marginal position of farmers in Italian history is a central motif in Italian rural sociology. For example, Barberis (1985) argues that the *contadino* has always been associated with images of backwardness and irrationality in Italian society, litera-

ture and social science, an association also indexed by the etymology of the term *contadino*. *Contadino* means *l'uomo del conte* (the man of the count) and thus defines not a type of activity (e.g. agricultural work), but social relations of subservience (unlike for example in French where *paysan* means 'the one who looks after the land'). In Italian, the term *contadino* is also defined in contradistinction to *cittadino* which means both the resident of the city and the citizen or political subject. Thus *contadino* marks the exclusion of the peasant from both the city (and with it culture and civilization) and the sphere of political rights associated with the position of the citizen.

5 Many were keen to talk about the 'entrepreneurial' activities they engaged in, such as finding buyers for crops; negotiating contracts, making plans and decisions about extension, land acquisition, renting, investment in machinery; negotiating loans with banks; finding shops that would sell their products directly rather than rely on intermediaries (and in the case of Rosi setting up her own shop); and for those engaged in agrotourism contacting and advertising with foreign travel agencies, and designing promotional materials.

6 See Lee and Brown 1994; Kappeler 1997; Höpfl 1997, 2000a; Hetherington and Lee 2000.

7 Although the postmodern celebration of differences is often associated with writers such as Lyotard, Lyotard (1984) seems to hold on to an idea of difference which is closer to what I want to articulate in this chapter as 'otherness'. For him, differences cannot be reduced to common measures, measures of the same, but rather are incommensurable. The differences envisaged by Lyotard are devoid of possible mediation, or mutual recognition. Thus the heterogeneity which for Lyotard marks the postmodern condition is not one where all differences are reconciled and recognized into an all-embracing world of difference, but rather is marked by an absence of common bond (see Hetherington and Lee 2000, for a similar reading).

Appendix

Table 4.1 Personal and farm characteristics of participants

Lazio

Name	Farm ownership	Source of farm labour	Main farm activities	Farm size	Personal characteristics
Lidia	Sole Inherited	Herself and contracted workers	Cereals and sugar beet	6 hectares owned, 4 hectares rented	33, single, higher eduction
Silvia	Sole Inherited	Herself, her parents, 1 full time employee	Dairy herd, hay, maize	45 cows 16 hectares	30, single, left school at 16
Angela	Sole Self-started	Herself, occasional help from husband	Calves breeding, asparagus	5–7 calves 1 hectare	45, married, 2 children, left school at 16
Isabella	Joint with husband Inherited	Herself, sister, husband, daughter, 5 full-time employees, seasonal workers	Carrots, courgettes, tomatoes Carrot packaging line	21 hectares	42, married, 5 children, left school at 16
Lisa	Sole Inherited	Herself only	Organic strawberries and cucumbers, sugar beet	3 hectares	38, married, 2 children, higher education
Rosi	Sole Inherited	Herself, her parents and sister, 4 full-time employees, occasional help from husband	Flower farm (in greenhouses) and shop	3 hectares	48, married, 2 children, left school at 16
Cecilia	Sole Self-started	Herself, 1 seasonal worker, occasional help from husband	Mushrooms in greenhouses	2 hectares	45, married, 2 children, left school at 16
Anna	Sole Inherited	Herself and her parents	Tomatoes and courgettes (some in greenhouses)	6 hectares	31, single, left school at 16

Umbria

Name	Ownership	Source of labour	Main farm activities	Farm size	Personal characteristics
Teresa	Sole Inherited	Herself, two full time employees, occasional help from husband and son	Sunflower, corn, olives, agrotourism (self-catering), small vineyard	20 hectares	51, married, 1 son, higher education
Natalia	Sole Inherited	Herself, 1 full-time worker, seasonal workers	Organic olives Agrotourism (self-catering)	6 hectares	45, married, 1 son, higher education
Marisa	Sole Inherited	Herself, 1 full-time worker, help of two sisters and mother	Olives, fruits, agrotourism (self-catering and catering for some groups, direct sale of olive oil and home made jam)	10 hectares	26, single, higher education
Francesca	Sole Self-started	Herself, help from neighbours, and boyfriend	Organic olive and fruit Agrotourism (bedrooms and catering), small vineyard	13 hectares	46, divorced, 1 daughter, higher education

Basilicata

Name	Ownership	Source of labour	Main farm activities	Farm size	Personal characteristics
Mina	Joint with husband Inherited	Herself, husband, 5 full-time employees, seasonal workers	Apricots, peaches, nectarines, oranges, small vineyard	13 hectares	43, married, 3 children, left school at 16
Roberta	Sole Inherited	Herself, help from sister and mother, contracted workers	Wheat, small production of cheese	3 hectares	58, single, left school at 14
Elena	Joint with husband Inherited	Herself and 1 full time worker, occasional help from son and husband	Strawberries, apricots, small vineyard	5 hectares	44, married, 2 children, left school at 14

Table 4.1 continued

Piemonte

Name	Ownership	Source of labour	Main farm activities	Farm size	Personal characteristics
Beatrice	Sole Inherited	Herself and her parents, part time workers	Kiwi and agrotourism (self-catering, catering, school visits), direct sale of home made preserves	7 hectares	33, married, no children, higher education
Carla and Joanna	Joint between the 2 sisters Self started	Themselves, part time workers for catering, help from parents	Organic fruit and vegetables, agrotourism (bedrooms, catering, school visits), sales of home made preserves, vineyard	4 hectares	34 and 36, one married and one divorced, both had one daughter, both had higher education
Albina	Sole Inherited	Herself, occasional help from husband and son	Calves breeding, hay	6 hectares 25 calves	45, married, 2 children, left school at 16
Giulia	Sole Inherited	Herself	Shepherd, production of cheese	12 dairy cows	44, married, 2 children, left school at 16
Paola	Joint with husband Inherited	Herself, her husband and mother, 1 full-time worker	Calves breeding, fruit and vegetables, hay	20 calves, 7 hectares	43, married, 1 son, left school at 16

5 Construction of gender in corporations

Ulla Eriksson-Zetterquist

Why do gender differences continue to exist in corporations, in spite of all the good intentions and attempts to change the situation? In this chapter, I will try to show how new employees are socialized into prevailing gender norms, and how the dominant gender construction is thereby reproduced.

Research in the field of gender discrimination has established a general awareness of structural gender inequalities (Kanter 1977; Wahl 1992), not only in terms of the financial advantages, but, first and foremost, of moral consequences (Billing and Alvesson 1989). By conducting a study of newcomers' socialization in a trainee programme, my aim is to develop the question further. An investigation of the social construction of gender in an organization may throw some light on the question why changes concerning gender inequalities seem to move so slowly.

Entering an organization is usually seen as the most influential event in an employee's occupational life (Van Maanen and Schein 1979). This phase thus says a lot about organizational socialization. Alvesson and Billing (1992) claim that, through scrutinizing socialization processes, the survival of gender differences in organizations can be studied.

An example of this kind of situation can be found in a trainee programme, i.e. a form of apprenticeship programme for young people who have recently graduated in Business Administration. The aim of the programme studied by the author was to find a position for each trainee in one of the management groups within an 8–10 year time frame. During the programme the trainees received on-the-job training and took take part in theoretical courses. A trainee programme is thus a distinct example of socialization that contains a structured and standardized adaptation process. It is therefore legitimate to expect that a study of what happened during this trainee programme, an observation of messages sent by the company, and the reactions of the newcomer, might reveal the nuances of gender re-construction in the company.

Gender construction in the first encounter

> Enter eight men managers in dark suits. Seeing them enter, the course coordinator, Leif, begins the meeting by welcoming everybody present. Introducing the managers, he says: 'This is a male gathering – a fact which we have discussed a lot. We still don't have any solutions as to how to get more women into the executive group'.
>
> (Fieldnotes)

This example creates the setting for the paper as it did for the trainee programme. The men in the leading positions in the company declare their intention to promote women but admit their failure in this goal. The question that interests me was relevant for them as well. Why was this?

In the very first sentence of the presentation of the course programme something was said about gender. No wonder that gender, as a topic of discussion, returned later on.

> 'Why do you recruit female trainees?', the trainee Erik asks as soon as the floor is free.
> 'What?', the trainee Annica gives a surprised cry.

It is hard to say whether Erik is admitting to being a male chauvinist, or indicating his understanding that there is something problematic with the combination of women and career. Annica believes that the first alternative is the correct one.

> As John (one of the managers) begins to explain, the remaining men whisper and squirm.
>
> JOHN: Over the last ten years, 55 per cent men and 45 per cent women have been recruited to the trainee programme.
> ERIK: How many of these continue their career after the programme?
> JOHN: There is a lack of women in the executive groups, and we have paid attention to this problem for some years now. The point is that both the company and the women themselves have to make sacrifices for their careers. It is a difficult problem.

Here is further evidence that the company was aware of equality issues. Statistics from the company showed that women managers earned less than men and even though as many women as men were employed over a period of ten years, the women ended at the second step of the career ladder (the executive group constitutes the third). Nevertheless, top managers still did not know how the company could support women in managerial careers.

In order to solve the problem of 'the manly company', a committee was appointed with the explicit purpose of finding solutions for women willing to engage in careers. The committee produced among other things a model composed of four fields: the 'organization', the 'culture', the 'family' and the 'women' themselves. Each field was said to be exhibiting different problems. The problems in the 'organization' could be, for example, prejudices and traditions, or lack of mentoring. In the field of 'family' the problem could be, for example, lack of support and back-up, or that parental leave for fathers was not accepted by the managers at the company. The company wished to increase the understanding of femininity and masculinity in the organization, and also to discuss a special, 'delayed' career path for women, which were two subjects in the field of 'culture'. The field of 'women' described women as persons who did not want to have a career and found a career too much of a responsibility. The model-makers emphasized that women themselves had to work out these issues.

Thus while the committee tried to solve the situation of women in careers, they inadvertently but clearly contributed to the re-construction of women in this company. Women were constructed as persons who were different from men. And as I learned from the managers themselves and from the statistics about the company, it was men who advanced (properly, normally) in their careers. They constituted the norm.

This interpretation might be seen as overly critical. The committee, after all, suggested several arenas where gender issues could be discussed, proposed that articles in the company magazine should be written about it, and recommended that the issue should be explicitly taken up in discussions for appraisal and on other occasions during the executive meetings. It needs to be said that the management's reaction to the lack of potential women managers was undoubtedly quick, problem-oriented and progressive.

> The introductory meeting ends with a speech from a finance executive, David. David is 60 and he introduces himself as 'a relic in the company'. For him there are no career lists, no 1- and 2-list, just the X-it-list. Everyone laughs. He also claims that he can explain what happens to the 'girls' in the company:
> 'We employ girls with good grades, who are both nice and good looking. I used to say that these girls get chased by the men in the company who try to put them into family bonds in order to keep them for themselves.' Everyone laughs again.

This humorous touch is another clue to the construction of gender at the company. One way to interpret David's joke is that beautiful women are in danger (or too dangerous?) when roaming freely in the company and therefore must be conquered, and kept safe in the home by men (Gutek 1989; Höök 1999).

Rite of passage

In order to describe socialization in the organization and the re-construction of gender that takes place within it, the anthropological concepts of enculturation and acculturation are used. Enculturation is the process during which people learn their culture (Herskovits 1972), and acculturation is when persons from one culture learn another culture (Redfield *et al.* 1936). The two concepts together offer an interesting way to describe socialization in organizations.

Robert Avery (1968) has actually used the concept of enculturation in the context of organization, to describe how young technicians learned the culture of an industrial laboratory. Simon Marcson (1968) used the concept of acculturation to describe how the professional worker and the organization impact on each other. Enculturation and acculturation can be found wherever cultural learning takes place, for example in myths, rites, rituals and ceremonies (Czarniawska 2001). One of the cultural events that are said to have an exceptionally strong learning or teaching power is the rite of passage. According to Trice and Beyer (1993) a trainee programme can be conceptualized as such a rite since it concerns the acquisition of a new social role.

One of the first to study rites of passage was Arnold Van Gennep (1908/ 1960) who divided them into rites of separation, transition and incorporation. According to Victor Turner (1969), rites of passage are the rites that accompany all changes in place, status, social position and age. It is the passage from a lower to a higher status that takes place through a 'limbo of statuslessness'. This liminal phase has the characteristics neither of the previous nor of the following condition. Consequently, I propose to call the rites of separation from a previous world 'preliminal rites', those executed during the transitional stage liminal (or threshold) rites, and ceremonies of incorporation into the new world postliminal rites (Van Gennep 1908/ 1960: 21).

The separation or the preliminal phase means that the persons let go of their present position and role to be able to learn new ones. The easiest separation is the physical, where one symbolically leaves the old environment, e.g. the world of the student (Trice and Beyer 1993). When a person has left her or his old role, but still has not acquired the new one, the transition – the liminal phase – takes place. This is the threshold to the new role. The phase is characterized by ambiguity, since people in this phase have no access to the schemes of classification that normally indicate everybody's place and position in a cultural space (Turner 1969). Incorporation is a rite that often is missing in the context of organization according to Trice and Beyer (1993). This part of the rite tells the newcomer that she or he is now 'one of us', and also, 'this is how it really is'.

Trice and Beyer (1993) wrote that the different phases of the rite of passage help to convince the newcomers, but also their colleagues, that the newcomers now are qualified, for example, to be managers. The passage through the different phases demonstrates that the newcomers' rise in status follows fair and impartial rules, and, above all, that both they and the others can now accept their new status as proper and suitable.

Are rites of passage a useful concept to apply to organizational settings, wondered Hallier and James (1999). One question is whether it is possible to compare rites in tribes and rites in modern organizations. It is also easier to find rites that mark differences in status than rites that mark a change in the role or a change in understanding. In spite of this, Hallier and James argued that the rite of passage is an excellent way of increasing our understanding of the presence, form and meaning of rituals in organizational contexts.

Besides offering a tool for interpretation, the concept of the rite of passage also offers a frame to structure the course of events in the trainee programme. Throughout the different phases of the rite of passage, enculturation and acculturation could be seen more distinctly, and with them even the construction of gender. In the next part of the paper I will describe the three phases of the trainee programme as the rite of passage.

The study and the programme

The study was carried out during a period of two years, that is, for as long as the trainee programme lasted. Five men and five women who took part in the trainee programme were repeatedly interviewed, in order to follow their enculturation and the concomitant gender construction as they developed and changed in time. Through observations of central events such as recruitment, trainee courses and trainee meetings, I constructed a picture of how the company enculturated the newcomers. Statistical material was used to supplement the description of the gendered career situation.

Gender was not explicitly asked for, since the study primarily focused on socialization. As patterns in the programme became visible during the study, the gender issues became clearer. This was one way to avoid some of the gender bias that often accompanies gender focused research (Alvesson and Sköldberg 1994).

About ten persons were recruited to the trainee programme each year, which means that about twenty persons were trainees at the same time. After recruitment, trainees began work in different training positions. As the company had eight subsidiaries, a trainee often worked in different organizations. Besides the on-the-job training, a trainee took part in two management courses and four trainee meetings during the programme. After finishing the programme a trainee assumed a position as a product manager at one of the subsidiaries.

Phase 1: Separation of 'the invited'

The first stage in the rite of passage of the trainee programme is recruitment. This is where the subject/object of the ritual, in this case a future trainee, becomes separated from the others. Turner writes:

The first phase (of separation) comprises symbolic behavior signifying the detachment of the individual or group either from an earlier fixed point in the social structure, from a set of social conditions (a 'state'), or from both.

(Turner 1969: 94)

Separation in a rite of passage is often both physical (geographical) and symbolic, where a person is moved to a new place but also might have to leave certain attributes behind (Turner 1982). In the case of the trainees, a trainee leaves the peers (students, non-managers) to enter a road leading to a management position (Schein 1978).

On recruitment, the trainees were symbolically separated from the others who applied for the programme and were not accepted, and also even from those who did not apply, and were moved from the status of student to that of an employee. By choosing to take part in the trainee programme, they set aside the time which was characteristic of student life and career. Since they as trainees chose to go in to yet another form of education, they partly renounced one particular attribute – that of having already a degree.

The recruitment process consisted of the advertisement, the first interview and the second interview. The advertisement offered a position as a trainee with on-the-job-training for two years, if the person had '*the will and strength to become a manager*'. About 1000 people applied for five trainee positions. Eighty of these were welcomed to a first interview, where they met the personnel manager, a division manager and a trainee for an hour of questioning. Sixteen persons went further to the second interview where the separation proceeded with the assistance of an assessment centre and another interview. This interview was conducted by the personnel manager in the presence and with the participation of six managers from the executive groups.

Throughout the recruitment, images of men and women at the company were often introduced. The different elements of the recruitment process permitted the trainees to meet eight to ten different examples of careers within the company. The gender picture at this stage showed women as either personnel managers or product managers while men were division heads or members of the top management group.

In contrast to other European countries, the question of the candidate's family plans can enter the recruitment interview in Sweden.[1] In fact, the question came up in both recruitment interviews, but it was asked only of women candidates. From the company point of view (as explained to me by participant observation of the discussion among the recruiters), the question was to reveal the candidate's awareness of future career. To become employed women have to plan their families. An acceptable version of the future is close to a traditional Swedish mother role where the mother has the main responsibility for her children. A daycare centre or a domestic help can take care of children during work time, but not all day long. If women candidates revealed that they did not desire to have children, they were seen as 'unfeminine' and too career-oriented to fit the company. Another reason for rejecting a candidate as suitable might have been the lack of a realistic picture of her future, or lack of a proper solution to future problems.

The women candidates reacted in different ways to the introduced models of management and the question of their future family. Only one (foreign) woman reacted to the fact that there were few women managers in the company. One woman trainee interpreted the question about the future family as a proof of the company's holistic view of the person, and its awareness of the fact that children and career must be combined. The company was thus perceived as a humane employer. Another woman said that the question about future family felt like a negative separation in terms of her career, indicating that she was and had to remain a 'woman'. Thus, the individual reactions of the women to the company's message differed.

It also appeared that there was a 'desirable' level of masculinity for men who wished to have career opportunities. In the second interview men could be rejected with the argument that they were too dominating, were self-centred and had no ability to listen. Together, these could be interpreted as stereotypically masculine traits (Alvesson and Billing 1997). One way of sorting out men who applied to the programme seemed to be to describe them as too masculine. There was no corresponding description of 'too feminine' which would be used to sort out women candidates. Apparently, 'not enough femininity' and 'too much masculinity' were traits that did not fit into the image of a desired member of the company's management.

This phase also showed that the trainees had different motives for choosing the programme. When asked why they applied for the company, women explained that they felt an affinity with the people who interviewed them, that they felt as though they were coming home, while men argued that it was a good first step in their careers. This turned out to be one of the few differences in the trainees' answers to the question concerning their socialization. The two answers could be seen as gender-differentiated, but it is difficult to see what it is that differentiates gender. One possibility is that women chose affinity and men chose career opportunities, while another is that all candidates were engaged in impression management and gave the interviewer an expected answer. People can be said to be socialized if they answer in a given way, or answer with a cliché, indicating something that is said but not necessarily thought (Anderson *et al.* 1998).

The reading of recruitment as a phase of separation shows that the representatives from the company used a gendered norm to decide whether the candidate was suitable for a career or not. Applicants were thus sorted by different criteria. The candidates themselves gave different reasons as to why they chose to enter the programme, but in every other respect – background, education, and family situation – they were strikingly similar.

Phase 2: Transition – on the threshold of a career

After having been separated the ten persons began work as trainees. If the trainee programme is seen as a rite of passage, this phase is a liminal one. The student leaves the structured life in the centre of the university institution to enter the more marginal one of the trainee programme. Turner writes:

> The attributes of liminality or of liminal personae ('threshold people') are necessarily ambiguous, since this condition and these persons elude or slip through the network of classifications that normally locate states and positions in cultural space. Liminal entities are neither here nor there; they are betwixt and between the positions assigned and arrayed by law, custom, convention, and ceremonial. As such, their ambiguous and indeterminate attributes are expressed by a rich variety of symbols in the many societies that ritualize social and cultural transitions. Thus, liminality is frequently likened to death, to being in the womb, to invisibility, to darkness, to bisexuality, to the wilderness, and to the eclipse of the sun or moon.
>
> (Turner 1969: 95)

This colourful description might not be the first that comes to mind in the context of a trainee programme. Such a context is more commonly associated with success, the start of a career, the end of school rewarded with a promising position. And yet there are many similarities between being in a trainee programme and being in darkness or in a wilderness, since the future is neither obvious or given.

During this phase, the trainee learned about daily life at the company. At this stage, of great importance were the interactions with colleagues, the first course discussed in the introduction, and the first trainee meetings. The career messages given in the advertisement for the position began to be clarified and accepted. Meanwhile, the gendered image of the Company and the gender construction among the trainees continued to develop.

The marginalizing of the trainees showed in many different ways. The trainees moved from the rather loosely structured daily life of a student to the routines of working life, but as they were not average employees but trainees, they remained at the threshold of real working life. The trainees discovered that they had too little to do. They would have liked to work harder but there was little room for that during the ordinary working day. At the same time the CEO gave a speech at a trainee meeting where he encouraged them to work harder. It was thus up to the trainees to solve the betwixt and between situation that came from wanting to work harder, being encouraged to work harder but having no space for it in the ordinary working day.

During the first course for the trainees (see the first section) and at the first trainee meetings, the gender construction at the company became more obvious in comparison with the picture from the recruitment. The descriptions of the company were permeated by a masculine discourse. The managers were described by the course leaders and the CEO as a group of people who were the company's investment (the human capital, in the latest jargon), and who had succeeded in their career because of sacrifices and/or rational planning of their private lives. This description is not surprising in the context of corporations (Collinson and Hearn 1996). Speeches given by (male) managers from the company and presenting a work area or a subsidiary always followed a certain pattern. They described their careers up to the present moment, the positions they had had and then their family. The latter was described as a source of harmony and balance in life.[2]

The trainees did not reflect upon the stereotypical character of the presentations, but they did reflect on the careers of men and women. It seemed to them that men who had small children were still in the office at the time when they should be at home. The career women with young children were perceived as efficient but asocial in their effort to combine both parts of their lives.

If one had to take stock of the state of enculturation at that point in time, one would notice that the trainees showed an increased self-awareness, increasingly similar views on career, and a stronger emotional orientation among the men. Self-awareness was somewhat different for men and women. For the women self-awareness meant that they knew why they chose to make a career at the company and they were more certain than before of what they wished to do. For the men, self-awareness meant that they became aware of the competition from others and that they realized that they still had many things to learn. The advancing enculturation also meant that women and men trainees acquired similar views on their current work and relationships. The male trainees deviated at this time from the standard image of a male manager in that they talked about family and career in a way that is usually associated with women. The emotional orientation seemed to be something that was reinforced during the programme, since it took about six months before men started to talk about their future children. After six months in the programme, both men and women declared that they wanted to have a family and were going to make use of the parental leave when it was time for that. At this point, both men and women believed that it would be harder for men than for women to combine the responsibility for work and for the family.

The increased similarity among the trainees in this phase makes division into the gendered categories impossible. This division is effaced by a feeling of community, where intensive comradeship and egalitarian thinking dominate. This again can be related to the liminal period. According to Turner (1969), the liminal period is characterized by the unstructured *communitas* (community) replacing the ordinary structured system. The structured and the unstructured are two human ways to interact. In the structured, differentiated and often hierarchical system, men are separated into 'more' or 'less', Turner wrote. In *communitas*, the group is more or less unstructured and relatively undifferentiated; homogeneity and comradeship prevail. The trainees seemed to form a *communitas* after they had been employed for a couple of months. The importance of the group relationship grew when the environment became less predictable and when the message received at the time of recruitment became transformed. The trainees began to feel that, taken together, they were selected because they were special; they were recruited as an elite and they all expected to be treated that way. However, daily life as a trainee abounded in counter-examples, both because there was no special treatment and because the situation in the company seemed to be changing. A 'we-against-them' feeling started to develop.

In the everyday structured life of the company a hierarchical system determined what was seen as an ordinary career. To follow Turner (1969), people are 'more' or 'less' in relation to each other in ordinary life. Thus a CEO is 'more' than a financial manager, that is, higher up on the career ladder. There were no traces of a corresponding system among the trainees after a time spent in the programme. They were all alike. Even if someone had been employed for six months longer, there was no corresponding 'more' on a career ladder. Rather, they were equals supporting each other in the unstructured daily life, where ordinary career thinking was not to be found.

There was, instead, an increased similarity among the trainees, which resembled the spirit of *communitas* (Turner 1969). In the ordinary structure that was activated during recruitment, the candidates could be separated into men and women. During the first period in the programme they were oriented towards each other, becoming homogenous, genderless persons, with the same career goal and similar views on how work and family should be taken care of. Also, their image of the gender construction within the company had become more complex.

Phase 3: Incorporation – or not?

After the transition and the renewal of the understanding of earlier cultural experiences that were taken for granted (in this case the understanding of the content of a career), the incorporation phase began. This is when the trainee got to know that 'she is one of us' and at the same time was introduced to 'how it really is'. Turner explains:

> The third phase . . . includes symbolic phenomena and actions which represent the return of the subjects to their new, relatively stable, well-defined position in the total society. For those undergoing life-cycle ritual this usually represents an enhanced status, a stage further along life's culturally prefabricated road.
>
> (Turner 1982: 24–25)

As I mentioned earlier, this part in the rite of passage seems to be often missing in the context of organization (Trice and Beyer 1993). The case of the trainee programme confirmed this observation. At the company, there were no institutionalized ceremonies at the point in time when a trainee finished the programme and started in his/her first real position. There was no event, ceremonial or not, to signal that, at this point, the trainee had finished the programme and entered his or her proper position. Therefore, the liminal stage and the stage of incorporation ran parallel for a while, and so does this section. The trainees were still marginal but they showed many signs of having been incorporated (and being incorporated) into the mainstream of the company's life.

The shared events during this period were the second course and the third and fourth trainee meeting. These contained new messages concerning career and gender. It was time for men and women in the trainee programme to learn how 'things really are' at the company.

During the study seven out of ten trainees chose to leave the company (mainly because of internal changes in career prospects): five men and two women. It could be seen as a rather obvious gender effect if more women left than men. In this case, however, the three women who chose to stay received better job proposals and higher salaries compared to men and women trainees before them. Another explanation for the departures is to see them as a sign of an incomplete incorporation. But a scrutiny of the view on careers among the trainees at that time, in contrast to the time when it was first communicated during the programme, revealed that the trainees had adopted the spoken norms. The trainees had developed a more hierarchical view on careers, which mirrored the descriptions of careers that were made by the successful managers during their presentations. When the company offered alternative careers, due to internal changes in the organization, the trainees were not interested anymore. They preferred to choose other companies, where the enculturated career pattern was in fact possible. The decision of the trainees can thus be related, paradoxically enough, to a successful incorporation of the norms for a career.

In this phase men continued to be the ones who best exemplified the successful patterns of work and career in the company. Monika Kostera and Maciej Wicha (1995) showed how 'being a man' was an important part in the role of the manager in communist Poland. The homogeneity among those who represented success at work in the company suggests that 'being a man' was important there as well.

At the same time as my picture of the gender construction in the company became more complex, the women trainees began to understand, too, that the company was not gender equal. Women might arrive at the top management level, but it became obvious that a career at the top was impossible to combine with a family. The company now appeared to be a career-focused place where it was difficult to have a family. One of the female trainees talked about it in general terms and she might have intended to say that it was difficult to have a family and a career, no matter which gender. Career no longer naturally contained children. At any rate, at least one woman and one man trainee understood by that time that men and women had different career conditions in this company. The male trainee expected his future wife to set her career aside during the early years of child bearing, while the female trainee expected that her career would be made easier if sacrifices were made by both her family and the company.

The fact that men were the norm for careers in the company was not particularly original. The idea of men as the norm in society can, for example, be found in ancient Greek and Latin literature (Höpfl 2000c). Simone de Beauvoir (1949), a theorist of normality and deviation, wrote about the problems resulting from placing man as the central point for normality and woman as the deviant. In the context of organizational theory, women are often seen as deviant from 'normal' leadership, which is intended for men (Nyberg and Sundin 1997). However, it is the theoretical norm concerning leadership rather than its practice, as the latter reveals no gender-related differences in management (Alvesson and Billing 1997).

The recruitment slogan of the trainee programme ('with will and strength to become a manager') and the traditional notion of 'making a career' (Collinson and Hearn 1996) seemed to suggest that the person who could make a career at the Company was a masculine man or woman. By now, however, it was becoming clear that the person who fitted into the company was, rather, a 'normally masculine man' and a 'normally feminine woman'.

It did not seem to be enough for a man to be normal and suitable in the company. Men could be excluded because they were too masculine. The male managers, who exchanged recipes and discussed diets, as they did, could hardly be seen as very masculine. The women trainees reacted negatively towards the manager who behaved in 'too masculine' a manner, but the absence of a reaction in other contexts suggest that they accepted the 'normal' masculinity of other men managers. It might be that 'normal masculinity' was acceptable to women, but 'too much masculinity' was a threat. It seemed as if 'man as the norm' did not extend to men and masculinity in general, but delimited a certain space for men at the company.

As we saw earlier, women were normal and capable of a career in the company if they already, by the time of recruitment, had a solution for their future family, and a solution that did not deviate from the traditional mother's role too much. Women who did not plan to have children were definitely seen as deviant in the company, as in the rest of Swedish society. Also, the reason that women trainees did not seem to be able to see the women who had succeeded in their careers, may well have been because women pursuing careers disappeared behind all men in careers. The minority is invisible also to the subordinates, as Kanter (1977) pointed out. Alternatively, it could be that the women trainees (who succeeded in building a career) were not different from men who built careers, but they were different from other women.

To belong to a group that constitutes the norm does not seem to mean that everything is justified because of gender. Rather, it delineates a certain frame of 'normalcy' that men have to observe. A corresponding frame seems to exist for women. Even if the women trainees deviated from 'man as a norm', they could not deviate from being 'a normal woman' – that is, if they wished to fit into the company and make a career there.

Thus, at least in this company, a man who wanted to have a career had to fit into a certain frame of 'normal masculinity'. A woman who wanted to have a career had to deviate – at least from a picture of 'normal femininity' that assumed having a family – but a woman accepted by the company had to be a 'normal woman'. From this one could conclude that women could not have careers in this company, even if both they and the company wanted it.

Conditions for the manly company

The study of socialization among newcomers from a gender perspective shows some of the complexity concerning gender in organizations. Even though the managers had the best intentions of changing the situation for women careerists, they reproduced the picture of a normal man and a normal woman. A normal man is the person who can build a career with support from his family – the source of balance and harmony. A normal woman is the person who bears children, but with that follows a responsibility that makes a top career impossible. For her, the family is no source of balance and harmony but rather something that takes all her attention, at least from the company's point of view.

This can be compared to Eräsaari's study of women architects and cleaners in Finland (Chapter 8, this volume). She writes that women in Finland today have symbolic rights and also access to the public space. In this sense they are visible, as were the women with the potential for management in the trainee programme. Eräsaari puts forward the view that other parts of women's lives, such as the care-taking duties of being a mother and a wife, are meanwhile rendered invisible and not public. Compared to the trainee programme, the situation seems to be the same in the sense that women's duties as mothers and wives are not put forward or accepted as a duty even when they are thought of as future managers.

It seems to have taken two years for a woman trainee to learn that career and family did not go together well at the company. Men trainees seemed to understand from the start of the programme that the women would have a problem with their careers. During the programme men learned that they needed to have a family in order to fit in with the normality of a career – a situation that raised the issue of heterosexuality and a business career (Borgström 1998). The norm was not just being a normal masculine man; it was also being a normal heterosexual man.

Gender messages

Thus, contradictory messages concerning gender were sent throughout the trainee programme. The creation and recreation of gender was carried out both by the representatives of the management and by the trainees. This happened both overtly and covertly, where gender could be read between the lines. The messages sent and received sometimes challenged the traditional gender roles and sometimes (more often) conformed to them. This complex situation can be schematically represented as follows:

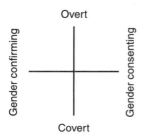

Figure 5.1 Gender messages in the company.

I have divided the messages into four categories:

1) *Overt gender contesting messages*: examples and signs of progressiveness. In the company studied, the management wanted to have women as managers. Among the trainees, both men and women wanted to have careers. Taken together, this kind of message showed a great potential for change of the current situation. At the same time, other messages were given:

2) *Overt gender confirming messages*: only men were managers in this company; women were the persons who had full responsibility for the family. After two years in the programme, the trainees constructed themselves after a traditional family responsibility model. The latter reveals a situation where the identity of a woman was not completely fulfilled within the organization (Ely 1995). As Gutek (1989) describes it, men could be seen as natural inhabitants of the organization, while women had to construct their own images. Messages in this category thereby preserved the stereotypes of the man as manager and the woman as the person having a child and, first and foremost, being different.

3) *Covert gender contesting messages* are not easily apparent but still progressive. An example of this is that work descriptions in the trainee programme contained both masculine and feminine elements. The trainees were enculturated in a similar way. This category also contained changed images of gender. Among the trainees this was not so surprising since the cultural construction of the woman and the man seldom was in accordance with the actual persons.

4) *Covert gender confirming messages* require a more critical reading of the examples from the study. The implicit picture of an employee successful in a career presented a woman who was feminine to a 'normal' degree and a man who was 'sufficiently masculine'; the trainees argued for choices in a gendered way. Here women and men belonged to two differ-

ent categories, one problematic in the context of organizations, while the other one was 'natural' in this context. The trainees adopted this 'natural' construction of gender in organizations, and most of the time they did not find it particularly strange in any way.

The model helps to explain how women managers can be wanted but at the same time nothing happens on the practical level. In Herskovits' (1978) terminology, the reason is that all employees take part in the same belief system. On the overt level, the signals of change are sent, which makes it possible to live with the covert level where the gendered construction is absorbed and internalized in a subconscious way. It can be seen as an example of decoupling (Meyer and Rowan 1977/1991). The institutional myth in society in general promotes talk about changes, which, however, are decoupled from everyday organizational practice. The message is a wish for change, even while the practice shows how impossible it is to make this wish come true. The covert level – the taken-for-granted – contains the absorbed and internalized messages that the members are unaware of. Thanks to that, both management and trainees continue to reproduce the covert level.

However, the figure in the model is a problem in itself. Höpfl (2001) describes how the formal form of the matrix leaves the body behind and instead regulates the text and words. The matrix appears to give definition and location within a structure, and also appears to make things intelligible, even though they are ambivalent within the text, Höpfl writes. This is also the case with the matrix used here. By structuring the different messages of gender I also order them, but according to the inherent message of the matrix, the different interpretations and meanings in the mediated action from the observations in the trainee programme, become excluded. Instead of opening up – as the open form of the matrix tries to – it formalizes the complex gender pattern that exists in the company to the same construction as in any management textbook. This allows the problematic gender issues into the same discourse as other managerial analysis, but it also simplifies the complex gender actions that often lie beyond language.

Notes

1 Questions concerning family and pregnancy have for example not been allowed in recruitment interviews in Germany since the beginning of 1990s. Since 1 January 2001 there is a new act in Sweden where questions like this can be seen as gender discriminating. According to interpretation of the act, the question is legal when asked of both women and men.

2 During the study thirty-eight male managers gave speeches, all following this structure. There were two women in leading positions: an information manager, and a young technician. These two women did not give a speech; instead they 'did' something, for example photographing (the information manager), or guiding the process of production (the young technician).

6 Individual vs collective action

Gender inequality and women's action strategies in German and Swedish business firms

Hildegard Theobald

Since the 1980s, the gendering of organizations, studied on the micro level, and the cross-national approach towards gender and employment, studied on the macro level, have occupied a prominent role on the research agenda. Studies conducted on the macro level have revealed different patterns of gender segregation and hierarchization in different labour markets. Although the pattern of segregation is basically the same in many countries, the form and extent of the segregation process varies and reveals the impact of gender policy at the societal level in cross-national variability.

The research on micro-level shows that organizational processes are not gender-neutral. Gender is a basic variable in organizational practice. Gendered structures and processes lead to a reproduction of patterns of gender segregation and hierarchization within organizations. The societal effects of this continuous reproduction, for example, weighty institutional features that, in turn, are a potential source of gendered practices in organizations, have only rarely been studied systematically on both micro- and macro-level, despite a considerable growth in scholarship.[1]

The aim of this chapter is to show the impact of societal factors on gendered processes in organizations. In terms of theory, the chapter draws on gendered welfare state approaches for the macro-level analysis and the research area 'gender and organization' for the micro-level analysis. The empirical basis of the chapter is grounded in the results of a study of middle-level female managers in private sector companies in Sweden and Germany. Despite the differences in gender policy in each country, women have made remarkable inroads into middle management. The results show the differences of gender political approaches in both countries and the concomitant process of the opening up of the labour market for women.

Welfare states and gender relations on the labour market

In recent years, an increasing number of studies has highlighted cross-national similarities and differences in the labour market position of women as compared to men. Among the main issues studied were the institutional and normative influences on the degree and forms of women's and men's labour force participation and the gendered division of labour along the lines of sectoral, occupational and vertical segregation.[2]

Studies in the compared countries show a pattern of gender segregation followed by a hierarchization of male and female labour market areas and the positions of men and women based on an on-going process of differentiation and 'hierarchization' between genders. Differentiation and hierarchization may be conceptualized as two sides of the same classification process (Gottschall 1999; Hirdman 1990). The resulting patterns of gender segregation and hierarchization however, differ in form and degree markedly among countries and periods of time.

The cross-national variability in women's and men's labour market positions is moulded by national institutions, societal structures and the prevailing norms and values. Current literature on the impact of the welfare state has addressed this societal reproduction of gender relations on the labour market as an important phenomenon (O'Connor 1996). In the 1980s, a distinct feminist debate developed on the issue of the variations in the welfare state and the accompanying variability of their influence on gender relations. Esping-Andersen's (1990) concept of welfare state regimes is useful for this discussion. He distinguishes three welfare state regimes: the liberal, the conservative and the social-democratic. Each is characterized by qualitatively different arrangements between the state, the family and the market. The distinct patterns of employment regimes are a consequence of the regime-specific regulations concerning the state, the family and the market. Each regime is also characterized by a specific pattern of female labour market integration and segregation between genders.

Feminist criticism has pointed out the negative consequences of the traditional focus on the situation of the implicitly male employee without family obligations. These critics demand that the impact of unpaid work in the family must also be included in analyses of gender relations in the labour market.[3] Crompton and Harris (1997: 196) argue that only an 'expanded version of "welfare state modelling" approach', which concerns welfare state regimes and gender equality policies and the encouragement and support given to women as mothers, has the capacity to develop a sufficiently detailed and dynamic account of national variations in gender relations and gender role attitudes. Their results coincide with Lane's (1995) earlier work which revealed how differently women's employment opportunities were affected, respectively, by the laissez-faire or interventionist ideology of the state towards family and employment policy.

Pfau-Effinger (1994, 1998a, b) developed an approach of her own, which reveals the connection between welfare states and gendered employment patterns. She uses three basic concepts – gender culture, gender order and gender arrangements to distinguish between norms, institutional regulations, gender structures in a society and the emerging forms of gender relations. The concept of gender culture is defined as 'common assumptions about the desirable "normal" form of gender relations and the division of labour between women and men' (Pfau-Effinger 1998b: 178). The concept of gender order refers to the structure of gender relationships, for example, the division of labour and power in a society and in different societal institutions. Societal institutions, for example, the welfare state, the family or the labour market, are important in relation to the gendered division of labour. The concept of gender arrangement is defined as 'generally binding forms' of gender relations which are made up of both gender culture and gender order. The distinction between gender culture and gender order on the one hand, and gender arrangement on the other, enables the exposure of inequalities, infringements and strains which develop between norms, societal institutions and their practice in society. Pfau-Effinger sees gender arrangements as resulting from on-going negotiations between male and female actors on different levels and in different areas of society. Thus this approach allows the inclusion of both the structural conditions for gender relations, underlying norms and the influence of male and female actors in the analysis.

Gendered processes in organizations

The development of gender relations within organizations in everyday working life, as one central area in a society, has become a major issue in feminist research since the 1980s. While early feminist studies often focused on the individual attributes of women and/or on the organizational structures, which contribute to gender specific opportunity structures (see e.g. Kanter 1977), the focus of more recent studies has been on 'how gendering is done' (Acker 1990, 1992) and on gender criticism of the fundamental theoretical assumptions in organization theory, such as hierarchy and bureaucracy (Witz and Savage 1992; Ferguson 1984), leadership (Calas and Smircich 1991) and the organization culture (Marshall 1984; Gherardi 1995). A common concern of a variety of feminist approaches is that organizations cannot be understood without analysing gender relations and the interactions by which males and females are established as different groups (and thus assigned to different types of work and jobs) and the ways in which male dominance is attained, maintained and reproduced through power relations.

Joan Acker (1990, 1992) has identified four ways in which persistent structuring along gender lines is reproduced within organizations. These four ways are 'components of the same reality; although, for purposes of description, they can be seen as analytically distinct' (Acker 1992: 252). They serve as different points of entry for the identification of gendered practices and processes within the ongoing flow of actions and interactions. Acker's inventory of general processes distinguishes between: a) the production of gender divisions through 'ordinary' procedures and decisions; b) the creation of symbols, images, and forms of consciousness that portray and give legitimacy to the divisions; c) the multitude of interactions that occur between individuals indicating dominance and subordination; and d) the gendered social construction of reality that forms the minds of individuals, for example, in terms of appropriate behaviour in the organization.

Both men and women participate actively in the construction of gendered practices within organizations. There are quite a few studies which deal with the action strategies of women in organizations.[4] The results of the studies show that despite the active participation of women in the construction of the dominant discourse and their resistance to oppression, a tendency towards individual and defensive action strategies remains. Researchers attribute these defensive action strategies to the male dominance in organizations along with the devaluation of women (Müller 1998). But there is still some form of variance concerning the preferred action strategies of women. On the one hand this tendency varies in accordance with varying situations in everyday organizational life. In informal situations, the women encourage and support each other, whereas they tend to avoid doing so publicly (Metz-Göckel 1993; Roggenkamp 1993). On the other hand, this tendency varies in accordance with societal contexts. In her research Czarniawska (1997b) observed local differences in the patterns of discrimination and action strategies in organizations in her country to country research. The national influences of the framework of common legislation and cultural differences are noticeable in the results.

The opening process in the private economy: women middle managers in German and Swedish business firms

Women working in a managerial position are seen as challenging prevailing gender norms and gender hierarchies, namely the predominance of male power in organizational contexts. Traditional norms and expectations relating to men and women, male and female positions and tasks are put to the question. But there is a great variance in how women are assessed and how they act within organizational and societal contexts. They may evoke manifest and latent expectations linked to traditional pictures of feminity in their male-dominated environment, but working as a woman in a male-dominated occupation may also offer a basis for change. They become actors challenging both the prevailing traditional feminine perceptions and the devaluation of female professionalism (Kirsch-Auwärter 1996a, b).

The research reported here focused on the work situation of women managers and their action strategies in Germany and Sweden. The results show how patterns of negative gender discrimination, women's action strategies and different societal contexts interact. The women studied by me worked at middle management level in private sector companies. The reason I chose this group is that, since the mid-1980s, women in both these countries have gained greater access to higher positions including middle management areas in private business companies. This development was stimulated by a growing demand for highly qualified personnel, which led to increased recruitment and promotion of women within the companies. In addition to this, there was a marked increase in the proportion of women studying economics or other related subjects in both countries in the 1980s. Despite their increased access to middle management positions, there are only a few cases in both countries where women actually reached the top management level (Theobald 1999).

This chapter examines the experience of these women during the initial process, when a large number of women entered middle management positions for the first time. The experience was probably rife with contradiction for many women as they noticed that the opening of some positions was offset by the closing of access into higher management levels – an ambiguous situation which necessitated interpretation of such contradictory experiences and the formulation of action strategies.

The initial process in both countries was accompanied by equally contradictory approaches to gender policy and corresponding gender norms and gender order (Pfau-Effinger 1994, 1998a,b). This concerns the question of maternal employment and of affirmative action policies on the labour market. While in Sweden the employment of mothers is both a norm and a reality supported on the basis of institutional regulations, in Germany the norm is that mothers have 'freedom of choice' between being employed on the labour market or being a housewife. The institutional regulations in Germany impede the labour market participation of mothers. In Sweden the equal opportunity legislation claims affirmative action in both the public and the private sectors, whereas in Germany this relates to the public sector only. In private sector firms there is considerable scepticism about obligatory affirmative action on the basis of legislation.

The research project proceeded on the assumption that it was not only the particular experiences of individual women and their situation in the company that had formed their assessments of their professional situations and the action-strategies they formulated. The framework of interpretation and the orientation of their action – so the thesis goes – was also determined by the societal context. These complex processes are at the centre of the argument that follows. The actual research consisted of two phases. First, a survey gathered information on the work situation and/or the progress of the women's careers. In the interviews which followed most interesting results were specifically targeted.[5]

Support and discrimination in everyday working life

Both in the interviews and in the answers to the questionnaire, the women in both countries describe the same contradictory experience of support and discrimination in their everyday working life. Acknowledgement and support are basic requirements for promotion to managerial positions. The descriptions given by the women show clearly that acknowledgement in their occupational environment is one important condition for the development or maintenance of the women's interest in having a career and reaching such positions of power and influence within the company. The interviews reveal the ambiguity of an environment that is simultaneously supportive and demanding. As an example of this, offers of involvement in certain tasks or opportunities to participate in training programmes made the women think about certain career positions in the first place or talk openly about what they envisaged.

Just how much such experiences could change a woman's way of thinking is shown in the following passage from an interview:

> I never really thought about going into management. But when [in the 1980s] they set up this programme for management trainees, they suggested that I should take part and so I did. I never thought that I could be thought of . . . I thought that that would be a fascinating possibility . . . I never thought that I could achieve that although I had always had an informal managerial position.
>
> (Sweden, 46 years old, insurance)

In both countries, the predominantly male superiors played a decisive role in women's developing interest in the advancement of their careers. In the few cases where women described overcoming the resistance of their direct superiors, further success or promotion was only possible with the support of other people who as a rule were higher up in the hierarchy than the immediate superiors. This support took very different forms. The superiors would, for instance, talk of a certain woman as an expert on specific questions, or suggest that she take on certain tasks, or offer her a vacant position, or even lend support in the planning of an individual career. A precondition for this support was, however, that from the perspective of the superiors, the women seemed to be interested in further career development. Such interest did not have to be declared explicitly: it could be deduced from some side remarks during a conversation, from a high commitment to their work but also in formal staff discussions. An example of the 'intentional signalling' is shown in the following interview passage:

> I gave clear signals that my job was important to me and that I wanted to get on . . . It's important that you do your job well and that you are present at certain discussions on certain subjects . . . I think if you don't do anything, you can't be gauged.
>
> (Germany, 32 years old, information technology)

This positive side – acknowledgement by the occupational environment and support of the superiors – was set against negative discrimination experiences. Such experiences were seen as barriers in career development, which women in both countries attributed to 'being a woman'. The results of the survey revealed how widespread this experience is. In their answers, 60.3 per cent of the German women and 64.2 per cent of the Swedish women stated that they experienced (negative) gender discrimination of some sort during the course of their careers.

In the interviews, the women in both countries related their experiences of gender discrimination. These results have been repeatedly confirmed in studies on the situation of female managers since the 1970s.[6] Women on the managerial level are spoken of as 'tokens', as members of a minority in a work situation imprinted with male norms. Such a work situation is characterized by the specific perception processes and behavioural patterns of men and women. The visibility of women within a male majority is linked to a marked control by their occupational environment. Individual women are perceived against a background of traditional gender stereotypes, which are contradictory to the demands and norms concerning behaviour on a managerial level. The women often tend to be excluded from the powerful informal networks and are like 'strangers in a male world'. The low status of women in the occupational environment makes it difficult for women to support each other openly.

Women's action strategies: individual versus collective action

Improving the career possibilities of women, and thus reducing gender-discrimination practices in the companies, proved to be an important issue for all the women in the study. Nevertheless, there were distinct differences in the kinds of statements the women made. Although they agreed about the experiences of women in managerial positions in both countries, they disagreed significantly in their assessment of the scale of gender-discrimination in their companies and in their strategies for change. These differences presumably reflect the impact of gender policy and the corresponding gender culture and gender order. In what follows, I illustrate the differences in women's statements first and then attempt to interpret the contradictions against the background of different gender policy approaches and the differences in individual experience.

The analysis of the questionnaire answers gave the first significant indication, revealing the difference in the estimated effects of gender on career development between both countries. While the female managers in Germany rated the effects as negligible, the Swedish women estimated that their gender had a significant influence on their own career development (see Table 6.1).

A second significant difference between the two countries concerned action strategies which the respondents suggested as ways of improving career possibilities for women. The Swedish women perceived affirmative action in the companies as a sensible approach to improve the promotion chances of women, but the German women did not (see Table 6.2).

The answers to both of these questions were discussed during the part of the interview concerning effective action strategies for improvement of women's career chances. In the course of the discussion the answers were linked to a number of ideas. The difference between the two countries con-

Table 6.1 The importance of the influence of gender on career development (percentage). The difference is significant (p ≤ 0.05)

	Germany	Sweden
No influence	9.0	0.0
Little influence	41.0	23.5
Some influence	21.8	23.5
Considerable influence	17.9	44.4
Strong influence	3.8	4.9
No details given	6.4	3.7

Table 6.2 The influence of affirmative action on career development (percentage). The difference between two countries is significant (p ≤ 0.01)

	Germany	Sweden
No influence	6.4	2.5
Little influence	42.3	7.4
Some influence	19.2	33.3
Considerable influence	12.8	23.5
Strong influence	2.6	8.6
No details given	16.7	24.7

cerned not only the issue of formal affirmative action but the possibility of a women's network (a network that would have any kind of influence), and the possibility of an open debate on gender policy in the company. Differences in views on those matters, as revealed by the women in the two countries, can be summarized in terms of 'individual' versus 'collective' approaches to change.

The majority of German interviewees opted for individual action, which in their opinion would target discrimination against women by the reduction of gender stereotypes in the occupational environment, and by doing so, improving women's career chances. It was postulated that the attitude towards women in higher qualified jobs, particularly that of superiors and male colleagues must be changed within the realities of everyday working life. The women wanted to prove to their superiors and male colleagues that they, in particular, and therefore women in general had skills and expertise which would make them capable of professional action. The women reported that when they felt discriminated against due to their gender, they tried to change this by having a private conversation with the person guilty of discrimination. This course of action was chosen as a result of the experience of the majority of the women which showed that prejudice lessens when colleagues and superiors are given an opportunity to work with women on highly skilled tasks. Furthermore, this was not just 'going to happen'. Women have to be continually prepared to act, as indicated in the following excerpt from an interview:

> I had two crucial experiences. My current boss was at first really a barrier for me . . . but at least after working with him for thirteen years he made sure that I would be his successor. And the second was my first boss who wrote to me and told me that at 55 years, I had given him food for thought. My continual effort and my readiness to work was important. I'm glad about things like that, breaking down the barriers . . . You have to do that individually, not in a group. In a group there is a blockage, they only achieve the opposite . . . Well, we had all that before. That's a long process and essentially it comes from the individual woman herself. Otherwise you get a reputation and they dismiss it as Women's Lib stuff and all the prejudice comes back again and then you can't say anything anymore.
>
> (Germany, 40 years old, bank)

The German women's preference for individual action was not only confined to a reduction in stereotypes in their occupational environment. It was their basic strategy for building up their careers. In the development of their own careers they were often able to get the position or the tasks they wanted if they talked to the superior who was responsible for those jobs. On an individual basis they were prepared to support other younger highly motivated women, but they disliked supporting just because they were women. This support and back-up of highly motivated women they see as significant for the general improvement of the career chances for women. Their women colleagues they value mostly because of their 'informal' professional discussion; but in public, for example at conferences, there is, as a rule, no mutual support among women, although some, if not many, would welcome it.

> Women could well support each other but we are too few . . . It would be better, for instance in public discussions, if a woman who talked was supported by other women. This would be an ideal case, but, of course, it's not always that way.
>
> (Germany, 33 years old, bank)

Other kinds of mutual support and affirmative action in the companies were viewed sceptically by the German women in the study. They saw co-operation with their male colleagues as more supportive of their careers than building women's networks. They explained this resistance to women's networks as being due to the lack of solidarity among women and to the fact that women generally have low placed jobs. Such positions do not make a good basis for any efficient support for the careers of other women. The idea of women's networks was only supported by the few women who were already integrated in such a network.

The following excerpts illustrate the argumentation of the female managers who tended to reject the idea of women's networks and permit insight into the contradictory experience of those women who endorsed the idea of women's mutual support:

> But there comes a time when I ask myself how much more I would have to do to set up a women's network in the company. I think I lack the talent to be a missionary ... Anyway, I haven't missed it up to now. I'm not obsessed with women just because I've male colleagues around me ... And it can have a negative touch, just like those 'buddy buddies'.
>
> (Germany, 37 years old, car industry)

> Yes, that's what I mean with these informal groups, that they function better with men. Men meet each other now and again for a chat and get together on something. I think that that doesn't work with women; people're more likely to say that the women gossip. Maybe that's because the women don't take enough time for these things. I think that's important.
>
> (Germany, 33 years old, bank)

The female managers in the German sample were more likely to expect disadvantages for women from an open debate on the gender question in the companies and the company's affirmative action programme. The lack of acceptance by their male colleagues of affirmative action would create yet another barrier for the career chances of women. The women supported an open debate on the gender question outside the company, in either the private or the political area. However, it should be pointed out that a negative or a positive attitude towards those anti-discriminatory measures seemed to depend on their acceptance or non-acceptance in a given company. The interviewees from the companies with a formal affirmative policy had a positive attitude towards affirmative action; those from companies without such a policy were negative. It was also common that only those measures already accepted by the company were seen as positive; the others were treated with scepticism.

The majority view on affirmative action in the companies and the perceived connection between the actual conditions in the company and the preferred action is shown in the following quotations:

> Such a debate would be likely to be negative. It's not good to talk to men about women's demands and I've never done it. I think it only does harm to make an issue of it and to tell tales ... We women agree, we don't want to be quota women, we want success on the basis of our own performance.
>
> (Germany, 49 years old, information technology)

> It would be good to be able to talk about it [women's discrimination], but you would need a lot of courage. Our company would defend itself strongly against any claim of discrimination against women. The women

do have chances . . . You have to look first and see; do the people who go along with it really think about these things so that you don't use up your energy for nothing . . . I'd be sceptical on a managerial level and there are so few and mostly on the lower levels. They're not really a mass of people who think about these things. Maybe two or three, but that doesn't make it a theme for women in general.

(Germany, 35 years old, information technology)

In addition, the majority of the Swedish women studied would prefer to improve women's chances by means of collective action, formal affirmative action programmes and open debates on the gender question within the companies. In their opinion, individual action has proved to be successful in building up their own careers, but it would not change the situation for all women. The basis for the collective action should be, in their opinion, a women's network.

I think that women need to know that we have to support one another if we are to change the prevailing patterns. Women are on the way there. There are some small networks already.

(Sweden, 43 years old, car industry)

By way of their networks, Swedish women have contact with other departments in the company and thus they can find out when there are vacancies, or render mutual support in difficult situations at work. One basic problem with the networks however, is that, even in Sweden, the women's jobs are usually on the middle or lower level of the hierarchy. Just as before, there are more likely to be men at the higher levels in the hierarchy and it is the men who make the decisions on the interesting positions in the company. This is why women prefer a double strategy: they not only participate in a women's network, but also try to gain access to the more powerful, informal networks of the male managers within the companies.

Formal affirmative action in the companies is welcomed by the majority of the Swedish women, some of whom have had a very good experience with it.

One of the interviewed persons who took part in an affirmative action project described her experiences thus:

It's important to be aware of the fact that there are always many excuses, and after all, why not? It's easier for men to work with men; they're playing the same game but the women are standing in the rain . . . Thus it is important that the employers themselves make a conscious effort. It has to be based on facts; they have to know why, and what the advantages are, just as with any other measures in the company . . . The firm has to develop a strategy and set out goals, control them and work out how we can reach them. As long as women don't do that, they'll be on their own . . . They did this in one company in a big concern and they got more female technologists. But as soon as you stop, it doesn't go any further. You have to have goals and give the reasons for them and ensure that they are being reached.

(Sweden, 43 years old, car industry)

The Swedish women interviewed emphasized that any approaches taken towards affirmative action policy have to be chosen with an actual problem as a target and with the aim of gaining acceptance for specific measures within the company. They recommended mentor programmes to promote career chances for women. Only a few of the female managers had any desire to have quotas in the workplace. The majority feared that positions earned that way would be too heavy a burden on the women because of the lack of acceptance in the companies, or from their male colleagues.

The Swedish interviewees stated that the participation of women in the networks and in affirmative action seminars not only reduces discrimination but offers women the chance to talk about their own experiences.

We have a women's network, and it's great when women go to conferences together and talk to one another; it's better than in the workplace.

(Sweden, 53 years old, insurance)

Just how important these meetings were in the everyday working life of the female managers could be seen in the way they described co-operation with their female colleagues. They made a distinction here between different work situations. Like their German colleagues, they found the more informal discussions on business problems effective and supportive. The different affirmative action programmes also offer the women a platform to support one another publicly within the companies, because it is still difficult for Swedish women to support one another in a public context.

A frequently mentioned example of this is the lack of endorsement for female speakers at conferences:

Men support one another more than women. Women support one another in everyday working life and when they talk to each other, but not in public at the leadership level. I'm disappointed about this. Men are more supportive when it comes to decision-making, and that's what's important. Women would get on further, if they were more supportive of each other.

(Sweden, 40 years old, insurance)

Action strategies and gender policy

The experiences of the women in everyday working-life in both countries show a pattern of acknowledgement and support as well as a devaluation of their professional competence, which they attribute to their gender. The acknowledgement and support, especially of their superiors, have proved to be a necessary precondition for the women's interest in pursuing a career and in their career advancement (Benshop and Doorewaard 1998; Tienari 1999). The active role the women play in the process can be seen in the many ways in which they demonstrate their professional competence and their interest in the advancement of their careers. Despite the acknowledgement and support, the women felt devalued as professionals and excluded from the important informal networks in the companies.

The Swedish women interviewed saw gender as having more influence on their career development than the German women. The recommended action strategies revealed two basically different approaches. German women wanted to overcome career barriers by individual strategies, for example, by convincing their male superiors and colleagues of their professional competence or by the support they gave to other younger highly motivated women on an individual basis. Swedish women favoured collective strategies: women's networks, open discussions on women's discrimination within the companies and formal affirmative action. They claimed that women's networks and seminars gave them the opportunity to make an issue of the gender question. But in everyday working life it was still difficult to discuss the discrimination of women openly even in Sweden.

At first the results seem to indicate a contradiction between the similar work experiences of the women in both countries and the difference relating to the estimated influence of gender and their preferred action strategies. This contrast can be more clearly explained by further statements on the part of the women studied.

The estimation of gender discrimination and the choice of collective action strategies of the Swedish respondents reveal the strong influence of gender policy and the corresponding gender culture and gender order. Gender equality, defined as an equal participation of women and men in family- and working life, has been an important goal on the political agenda in Sweden since the 1970s. Despite this, the labour market in Sweden is highly sex-segregated. The limited access of women to (top) managerial positions has been a central issue in the feminist debate since the 1980s. The Swedish respondents interpreted their work situation against the background of the goals of gender policy and a public debate that emphasizes the contrast between the high rate of female employment and the minor participation of women in management. This contrast, which the women themselves stressed, results in the emphasis on the influence of their gender on their career development.

The approaches to affirmative action policy accepted in society are decisive for the action strategies the women choose. There is a large consensus in Swedish politics concerning the necessity for formal affirmative action in organizations, opportunities for collective change strategies and open debates in organizations on the gender question. Thus, the women acquire a type of common and even public space for collective action within the organizations, through, for example, the women's networks. But it is difficult to transfer the debates and issues to their everyday working situations. The women studied stated that the question of discrimination against women is seldom an issue in everyday working life. Further evidence of this is shown in the difficulties, already described, which women experience in publicly supporting each other in their everyday occupational environment.

In line with gender policies in Germany, the women studied assessed the decision of women to seek gainful employment as their own individual choice. Indeed, the majority of the German interviewees explained the minimal representation of women at managerial level as being primarily due to the break most of the women take to bring up a family and not as a result of conditions within the companies. Despite the fact that gender equality is anchored in the constitution, there is a widespread scepticism in Germany towards affirmative action especially in private sector firms. Women have to prevail on the basis of their own professional competence. This attitude is evident in the interviews with the women. One example of this is the attitude of the women towards affirmative action in their firms. Also, the women reported that they were often able to overcome the prejudice and resistance of their male superiors and colleagues. The gender policies and the women's individual experience result in their low estimate of the influence of their gender on their career development. This leads to the choice of individual action strategies, a strategy of convincing their male superiors or colleagues of their professional competence or of supporting other highly motivated women on an individual basis. This strategy might lead to the defining of these women as 'exceptional' and to isolating them, as Cynthia Cockburn has demonstrated (1991).

Conclusion

This chapter shows how different approaches to gender policies in two countries are moulding gendered practices in organizations. Differences in gender order and gender culture influence how women assess their work situation and their individual experiences and determine their choice of action strategies. In both countries different patterns of gender arrangements are emerging within (working) organizations.

The research results present the organization from the women's point of view. But action strategies and interpretation processes are developed in the everyday social interaction of men and women. There is a necessity for further studies which will include the male superiors and colleagues in order to obtain an overall view of the on-going gendered processes in organizations and their societal impact. Interviews with men in organizations could give new insight into men's interpretation processes and action strategies and, with that, a reference point for effective strategies for change within organizations and on the societal level.

As organizational processes are always embedded in a specific societal context, the question arises as to the transferability of affirmative action programmes or, in a wider sense, strategies to counteract gender discrimination in organizations in different countries. The apparently necessary conformity to societal norms, approaches and initiatives in organizations does not imply a non-transferability of models and experience between countries. A double strategy of change is important: gender policies embedded in societal debates on the national level and adequate action-strategies, for example, affirmative action programmes on the organizational level. No matter how varied the women's strategies for change in both countries appear, their similar experiences could lead to the formulation of common goals. In everyday working life, we all need a culture which not only encourages and supports women but allows them to show their interest and their competence. We have to create a context of valuation to counteract the prevailing cultural pattern of the devaluation of women. A precondition for this is that the gendered processes in organizations and the practice of discriminating against women are named.

Notes

1 Some examples can be found in Crompton and Le Feuvre 1992; Czarniawska 1997b and Tienari *et al.* 1998.
2 For reviews, see for example Duncan 1998; Fagan and O'Reilly 1998.
3 See, for instance, Lewis 1992; Lewis and Ostner 1994; Sainsbury *et al.* 1994.
4 See e.g. Kanter 1977; Edding 1983; Ferguson 1984; Lindgren 1985; Acker 1990, 1992; Cockburn 1991; Wahl 1992; Witz and Savage 1992; Gherardi 1995; Czarniawska 1997b; Benshop and Doorewaard 1998b; Wahl,Holgersson and Höök 1998; Billing 1999.
5 The research was carried out in 1992–93 in seventeen companies in both countries in four branches of private economy: banking, insurance, the car industry and information technology. Eighty-one Swedish women and 78 German women answered the questionnaire. The response rates were 62.9 per cent in Germany and 74.3 per cent in Sweden. Twenty-two women in each of these groups were chosen for the interviews.
6 See Kanter 1977; Preuss 1987; Ressner 1987; Friedel-Howe 1990; Wahl 1992; Benshop and Dooreward 1998b.

7 Gender–neutral gender and denial of the difference[1]

Päivi Korvajärvi

The understanding of gender varies considerably within organizational studies. One of the lines of argumentation has it that gender is one of the most profound relationships in societal life (Gherardi 1994). However, other scholars have warned us about the risks of seeing gender as 'relevant and decisive everywhere'. The risk then is to reduce organizational issues solely to the question of women or men, and deny other possible standpoints and explanations (Alvesson and Billing 1997: 12). Indeed, in the course of my research on transformations in white-collar and clerical work organizations, gender seemed to be disappearing from my research material. As I interviewed clerical employees in several different workplaces and followed the transformations of their work over a long period of time, I have become more and more confused myself.

During fieldwork in several white-collar workplaces, it became clear that some gender differences were salient and easily found – like different places in the hierarchies of organizational positions or the sizes of office rooms, for example. Some other distinctions, including devaluation of women or their work, were formulated in comments like, 'why demand better positions for women if they are not interested in them?' (a male supervisor talking to me about his experiences in a social work office), or, 'if you ask me, the management are doing nothing; many of them have posh titles and important jobs, but somehow I feel that the real work is done somewhere else' (as one female insurance clerk put it). Yet other distinctions were quite simply matters of course, for instance how clerical employees created space for themselves at meetings; there were people who served coffee, people who made suggestions, and people who made decisions. Thus gender issues seemed to appear in hierarchies and appreciations of either organizational positions or everyday practices at work.

As I read and re-read the interview protocols and the observation material, however, gender issues seemed to take on a more contradictory nature than my fieldwork experiences indicated. The evidence of the presence of gender issues was no longer as clear-cut and visible as I had thought; indeed in its written form the research material seemed to have lost its gender aspects altogether – a phenomenon noticed also by Barbara Czarniawska-Joerges (1994) in her study. In fact, my first impression from my reading was that the written research material – and therefore work organizations I studied – were quite void of explicit gender-related issues. True, there existed occasional statements that provided good material for quotations as presented above, but these seemed to be more or less isolated rather than being an integral part of the broader picture.

I had to admit that this was in line with some other research results. In Finland, where I collected and produced my research material, the debate on issues concerning work seems to be silent on gender issues, maintaining a culture of gender neutrality. Indeed, as has been suggested by Julkunen (1994: 20–21), it is only very rarely that there has been any heated political debate about gender topics at work. Sexual difference at work does not appear as a collection or a mosaic of differences, but as a vertical structure which includes the hierarchic dichotomy between women and men, complemented by a combination of a self-evident heterosexist culture and rather non-eroticized relationships at work (Rantalaiho 1997: 21). Thus both my actual experiences at clerical workplaces and other research results supported organizational patterns where sexual difference had a visible hierarchic form but otherwise an obscure content.

The problem I want to tackle in this chapter is the paradox of simultaneous gender visibility and invisibility in clerical work organizations. The hierarchies as static structures in work organizations are clearly visible whereas the practices and processes in which they are produced and reproduced are practically invisible. Therefore my aim here is to move beyond the issues of hierarchic divisions between women and men at work and to explore in closer detail the dynamics of producing gender differences and the consequences of this in four service-type organizations in both the public and the private sector. How, if at all, was gender expressed in these work organizations? and how, if at all, did the gendering dynamics change in the period between 1986 and 1996? What, if any, are the challenges for the analysis of gendering processes as they appear at the beginning of the new millennium?

The research process

The study was carried out in the context of a long-term research project on transformations in work organizations. Consequently, gendering was just one topic among others such as transformations in the division of labour in the wake of the introduction of computer technology, or changes in management strategies and recruitment practices. That is to say, studying gendering did not simply mean collecting material on gender issues; rather, it was more a matter of close and sensitive reading of all the written research material concerning other issues also.

The fieldwork in four clerical work organizations was conducted by three female researchers on three separate occasions between 1986 and 1996. We went through more or less the same procedures to collect the research material in all three rounds of fieldwork in 1986, 1988–9 and 1996.[2] We started by visiting workplaces and by interviewing the contact persons who were more or less informally chosen – in some cases by one of the managers of the organization and in some cases through a discussion between the local shop-steward and the managers. At the same time we either informed the employees about the study in joint meetings, or the contact person informed the employees via Intranet, especially in the 1990s. The study was financed by The Finnish Work Environment Fund.[3] Having conducted a survey, we made observations in day-to-day work situations. Finally, we conducted interviews with the clerical employees, representatives of management and trade union people and gathered all the documented material we could lay our hands on.

In the studies of gendering, the most important material comes from field-notes and interview protocols. Given the long time span covered by our fieldwork, the conceptual frameworks, both in the work organizations and in our thinking, changed. Consequently, the research material was not exactly the same and the focus varied at different stages.

I was confident at first that I had adequate material for an analysis of gendering processes in these workplaces. The gendered structures which materialized in both concrete and symbolic differences and distinctions between women's and men's activities at the workplace were usually visible. This was what I thought at the time of the study. However, our understanding of the content of gender issues changed. In the mid-1980s we stressed occu-pational hierarchies between women and men. We mostly looked for (unequal) divisions between women and men. In addition, in the reports we wanted to be sensitive to what our interviewees had to say on gender issues. We wanted to work on their terms. Later we began to question the idea that a researcher is able to grasp the authentic voices of the researched. We realized that the researcher produces both the research material and the analysis.

During the course of the study we understood clearly that gender issues are not only about hierarchical divisions. We started to conceive of gender issues as practices performed in everyday activities at work. The shift in the under-standing of both the production of the research material and the content of gender made no big changes to the observation and interview practices in the work organizations. However, during the fieldwork of 1988–9 and 1996 we tried to be sensitive to the implicit gender aspects of different activities and transformations at work. Consequently, the analysis in this chapter is done through the lens of the latter understanding that focuses on the practices of the employees in everyday activities at work.

The organizations under study were an employment office, a unit of a social work office, a call centre of an insurance company and the administra-tive personnel of a metal company. The employment office was a small work organization that changed during the research period from a clearly female-dominated site into a workplace where in numerical terms women and men were almost equally represented. The office was headed all the time by the same man. The most striking feature of its activities during the research period was the continuous tension between the goals of service and efficiency, due to a growing market orientation. In the employment office I realized for the first time that it was not at all self-evident where the employees located equal opportunities and discrimination. It was a surprise to me that the employees saw that the real problems of equal opportunities between women and men were located in society at large, not in their own office.

The unit within the municipal social services office was even smaller than the employment office. The clerical workers here were women and the supervisor was a man. The activities in the office were framed by bureaucratic order. It was this case which presented in a pure form the basic problem discussed here: gender issues were hardly discussed at all. At the same time, women created hierarchies among themselves – on the basis of age, type of job contract, and pay. This was the organization that turned my attention to non-explicit gendering activities at work, and made me scrutinize gendering processes in relationships between women.

The call centre of the insurance office, which earlier, in the 1980s, was more accurately described as a telephone support and sales unit, was a growing workplace. It was a women-dominated unit, although the number of men increased considerably during the research period. The transformation of the unit into a call centre also implied a profound transformation of work from service to selling. This was a workplace where interactions with customers took on clearly gendered content.

The metal company differed from the other organizations under study in that here we focused on no specific unit but covered all the company's clerical employees and their supervisors. The clerks were women and their bosses, with just a few exceptions, were men. Surprisingly, the management had an equal opportunity policy, although it was only informally applied in recruitment situations and was not accompanied by an equal opportunity plan.

The vast majority of the employees with whom we had contact during our research were middle-aged women, working on a full-time basis with permanent job contracts. Educational background varied, but all the clerical and white-collar employees had relatively high vocational qualifications. By the end of the research period in 1996, most employees who had children did not have children at home anymore.

I begin with an example – of the purchasing assistants in the metal factory – and raise both methodological and conceptual questions that are crucial to studies of gendering processes in organizations. After that, I proceed with an analysis of gendered practices in the organizations I studied. According to my interpretation, gendering was embedded in and produced within five areas concerning:

1   Differences between individual women and men in promotion.
2   Differences between the work communities of women and men.
3   Differences between spheres of life.

4   Sexuality.
5   Skills and their appreciation in work organizations.

The central conclusion is that in the course of the study, that is between 1986 and 1996, the cultural construction of social skills became more and more salient. I end with a conjecture that social skills and the construction of social skills will be more and more important for understanding gendering processes in clerical work organizations in the future.

Let me now turn to the concrete example of what happened in the group of purchasing assistants at a metal factory between the 1970s and the 1990s.

Dynamics of permanence and change[4]

In the 1970s, women could not apply for the job of purchasing assistant at the metal factory I studied. As formulated by a male supervisor at the company, this was a 'no-go' territory for women: 'It was felt that women didn't have what it takes, that they'd just burst into tears when the going got tough, that they'd spend all their time chatting to one another.' The job involved the purchase of materials and equipment needed in production as well as responsibility for scheduling and cost containment. The first women succeeded in landing a job in purchasing in the 1980s. This was a major challenge for them: they wanted to show that they could cope and do well in the job. For men, the recruitment of female colleagues signified a threat to their position and their prestige, which, they felt, had been dealt a severe blow. However, ever since the mid 1980s, there has been a growing recognition at the workplace that both women and men can cope with the job equally well.

As the first women were given the job of a purchasing assistant, a new position was opened up, that of 'senior purchasing assistant'. This job was exclusively carried on by men. The job description included the delegation of tasks to purchasing assistants. In other words, a new level in hierarchy was created, to re-introduce a difference between men and women. As soon as women gained access to a new job, the men received more authority, a better salary package and a new job title.

By the end of the 1980s, the situation had changed yet again. The position of senior purchasing assistant was replaced by two supervisors. One of these two new posts was taken up by a woman who used to work as a purchasing assistant. This, in the women's own words, was 'an historic appointment' which had caused much resentment among male colleagues. The manager who made the appointment decision had talked with group members in advance to find out what they would think if the job went to a woman. This preparatory talk was something that, the women felt, he would not have had to do had he decided in favour of a male candidate for the job. Obviously, the appointment was a huge challenge for the woman concerned; it was crucial that she could show that she had what it took to do well in a supervisory job.

By the end of the 1980s, the feeling was that the whole controversy had died down and that the woman was coping perfectly well.

In 1996 the purchasing assistants at the company worked as a group in which there was only one man. The group supervisor was a woman. This marked a complete turnaround in terms of the group's gender composition. The company was severely hit by the recession of the early 1990s, which caused some redundancies, of purchasing assistants among others. Some of them (both women and men) re-acquired their jobs later on. There were deep-seated feelings after this episode, however: a feeling of a split among those purchasing assistants who had been made redundant and then brought back, and the rest. The former reported that they felt very much like outsiders.

The female supervisor spoke about 'awful and hard decisions'. She felt involved in these, although the decisions on redundancies were officially made by a senior manager. She considered hers to be a good team: they worked well together to solve any problems they had, even though they were different personalities and had different ways of thinking. The supervisor said that the last time she was about to recruit a new team member, she wanted a man, but there was none among the candidates. On the other hand, she felt the job was well suited for women as it involved working with details. The female supervisor herself acted as a secretary at the regular meetings she had with the male supervisors from the other units.

As well as illustrating the complications of the entry of women into new jobs over a fairly long period of time, this account also tells us about other things. The gender label of the group of purchasing assistants was changed so much that when new vacancies were opened, there were no men among the candidates. This was not the result of a conscious struggle on the part of women. Women were simply making use of an opportunity that presented itself, applying for jobs that were vacant. As it appears, however, the hierarchic difference between women and men was re-created over and over again, even though it assumed different forms. Finally, when the job was dominated by women, the female supervisor still served as secretary to her male supervisor colleagues. At the same time, somewhat paradoxically, she had wanted to offer more space for men in her group.

The division along gender lines was not the only dividing line: in addition, the purchasing assistants became separated from one another by redundancies. There were shifting assumptions not only about what kinds of skills were required for this job but also concerning what kinds of jobs were suitable for a woman. In the 1970s, the accent was on a tough and uncompromising attitude in negotiations concerning costs and scheduling, which gave the job a male label. In the 1990s, when the job was mostly performed by women, the stress was on fluent team-working. The shift from male to female domination also included a change in the perception of key skills required in the job, although the women's original idea had been to show that they could be tough when toughness was called for. There were, however, no decisive changes in the concrete work tasks during the period in question. Thus, apparently, the gendering at work was related to the shifting assumptions concerning required skills.

My example was intended to show that differences between women and men at work are not fixed and constant, but local and changeable (see also Leidner 1993: 209; Weedon 1999: 102). It also illustrated the fact that gendering processes might be obscure – as has been suggested earlier (Gherardi 1994: 593). This raises the question as to how we should analyze the pervasiveness, elusiveness and ambiguity of gender processes in concrete settings.

In this chapter I have chosen to examine and to reveal processes that appeared to include and to result in gender aspects in the clerical and white-collar work organizations under study. They are based on a close reading of the texts resulting from the process of the fieldwork (that is, interview protocols and field notes) on the assumption that they bear traces of everyday work activities. The aim of such a close reading was to look for social practices that result in implicit or explicit gender divisions or distinctions. The approach resembles that of Joan Acker (1990 and 1992) who has suggested a distinction of four sets of gendering processes in organizations. According to her, the processes concern: the production of gender divisions; the creation of symbols that explicate, justify or oppose gender divisions; the interaction patterns between women and men; and the internal mental work in which people construct their gender-appropriate behaviours in organizations. Compared with Joan Acker's suggestion my aim is to look for the topics that the clerical employees use when they explicitly or implicitly express issues that can be interpreted as gendering processes. The gendering processes may be interaction, symbols or something else; I simply focus on topics where gender is either expressed or embedded.

Such an approach also required a re-examination of all observations unfolding in the reading process: in particular, I paid special attention to the contradictory elements that surfaced from the research material. In addition, I made comparisons between organizations I studied and related them to the other cases of gender at work reported in the literature. Sifting out those aspects of the topics in everyday work that can be seen as relevant for gendering processes meant juxtaposing the empirical research material and information from other studies.

The process of relating my research material and results to other studies makes possible a reading and an interpretation of the concrete activities in terms that are not explicitly available in the research material. For example, it has been shown in a North American context that women at work are evaluated through their family duties whereas men at work are seen as employees without a life outside work. Women's activities at work are related to their family, but men's activities are related only to the work (Feldberg and Glenn 1979). In addition, it has been suggested that women in UK workplaces have strong domestic ties, especially because of motherhood, but men do not (Cockburn 1991: 76–104). The reasoning concerning women's place among the purchasing assistants contained only implicit references to their families.

However, the reasoning was not limited to work, as if the world of work defined the world of the family and home, as was the case in Hochschild's study (1997: 51). Activities at home, including Taylorized time-schedules and parents providing quality time for their children that sounded like office appointments at work, were not to be found in the talk of the purchasing assistants. Furthermore, sexuality in organizations has appeared to be a complex phenomenon including both positive and negative aspects at work (Hearn and Parkin 1995). Again, explicit references to sexuality seemed to be absent in the workplaces I studied.

This absence of family and sexuality topics in the organizations under study raised doubts in my mind about the relevance of categories constructed outside the sites I studied, and in altogether different kinds of societies. In addition, it drew me to reflect in more detail upon the implicit and symbolic gendering that happens in distinctions between work and home and leisure, and in relation to sexual tensions.

The different organizations are used here as sites where the production of gendering was examined. On the basis of the concrete and symbolic aspects that emerged in the process of analysis I have constructed a more comprehensive picture of gendering phenomena. Some organizations 'offered' examples of certain topics, but I argue that such topics could be found in all organizations we studied, even though the topics have their local form and content.

Practices and locations of gender

Different as individuals

Throughout our fieldwork, the clerical employees and their superiors, whether women or men, rarely saw themselves specifically as women or as men. There were no expressions like 'as a woman I am of the opinion . . .' or 'as a man I'd like to say that . . .'. In the organizations under study, the self-definitions of women and men as individuals or members of groups with certain types of characteristics, or participants in certain situations in society, criss-crossed one another. One way for clerical employees to place themselves was to see themselves as gender-neutral individuals doing their job in a gender-neutral environment. Thus gender was not totally absent but its role was not admitted (Hanmer and Hearn 1999). However, the recognition of gender issues related to one's own experiences of the promotion chances in the organization.

The women related their gender to promotion prospects in a variety of ways, however. In some cases they characterized the relationship between their gender and their work as a matter of individual choice. One secretary said: 'You can still sometimes hear people say that a woman's place is at home. But I think that I'm equal to men. If I want to get ahead and move up, that depends on me alone, not my gender.' In other words, this opinion expressed a denial of any gendering of career prospects, supported by a statement that everybody has the same opportunities and that it all depends on the individual's will. A moment later, however, the same secretary admitted that 'of course women are always torn into two parts, because they have to look after the family'. In her account then, family matters connected women, making them into a social category.

I also met women who for the first time in their lives noted their gender when filling out our questionnaire. An insurance clerk with a university degree said she had never thought about jobs as being 'women's' or 'men's': 'This is completely unimportant.' A male top insurance seller said that 'we are women or men here and we are all equal. A sales agent is a sales agent.'

For some other women, however, a strive for promotion meant a possibility of hitting the glass ceiling. One woman manager had designed and successfully run a new unit for seven years. It had been hard work, with long, 12-hour working days. She was sure that a man would have had less of a struggle. 'As a man I would also have got a new job description.' When her last plans, which included the expansion of the organization into a nationwide operation, were put into effect, she had learned, much to her surprise, that the unit was not to be headed by herself but by a man. This was a hard blow to her, but she took it all in her stride: 'Perhaps it's the destiny of us women.' Despite the discrimination, she wanted to express her contribution in the development of the unit and to be proud of it. 'This [unit] is my thing, it's nothing else.' She did not want just meekly to fulfil the 'destiny of women' but appreciated her own activities.

Another, similar story was told by a secretary with a university degree. She said that were she a man, she would have been promoted. She continued: 'But I'm not the manager type. I'm usually always the one who is a cooperative mediator.' Yet another woman decided not to apply for a senior post which was at that time filled by a man. As she had some experience of that position, she was able to compare her working style with his, and concluded that he 'was not drawn into the same sort of things as I was . . . He delegated much of the responsibility . . . to other employees, and quite rightly so.'

These women had very concrete experiences of being treated differently from men in the same situations because of their female bodies. At the same time, they were looking for some other explanations than their bodies for these processes. In the first case, it was the 'destiny of all women', in the second the demand of unpleasant, authoritative behaviour, attributed to managers (usually men), and in the third a different managing style which was acceptable to a man but not to a woman, which made promotion an unattractive proposition.

Thus, women in the clerical organizations saw themselves as individuals who either thought that gender did not matter or had personal experiences of hitting a glass ceiling. In the latter cases, one explanation referred to women's position in society, another to their personal skills and abilities. This led to two distinct ways of producing gender: one of constructing women and men as individuals, the other presenting women as individual members of the social category of women. Women and men were understood and generalized as either gender-neutral individuals (in the case of women), or as an abstract person with the exclusive right to promotion (in the case of men). Only women were seen as a category sharing an inevitable experience of not succeeding on career ladders.

Differences within communities

There existed a line of presentation that depicted women as work communities where women shared something in common at work. Again, there was much diversity. The old stereotype of women who gossip and form cliques and who are envious of one another is very much alive and kicking (see also Benschop and Doorewaard 1998a). People I interviewed were of the opinion that workplaces dominated by women must suffer from quarrels. They usually added, however, that the social atmosphere in their own workplace was excellent, and that their workplace differed from a 'typical' women's workplace.

The insurance clerk quoted above said that her workplace was not a 'typical women's workplace' and continued: 'I've never worked in a female-dominated workplace, I do not know whether or not the gossiping is true.' Still, as in the case of purchasing assistants, the idea of women as a group that gossips framed the accounts of female-dominated workplaces. Interestingly enough, I did not find anywhere either men or a man who would have described women as gossip groups, or else suggested that their actions were based on envy. The idea of women as a gossip group seemed to be a frame of reference applied by women even when they had no personal experience of this.

In one organization under study women did create differences and even hierarchies among themselves. Practically all of the interviewed there said that there existed cliques in their workplace. According to the supervisor, older and younger (in terms of their age and experience) clerical employees were doing the same job. Nevertheless, an older employee in an interview presented her younger colleague as a personal assistant of hers. She felt that the rules of co-operation between herself and her 'assistant' were not quite clear. The younger employees said they felt obliged to listen to their older colleagues and take into account what mood they were in, although, in their opinion, the jobs were all the same. This situation gave rise to a split and a hierarchy between the older and younger employees: as far as the younger employees were concerned, there were 'us' and 'them'. The differences concerned both control (usurped by the older employees) and resistance (revealed by the younger employees); also, both older and younger employees created distinctions and differences in the way they talked. It has been suggested that this type of negative, informal talk behind the backs of the people whom it concerns highlights women's inability to show solidarity and their need for men to introduce order (Pringle 1988: 231–49). In this case it served to produce hierarchical order among women; it was not only about divisions between younger and older employees but about creating a hierarchy.

Later, when this division became outdated, new hierarchic divisions were created through the same type of mundane talk. The new differences were based on distinctions between permanent and temporary employees and the size of the monthly pay packet. I would interpret the distinctions to indicate that in this workplace the work community was creating identities which fitted perfectly with the bureaucratic structure of the organization. In the longer run it isolated the clerical employees from one another, effectively reducing their co-operation (see also Sotirin and Gottfried 1999).

If the issue of gender in relation to the work communities was raised in the interviews or during the observations by the clerical employees without any encouragement from the researcher, it was to point out that the female gender was perceived by women as something negative in relation to the male gender. In the accounts of these women, however, 'the men' were seldom concrete and known people, for instance managers from one's own work organization.

However, during the observations I could see and hear that there were also communities of clerical women who supported each other in many ways. If somebody did not know what to do, the colleagues helped and gave advice. If something new came up at work, the clerical women discussed with each other and aimed to solve how to handle the new issues. Thus the social life in work communities was not as quarrelsome as some descriptions seemed to suggest. Yet it is important to note that gender was not expressed in terms of a good and positive atmosphere among female clerical employees.

Spheres of life

People I studied did not connect different spheres of life explicitly to gender issues. To me, however, it was clear that the situation of women and men at work was differentiated by the division between work and family. Women and men differed very clearly from one another in terms of how they situated themselves in the domain of family matters. In short, men tended to see women at work as members of the women's families, as somebody's mother and wife, whereas women took the opposite view: family and household matters had no impact on the way they did their job. They saw themselves (and others) as waged employees at work.

One department manager in the insurance company was clearly aware of the gendered vertical segregation of employees in the company. He pointed out that female and male employees often have different problems at work. In his experience, women's problems were usually related to children and their illnesses, which made them handicapped at work. A male manager in the metal company thought that women were too kind at work:

> I think that kindness means taking on so much responsibility that you work more than is fair and reasonable. In this sense this is an individual

question. We have many people here who are willing to kill themselves at work. They do not realize their limits. Both women and men. . . . This is not a sensible thing to do. . . . They sit here all night filing papers and then run around with their mobile phones. They leave their children at home to look after themselves. In that sense women's kindness is a punishment on the family. It is easier for men to be flexible than it is for women. Men are flexible with themselves; women have to fit in other things as well. It is not the employer's fault that we have these traditional roles in society.

Gender, according to the manager, was a personal and individual issue as far as one's job was concerned. According to him, it was the employees who worked too hard; neither the employer nor the organization had much to do with the pace of work. The manager emphasized here only the voluntary consent of the employees. Thus from his point of view the organization did not directly appear to be a 'greedy institution' (Coser 1974: 4–6) that presupposes total commitment from its members. The other side of the coin was that the employees took responsibilities voluntarily and they saw their killing work pace as necessary culturally, as Arlie Hochschild has suggested (1997: 14–19). The employees had no other choice than to involve themselves in the flow of everyday work without having resources to reflect on or change their working style (see also Rasmussen 1999: 48). With clear moral undertones, the manager stressed the demands of the family and found the working style of the employees, especially that of women, harsh towards the families. In his view, the organization is a meeting place for individuals and identities produced by society, but in fact the work organization has nothing to do with them. The organization or the manager certainly does not interfere in gender questions, although at the same time the manager held clear opinions on the women's and men's different situations in relation to work and to the family.

The secretary whom I quoted earlier and who said that all depended on her own will, considered it a matter of course that women 'have to look after the family', and equally as a matter of course that this was separate from waged work. In addition, a supervisor in the insurance company separated work and family issues from each other. She said she was extremely committed to the job and therefore took only one month's maternity leave.[5] She had earlier been at home for eighteen months looking after her older child, but 'I was climbing the walls'. At the end of the interview she said in passing that 'of course children are more important than anything else'. It seemed to me that she lived in two worlds, that of making money and that of being a mother, performing effectively at work, and also at home – through getting her own mother to take care of home. There were also examples of women who had returned to work before the end of their maternity leave quite simply because they were bored being stuck at home with the baby. A woman who had stayed at home for a long time when her child was seriously ill, said that 'being at home is boring and depressing'. In one office a man took a three-month paternity leave which in the late 1980s and even today is very rare. The women in the office thought very highly of this decision.

Family issues were also raised in relation to more general questions and not just in relation to one's own family. Some of my informants believed that some married women were simply earning extra money for the family's consumption, and that these women were not at all interested in advancing women's position in society. The insurance company seemed to be the only work organization where having a family or being a mother also took on very positive meanings. The call-centre's information bulletin boasted of having on its staff a mother – the same woman manager who had introduced the whole concept of the call centre and advocated the idea for years before the plans materialized but who did not get the head position when the call centre expanded into a nationwide operation. The bulletin introduced not only the mother, but also her 'warm-hearted personnel'. A father was missing from this symbolism. However, as noted earlier, a patriarchal father who neglected to promote the 'mother' was doing very well in the company. In addition, in active selling interactions with customers, family issues were crucial in that the clerks had to present them as involving risks for the client.

The relationship between work and family life was seldom mentioned in the interviews, except in symbolic ways, in the case of the insurance company. I would interpret the going back to work before the end of maternity leave to signify that work was giving something positive to the family, but not the other way round. According to the same line of thought, outside work, people did not gain any skills that might be useful in the workplace. The decision-makers, usually men, felt that family matters were a source of trouble to women, but not to men, at work. The female clerks wished to separate work and family life, and they seemed to prefer work. They felt that work gave them more interesting content than home, an observation that Arlie Hochschild (1997) has shown to prevail in North American companies.

Thus, in the eyes of women themselves, their citizenship in organizations, that is, the practices and duties that 'individuals must fulfil if they are to be granted the status of citizens' (Gherardi 1995: 169) was closely related to waged work, whereas men viewed women more as family-oriented people. The latter standpoint is a salient paradox in the country where women's waged work has long traditions and where the housewife institution has practically never existed. There was no discussion of any other way of organizing one's life except to have a heterosexual family and work. In such a frame the female gender was seen as something negative because of its close relation to the family. As far as work organizations were concerned, family was a private matter that had nothing to do with the employer. Families only entered into the work organizations through laws which regulated the length of parental leave or leave for taking care of a sick child at home.

Sexuality

The concept of organization sexuality (Hearn and Parkin 1995: 133–50) is defined as movement and proximity, as feelings and emotions, as ideology and consciousness and as language and imagery. There is no material in my study that directly sheds light on emotional bonds between people in the case study organizations. Therefore I define sexuality in a much narrower sense, as body-related expressions and activities that can be both about positive attraction and seduction on the one hand, and negative and uncomfortable harassment, on the other hand. From such a perspective, the culture of these organizations can be described as de-sexualized. Sexuality was not discussed and, according to my interpretation, it was not expressed in dress or make-up, for example. Female supervisors and managers seemed to have a 'uniform' of their own: a jacket suit, or at least a jacket and a skirt or trousers, and comfortable shoes. It has been suggested before that for instance female civil engineers in Finland had a strategy of not dressing too elegantly and of not putting on too much make-up in order to maintain their occupational credibility (Haavio-Mannila 1986).

Interestingly enough, women whom I interviewed were eager to see more men in their workplaces. In the employment office, for example, women felt that this would have a stimulating effect Such a belief was not unique, as shown by studies conducted by Pringle (1988: 108) and Alvesson and Billing (1997: 123). As one clerical employee put it: 'it would create positive tension and invigorate people'. The women used to add that men's arrival would help to push up their wages, too. In the employment office, men had indeed entered the organization, and the female employees said that men created both a more easy-going atmosphere and inspired more discussion about work-related topics. Men, for their part, also preferred gender-mixed workplaces, although their arguments were not so clearly formulated as those of women. Men were very careful or neutral in their estimations. One male employee said that a gender-mix is 'good for customers and it's good for the image of our job'. This latter opinion appeared very rarely, possibly implying that men bring something good to the image of the organization in the eyes of others (customers and higher decision-making authorities) rather than that equal numbers of women and men would as such be preferable.

Body-related definitions were also used of women at the workplaces. One male manager said that it would have been unfortunate to have 'a feather-brained, narrow-minded bank-clerk type of person' working in the office – an old-fashioned but widely used stereotype of a female bank clerk in the Nordic context. In the insurance company in the mid-1980s the female clerks were described by their male managers as 'quick girls' who did not think too much. At the metal factory, male workers told chauvinist jokes, but clerical women said that they did not take them too seriously. As a female shop-steward of the clerks said: 'There is clearly this chauvinist side here. I've heard others say the same things as well. But as far as I'm aware no one has actually suffered. At least, this is my opinion.' Thus clerical women seemed to ignore the crude jokes and wanted to give the impression that they were not offended.

It is not necessarily surprising that the interpretation of the sexual joking takes place within an organizational structure with its dependency relations. Konecki (1990) has suggested that worker flirting including sexual joking follows certain rules and limits in the interaction process at work. Women did not, according to his study, feel hurt when sexual joking between women and men took place in the frame where they were structurally dependent on each other. The dependency consisted of informal power hierarchies, or each other's performances in the flow of work. In the metal factory, the male workers were dependent on female clerical workers, in this case the purchasing assistants, who purchased the material and equipment that the male workers needed.

A topic often associated with sexuality at work is that of sexual harassment. In the organizations I studied, open sexual encounters were said to be non-existent. Nonetheless there were occasional episodes when women appeared both as sexual objects (in jokes, for example) and as sexual subjects (for instance, when expressing their preference for more men at work). When I asked women specifically about sexual harassment, all the women said that in their workplace it was not a problem. However, they often continued pointing out that a friend of theirs, at another workplace, had been so affected, or they told stories about what they knew had happened in another workplace. Thus sexual harassment was something that took place elsewhere.

It seemed that social norms kept sexuality in check; with the exception of the chauvinist jokes, it was not part of the work organizations studied. One's own workplace was seen as exempt from any unpleasant sexuality; that was something that only took place in some other places of work or in the accounts of other people. When sexuality was mentioned in the accounts, women either mentioned it positively or did not mention it at all. Men either said that they did not consider any issues at the workplace as sexual, or told chauvinist jokes as a normal part of everyday interaction at work.

Skills

Skills, and especially the appreciation of women's contribution at work, appeared as the most salient topic in the organizations under study. Bearing in mind the research setting (the original frame was that of work transformation) and the previously reported discussions showing the neglect of family and sexuality issues, this was to be expected. The case of purchasing assistants showed how the image of the job can change without any change in the actual content. When the gender of people on the job changes, so do the formal requirements. The image of the job itself does not attract any label of a female or male job, but 'job features are resources for interpretation' (Leidner 1991). Rather than job content, it seemed that new ideologies of running the organizations were now defining the formal job requirements. The accounts concerning skills were fragmented in the same way as the topic concerning individuals, categories and work communities. There were at least two kinds of accounts that emerged during the research period: one concerned the recognition and appreciation of women's social skills in customer service, and it was particularly salient in the 1980s; the other concerned a shift in the meaning of social skills towards personal performance and results, typical for the 1990s.

In the mid-1980s women's service skills seemed to be highly valued and women appeared to have won space within organizations as developers of different forms of customer service in the public sector organizations. In the private sector organizations, however, women's ways of doing their work in clerical positions was not much valued and the cultural barriers between women and men were high (see the quotation from the interview with an insurance clerk earlier in the chapter). In the mid-1990s, there was a growing tendency for management in both the public and the private sector to emphasize the importance of customer service, although the ideological content of customer service was different from that in the mid-1980s. In the 1990s, interaction with customers was no longer seen by the management simply in terms of interaction between female clerical workers and customers. This interaction was now set in new frames which were termed 'effectiveness' in the public sector and 'marketing and sales' in the private sector. This meant that management tended to set certain concrete targets, and even specific models, for providing customer service. This also meant that management tried in some sense to redefine the work orientations and identities of clerical employees.

According to this redefinition, customer service was no longer to consist simply of providing helpful advice, but had to be effective and driven towards selling. In the 1980s, service work in the form of providing advice and listening to customers had a distinctly female label: this was work that was regarded as suitable exclusively for women. In the 1990s, this construction has been revised. The director of the employment office explained that his office needed to have outgoing people with a close involvement either through experience or good contacts in business life. I would not, however, say that sales, marketing or efficient work are seen exclusively as men's work: there were service jobs occupied by women both in the insurance company and in the employment office. New requirements were now attached to interaction itself, as it was no longer enough to show empathy and follow the lead of the customer. More and more weight was placed on an aggressive approach and on knowing how to lead and direct the discussion with customers. These are requirements that are rarely seen as women's ways of performing the service.

During the study period, the demonstration of personal skills became more and more important in the organizations I studied. Instead of formal qualifications or work experience, personal skills and characteristics were emphasized, especially the skill to convince customers to orientate according to the aims of the organizations either in terms of selling and marketing, for example. This means that gendering processes more and more often took place in the informal areas of organizations where the important skills at work were constructed as individual characteristics. It seems that formal qualifications are less important today than they used to be in the Finnish workplace. This is reflected in legislation that in recent years lowered the qualification requirements for official posts. This may lead to women losing their educational dominance, and perhaps also to the nullification of women's most important successful employment strategy, i.e. that of gaining education. Every middle-aged woman in Finland has learned one major lesson from her parents: education gives you the opportunity to get a good job, and therefore it comes first; spouse and children come second.

Today, it seems that personal qualities and orientation to work have assumed greater significance than formal qualifications. Companies are seeking for 'personalities', and they are less concerned as to whether a candidate has a certain formal qualification. For example, the manager in the metal firm told me that they want to recruit personalities whose most important characteristics are the abilities to be co-operative, flexible and social. My study shows that social skills and social performance in particular are becoming more and more important in the recruitment of new labour. This means that culturally gendered codes of what is suitable for women and what is suitable for men in working life might become more and more often a basis for promotion and a determinant of pay level. At the moment it seems that the social skills required are changing in regard to what they require from femininity and masculinity.

Everyday activities instead of hierarchies

In the everyday understanding of the people in the work organizations I studied, gender was explicitly a matter of promotion opportunities and pay in general. Women and men were, however, conceived as separate categories in society at large, where differences were seen to prevail. Workplaces and the activities of the employees there close at hand were supposed to be gender-neutral. Gender was produced in practices including certain topics related to work. These topics were as follows:

1   Introducing distinctions between individuals with no relation to gender in terms of promotion.
2   Introducing distinctions between the work communities of women and men.
3   Introducing divisions between spheres of life.
4   De-sexualization of one's one workplace, especially in relation to sexual harassment.
5   A change in the content of skills appreciated in customer service work.

There was some mobility and fluidity in gendering practices at the workplaces. However, when women and men were perceived simply in terms of separate categories with different hierarchic positions in society, gender appeared as abstract and distant.

When not seen as categories, the dominant image of women and men was that they were physical bodies with a heterosexual relationship to each other. This model of thought pushes gender issues far away and prohibits, or even denies, the agency that operates in everyday working life. It includes the idea of gendering harmony that supposedly characterizes the immediate working environment in contrast to conflict at a distance in society at large, beyond individual reach.

Such a distant location of gender hides the cultural and symbolic aspects of gendering processes. This is supported by the self-evident culture of gender neutrality, which includes naturalized heterosexuality. Numerically, this is also manifested in gender segregation at work, although gender segregation includes inner mobility and dynamics (Kolehmainen 1999). My analysis suggests a future direction of exploring skills as complex phenomena where the actual requirements of work are more and more closely related to orientations and to ways of acting. It could be that, in the 2000s, the cultures and ideologies that have been seen as frames and conditions for work will be recognized as actual skills necessary to do the job.

The simultaneous taken-for-granted gender neutrality in everyday activities and the construction of women and men as social categories in society prohibits the recognition of hierarchic and non-hierarchic differences between and among women and men at work. My results reveal work organizations as sites where both women and men make sense in more personal ways of their relationships to the world.

The crucial question for further studies is whether the importance of social skills could open up opportunities for more diverse gendered subjectivities and under what kind of conditions. Do the multiple forms of social activities both within the companies and workplaces and outside them with individual and company-based service recipients, customers and clients, provide new spaces for non-hierarchic gender differences in work organizations? Seeing gendering as an everyday phenomenon embedded in organizational activities might provide an opportunity for a more subtle analysis of gender inequalities and equalities.

Notes

1 I highly appreciate the suggestions made by Barbara Czarniawska, Liisa Rantalaiho and Jeff Hearn. The writing of the chapter took place at the Five College Women's Studies Research Center in Mount Holyoke College. I thank the Finnish Academy and the Finnish Work Environment Fund for funding my stay there.

2 During the first and second fieldwork rounds I worked with Riitta Järvinen and Merja Kinnunen. During the third fieldwork round my colleagues were Merja Kinnunen and Susan Eriksson.

3 The purpose of the Finnish Environment Fund is to finance research and development work that improves working conditions and promotes the safety and productivity aspects of the workplace activities. In line with the Employment Accidents Insurance Act two per cent of the insurance premiums of employers who have a legal obligation to insure is given to the Finnish Work Environment Fund. The fund is managed by the social partners and the Ministry of Social Affairs and Health.

4 I have presented this case in Korvajärvi 1998.

5 In Finland women have a statutory right to a 263-day parental leave. The first 105 days are defined as maternity leave and after 105 days the couple can decide which of the parents should take the rest of the leave.

8   The Black Engel

Women from the ruins of the National Board of Building

Leena Eräsaari

Jelly and Ice Cream Party

Jelly and ice cream party, had an unhappy ending
The Black Angel took away the birthday boy

Mother's screaming on the balcony, her hair's a mess
And she's screaming for the janitor, she's out of her mind
The little guests all still whimpering in fright
Father's telling something confused to the police

Who told him to eat too much birthday cake
And pour cold juice down the other kid's necks
That puts you into the Devil's pan to fry
Not even the most innocent is safe in this world

Who's to protect the child? Who's to love the child?
And protect the child from hurting those little feet?
The bad Black Angel takes whomever it wants
And that's the only angel there is

The bad Black Angel took the birthday boy
The bad Black Angel took the vacuum cleaner
The bad Black Angel took the little tyrant
The bad Black Angel took the birthday boy
                    (translated from Tuomari Nurmio's 'Lasten mehuhetki')

The text is translated verbatim from a very popular Finnish song of the
1980s. The song has maintained its popularity over the years because of its
somewhat vague or symbolic message and an easy singalong tune, which adds
to the song's contradictory messages. When the song was first released one
popular interpretation of its protagonist, the Black Angel, was that it represented capitalism. It was easy to arrive at such a conclusion, since the singer/
songwriter was indirectly connected with 1970s left-wing radicalism. Thus
when a former cleaner from the National Board of Building and an active
trade union member spoke the following words, I could hear the Black Angel
soaring in the background:

A member of parliament I know asked me what should be done with that Engel, should we sell it and put it in the stock market. I said go ahead, sell the lot, so that they'll get the Black Engel for Christmas just as we did back then.

Re-organizing the State

I am presently working on a study centred around one example of the changes that have been taking place in Finnish public administration: the close-down of the former National Board of Building (NBB). From the ruins of the NBB grew the State Real Estate Agency (SREA) and the Engel concern. Here my main emphasis is on the point I call the translation process, i.e. the change itself. The question is: how the global vocabulary of privatization is translated into the local dialect or practices. When the NBB was closed down at the end of 1994/beginning of 1995 it was an organization which employed 2083 women and 1153 men (on July 1, 1994, the number was 3400 people in total). The largest single group of workers within these numbers were the cleaning personnel: some 1500 people, all but a few of them women. The SREA employed just over 200 people and Engel, in the beginning, employed 660; some also found employment in other public bureaux. Yet about 1500 people had to find something else; most of them found unemployment or early retirement. Among the people forced out, the cleaners were again the largest single group, almost 1000 people.

Many of the central bureaux or ministries that were part of public administration had experienced the same fate, that is, they had gone through various changes during the 1980s and 1990s. Yet the close-down of the NBB and its metamorphosis into new organizations had no parallel among the already realized rationalizations. The NBB was one of the few state institutions that were completely closed down; others were mainly re-organized. Its size alone made the NBB a 'Titanic' compared to the other central bureaux, for in addition to the planners, administrative officials and experts it had also employed 'workers'. In numerical terms the uncertainty and/or despair experienced during the changes was also unparalleled, as was the number of people who became unemployed or were forced into early retirement. The uncertainty grew particularly great, since planning and talking about the forthcoming change took an exceptionally long period of time. The future organizational change was discussed throughout the 1990s (till 1995) and had already begun in the late 1980s. Discussion concerning administrative reform or structural change became a routine. Decisions concerning the new organizations were made at such a late stage that the waiting seemed quite endless, and no-one knew what they were waiting for. The waiting that took place at the NBB, however, ended with the arrival of change which was rapid, like a great leap or Titanic's collision with the iceberg. In the 1980s, the term 'controlled structural change' was applied to any changes in public administration or labour market. The term also appeared in some early drafts for the changes that were to take place in the NBB. Yet what happened to the NBB was far from a 'controlled structural change'.

The NBB was split into two separate organizations, the SREA and the Engel concern. Not only was the number of employees dismissed during the process radically greater than during any previous change in public administration, but also no administrative reform had brought about such a complete change. The previous 'company-izations' of state administrative organs had been carried out so that they first became state organizations which the state could subsidize, whereas the Engel concern was turned into an enterprise which was intended to be profitable right from the start. In other words the metamorphosis of the NBB was both quantitatively and qualitatively more radical than the previous company-izations. Within public administration such a change was unparalleled.

One thing that contributed to the social setting which brought about the change in question was an economic depression also unseen in Finnish history. Unlike other European countries or the United States, the Finnish economy had prospered up to the end of the 1980s, largely due to export to the former Soviet Union. In the late 1980s banking had been freed from restrictions, whereas before it had been strictly controlled by the Bank of Finland. Finland was known as Europe's Japan. Thus when the economic depression began, the crises in Finnish export and industry were made worse by a serious banking and loan crisis. When the depression started, a relatively inexperienced centrist-conservative government was formed to run the country. One of its most important ministers was the Minister of Finance, Iiro Viinanen, who has been characterized as a Thatcherite, and not without cause. The NBB for its part was subject to the Ministry of Finance, and its future reform was planned at different stages by various committees and groups: sometimes these were formed solely from officials working in the NBB, sometimes from those who worked both for the NBB and the Ministry of Finance, and in the end the Ministry of Finance dictated the decisions all by itself. Altogether, there was a serious organizational conflict between the NBB and the Ministry of Finance. This was nothing new; throughout the history of these institutions they had had opposite opinions about the resources – money and architectural effort – invested in public buildings. This had also previously taken the form of political and hierarchical rivalry. In the re-organizing process the price for this organizational rivalry was paid by the 3400 employees.

Decisions concerning the new organizations were made very late – or at least brought to the NBB's attention at a late stage. The NBB had insisted that the bureau should be kept in one piece, or that it should keep certain tasks, from planning to maintenance. This was not, however, the Ministry of Finance's plan, for it was interested in reserving to the future bureau merely the 'ownership and property management'. 'Ownership and managing the property mass' means that almost all of the concrete work is ordered from consultants and subcontractors.

The decision about two separate organizations was made very late in the process, but it took even longer before anyone was summoned to draw up plans for the future organizations. The whole matter was not discussed in the parliament, and apparently not even within the government, for the State Economy Controller's Office report on the reform states that 'the Ministry of Finance should have discussed the matter with those administrative bodies who already had experience of organizational reformation' (*Tarkastusker-tomus* 1998: 144). Approximately eighteen months after the organizational reform the Supreme Administrative Court decided that the dismissals that had taken place during the reform were illegal. When the Ministry of Finance founded the Engel concern, the event was regarded on the one hand as closing down the old organization, on the other hand as the beginning of a new one. The cleaners who took the case to the Supreme Administrative Court regarded it as a 'transfer'. One of the cleaners stated the case: 'How could this Engel have been a new firm when the cleaners took up the brushes and buckets brought there from the NBB? They took them from where they'd left them the previous year'.

The Court decided that the cleaners were right and the beginning of Engel was a 'transfer'; it also ruled that the state should pay compensation for the illegal dismissals, which was also done. The manner in which the NBB was privatized was not merely illegal; it was also illegitimate in the sense that the Ministry of Finance had known about the 'illegality' but decided not to inform parliament of the matter. Also, the highest-ranking official in the Ministry of Finance, who played a central role in preparing for and carrying out the reform, stated publicly in a TV documentary that 'the people in the Ministry of Finance knew well enough that the reform in question was illegal, but they tried to "trim it of illegal characteristics" enough so that it would fall short of the "essential elements of illegality"' (from a TV document called *Lost Case*). The Finnish constitution states that officials are under obligation to follow Finnish laws and statutes, but as far as the privatization of state utilities is concerned, these laws are apparently invalid. Perhaps the greatest illegitimacy in the whole matter is, that the official in the Ministry of Finance who played a central part in the reform could publicly announce that he knew the process would (probably) be illegal, but that it was still worth carrying out because it saved state money. Although I focus in this chapter on what happened to the women who were dismissed from the National Board of Building, I would still like to emphasize the fact that the legitimacy of the whole reform process was questionable.

The NBB was closed down during the deepest depression, which made people's chances of finding employment 'elsewhere' difficult, as it still is for many in the present decade. There are jobs available for cleaners at Engel too, but many of them are so bitter towards their old employer that they would not work for it even if it meant starving. Also, the cleaners went on strike right after the reform had been carried out, and either refused the new terms of employment they were offered after the strike or would not seek employment. Engel, for its part, has offered its cleaning personnel wages which are more or less equal to unemployment benefits (linked to the earlier earnings). The cleaners' workload has multiplied, in that the area to be kept clean has increased. It is also more than likely that many of the former employees of the NBB are simply unable to work after the tumult they have been through. There are no statistics of mental problems, suicides, etc., but all of the people whom I interviewed mentioned mental problems. One of the employees who got a new job at Engel said the reform process felt 'as if somebody had been sawing at my throat for six years'.

In ancient Greece the *polis* and the *agora* were reserved for free men; women and slaves had no access to them. Richard Sennett (1994) describes women's participation in the use of public space in Athens during the classic period, pointing out that women organized their public or common events at night and/or in places altogether different from the men's *agora*. In Finland, women got the right to vote at the turn of the century in 1906, the second country in the world where this was achieved. The number of women in parliament has been considerable throughout the history of Finnish independence, and women also gained the right to study at university level or to enter various public posts at an early stage, and relatively painlessly. Thus, as citizens, they have had symbolic rights of access to public spaces. The vote and formal access to different posts has been of great symbolic value in rhetorical terms. There is a well known figure called 'the strong Finnish woman'. Part of the rhetoric of the figure consists of the early access to political arena (Keränen 1993).

Usually organizational changes are studied from the point of view of the people who remain in the new or changed organization, or at least remain in working life. But since the present changes and the economic depression force many people outside the scope of working life, I consider their 'exit' a part of organizational change. Here I concentrate on the question of the women who were driven out, became unemployed or were forced into early retirement. How were the women who worked in various organizational positions driven out? What have the unemployment benefits and/or early retirement meant to them, or the state compensations that were paid to the former cleaners as a consequence of the illegal dismissals? How do these women get by? What do they expect of their futures?

My aim is to use a few individuals' fates to illustrate what happened to these women. The qualitative part of my paper is based on these women's biographic interviews. I have interviewed some of them only once, others several times. My group of interviewees consists of five women. Two of them are unemployed cleaners, the other one had retired by the time of the inter-view. Two of the interviewees are architects, one of whom first worked for Engel but then moved to a private agency. The other architect has been unemployed ever since the NBB was closed down. The fifth interviewee is a secretary who obtained employment at the SREA.

Women in the NBB

The cleaners

The largest single group of workers in the former NBB were the cleaners, almost all of whom were women. Actually the cleaners were even presented as a cause for closing down the NBB: 'the state should not worry about cleaning'. The high number of cleaners among the 'civil servants' was also singled out with the derogatory remark that 'the NBB had become just a National Board of Cleaning'. The cleaners' salaries and other benefits like seniority bonuses, occupational health service, and permanent employment were so 'good' that cleaning did not 'compete well'. From a cleaner's point of view it was a good thing to work for the state, if cleaning was how you made your living. Many of the cleaners who worked for the former NBB had had previous jobs in various areas of industry, such as factories or dressmaking departments. In other words they were familiar with infrequent working hours, uncertainty of employment and low salaries; the NBB was an improvement compared to their previous jobs.

One of the benefits the NBB offered to all of its employees was continuous education. Those who were employed by the NBB were encouraged to educate themselves, and advanced training was often rewarded with a better position or more meaningful job. In architecture this meant that the NBB became a kind of second institute of higher education, alongside the universities of technology. The last director made education an even more valued asset. When the organizational change was being planned in the 1990s, education was emphasized even more strongly, since it was regarded as a means of improving people's labour market qualifications. Again education was for all groups of workers.

To the cleaners the NBB also meant, in addition to better benefits and working hours, a rise in the 'status' of the cleaning. One aim of the training organized by the employer was to improve the self-regard of the cleaners. Among other things this training emphasized social relations and interaction skills; the idea was to improve their negotiating skills and their visibility in their workplaces. Since the cleaners working for the NBB worked during office hours (7am to 5pm) instead of the evenings and nights when the bureaux and other similar workplaces are empty, it was important that they should be able to negotiate with the other employees. Their work clothes and outer appearance were improved, and generally speaking the training aimed to teach them to 'act smart'. Central themes in building up the cleaners' identities were, for example, that 'cleaning is a job which requires professional skill', 'cleaning is a remarkable job', or 'cleaning is independent'. There were also attempts to improve the status of their job by making it more visible: 'There is nothing to be ashamed of in cleaning; there is no need to do it in hiding'.

The cleaners' visibility in public buildings has a considerable symbolic value. Historically the public buildings owned by the NBB can be considered as an extension of the *agora*, the symbolic heart of the ancient *polis*. The buildings owned by the NBB were not the *agora* or holiest theatrons of political activity like the parliament house. Most of the buildings built and owned by the NBB were ones in which public life takes place, where the citizens negotiate and mould their own share of citizenship, mainly in relation to public administration, officials or teachers, etc. In addition to access to the political *agora* women have also kept it clean and in order, and done this 'visibly' during the daytime, a symbolically significant act. Thus while the cleaners' jobs have been privatized, the terms of their employment have become worse, but their work also becomes less visible. It is increasingly the case that public space is kept clean and in order 'outside business hours'.

The cleaners of the NBB were visible in the state offices but not in the written histories of the organization, where cleaning was not named. The official histories of the NBB concern on the one hand the finished buildings, their creators and designers and on the other hand the leading persons of these organizations. The cleaning was also invisible during the reconstruction period of the 1990s in terms of functions. When the NBB for example tried to envisage the future during the reforming process there was no mention of cleanliness being necessary to the future working spaces. As the head of cleaning in Engel said: 'Cleaning was not that well appreciated in the NBB neither.' During the period of reform, the messages concerning cleaning concentrated on the costs, 'too expensive to compete well'. It was only after the organizational change that people working within the management of public buildings admitted that the quality of the cleaning was exceptionally high.

To the women employed by the NBB, work during the daytime meant that they were able to act as mothers in the evenings and during the weekends. There are no statistics on the backgrounds of the cleaners who worked for the NBB, but many were divorced single parents. Many interviewees also thought that the percentage of single parents among the cleaners working for the NBB was above that of the average workplace dominated by women.

Finnish sociological women's studies have dealt with and studied the relationship between the state, or welfare state, and women. One of the constant themes in this discourse has been that the state has provided safety in women's lives in two important ways: the welfare state has offered jobs to women and created services which make wage earning possible when women who are also mothers have not left the labour market. Often the functions of getting the job and getting social services are combined in the lives of working women, as in various caring professions. Children's day-care, education, health care, etc., are publicly administered and funded services although formally arranged by the municipalities. Thus the women employed by the NBB were among those women who benefited from having the state as an employer and provider of services for dependent family members.

The architects

In the sociology of organizations the term 'profession' is reserved for those jobs that were formerly considered vocational. A vocation or calling refers to the fact that such jobs demand full commitment from their practitioners – the practitioner of a profession is expected to be at the job's or organization's disposal all the time. Profession implies extensive university studies, the crucial thing being to get a certificate or diploma, which permits entrance to the field. One of the central contributions feminist studies in management have offered with regard to professions is the idea of the 'glass ceiling' – an invisible barrier between women and the professional 'elite' or the hierarchically superior. Some committees have based their recommendations, to improve women's situation in the labour market, on the concept of the glass ceiling. David and Woodward (1998) think that the concept of the glass ceiling is inadequate for analysing the situation. But I shall use it nonetheless to describe the situation of Finnish women architects, the ceiling being appropriate when talking about people who design and create buildings.

In Finland approximately one third of all architects are women – an exceptional number compared to, say, 10–20 per cent in other western societies (Fiona Wilson 2000). About half of the students of architecture at the moment are women. But since private employment has been more desirable than public employment, women have been employed by the public sector more often than men. Private architect agencies offer more of the actual work of architecture (planning, design, and implementation), as well as fame, status and riches. The most famous male architects have offices of their own and have been called maestros (Alvar Aalto is a famous example). The glass ceiling keeps women out of private agencies as well as explaining why men advance higher in the hierarchy than women, whether they work for private or public employers.

What, among other things, creates the glass ceiling and the walls are those official and unofficial societies and meetings in which all the new posts and tasks, as well as the persons suitable for these, are discussed. The expression 'professional closure' is also used and may be a better expression for locking people out. The posts that are available on the private side are filled solely through unofficial channels; the employers are under no obligation to announce them publicly, or they can set the terms for the open posts so that there is only one applicant to fill them. On the public side the posts are generally more open to all applicants and therefore also reachable by the women who have no access to men's circles and clubs.

Harriet Silius has conducted research on Finnish women lawyers (1992), who are comparable to the architects in professional terms. Both lawyers and architects share an extensive university-level education, and acquiring this education or entering the profession is relatively difficult. On graduation, the practitioners can work either in the private or the public sector. It is typical of the professional women that they tend to emphasize their 'genderlessness', or do not consider gender a relevant issue for their career or profession. Silius (1995: 49) writes about the female lawyers: ' "I have consciously chosen a field in which gender plays hardly any role", assured one of the women lawyers in the research. According to another, men and women are "remarkably equal" in her profession. A third one believes that the concept of "woman lawyer" will disappear in time, which makes it "unnecessary to emphasize being a woman lawyer". Several of the hundreds of women lawyers who participated in the study emphasized, assured and underlined the fact that theirs is a profession in which gender "doesn't count" '.

No-one has specifically studied women architects' views on the professional effects of gender, but my own interviews seem to imply an attitude similar to that of the women lawyers. An exceptionally high percentage of women architects in comparison with other countries does easily give the impression of normality. The Association of Finnish Women Architects, *Architecta* (founded in 1942), has worked within the Finnish Association of Architects (SAFA), but many of the women architects I interviewed saw it just as an 'old ladies sewing circle' which looks back on its glorious past. The existence of such an association however would seem to imply that the gender issue was at one time regarded as important, if not central, for working in the profession, whereas in the 1990s the issue was considered unimportant.

In 1982 the Museum of Finnish Architecture organized an exhibition of Finnish women architects, where the exhibition brochure stated in the introduction that 'The pioneers worked in conformity with the spirit of the times, at the same time fighting to achieve for our country's women a permanent place in the architectural profession. For this reason women architects in Finland today face no particular problems in practising their profession' (*Profiles* 1983: 5). Thus when the NBB was dismantled and renewed, neither Architecta nor any other women's organization or unofficial coalition took up the gender issue. Therefore among the official documents concerning the organizational change in the NBB there are none that would mention equality between the sexes. It is uncertain whether Finnish law on equality would have made a difference during the organizational reform in question, for the law does not recognize the so-called 'positive discrimination'; the law forbids discrimination among equals, but does not demand the selection of women or other minority groups when the scales are even. As far as I have understood it, during the organizational reform none of the women architects or engineers even unofficially took up gender issues.

Men's rooms and clubs

Silius (1995: 153) writes about the conditions that dictate women lawyers' careers: 'In the future it may become even more difficult for women lawyers to advance in the hierarchy. The problems stem from the fact that they have no free access to the colleagues and researchers, to the clubs and associations, or generally to the circles in which potential employment is made known and unofficial recommendations given. In other words the gatekeeper system works against them'. The situation is similar with women architects. When work in the public sector grows scarcer, so do women's chances.

Caroline Pateman writes in *The Sexual Contract* (1988), about the union of fathers and brothers in a patriarchal society. When one talks about Freedom, Equality and Fraternity, one generally does not stop to think about what, literally, 'fraternity' means. Where political science has regarded fraternity as a general type of solidarity, which applies to all regardless of gender or other characteristics, Pateman takes up the fact that sons and brothers fight the father and deal the power amongst themselves. The sons and brothers take it as a matter of fact that sisters are not mentioned or addressed when power is shared. This usurpation of power is taken as democracy because the absolute power of the father is divided between several males. Now since the 'brothers' divide the legacies amidst themselves, sisters have to go without. The last thing the NBB ever published was a work titled 'Engel's Legacy' (*Engelin perintö* 1995), which includes an article called 'Change of men – but work goes on'. In the article all of the still surviving male directors of the NBB discuss its past and future. The union of fathers and brothers is beautifully illustrated by the photograph (from NBB bulletin 21/91) below, supplied with the text: 'WE DO IT OURSELVES'. The ancestors on the wall emphasizing the brothers' worthiness are worth a special mention.

The bulletin mentioned above, which tries to tell its readers that 'we do it ourselves', goes on in the next page to talk about the so-called controlled

Figure 8.1 'We do it ourselves': The bosses of the NBB in their uniforms (1991). From left to right: Jukka Liede, Pertti Tuominen, Matti K. Mäkinen, Jorma Yrjö-Koskinen, J. K. Väänänen. (Photo: Pressfoto/Esa Pyysalo.)

structural change. Neither of the claims was justified: the officials working for the NBB had no authority in the organizational change, which, furthermore, was not controlled. Instead, the fathers and brothers, depicted in the photograph, saved themselves and their legacies. None of the officials in the photo became unemployed; the father was replaced but was made a professor until his retirement. One of the brothers headed the SREA until his retirement, and all except one received high-level posts in the SREA. That one exception is a boss in the Engel organization. The stage during which the reform was planned from within the NBB took up approximately eighteen months. Some of the interviewees are of the opinion that the Ministry of Finance had already made the necessary decisions before the 'we do it ourselves' stage, but had given the NBB the illusion of 'doing themselves'. And when the NBB could not do it 'itself', the Ministry of Finance took the reins and handled the whole change, making plans as well as carrying them out. Various committees sat mulling over the reform throughout the 1990s, making reports and plans. But genderwise they were, just as in the picture above, all men.

The appointment of these committees was made in public to the extent that the nominations were published with the Ministry of Finance's decrees as well as in the NBB bulletins. Information concerning the future organizations' 'timings' and the number of officials planned for the future SREA was also freely handed out. But the actual nominations for the organizations were done without any public application and the employees were recruited from within the NBB. Recently universities have also moved towards a similar 'invitational' basis. Chairs are no longer officially open for applicants, but rather a 'suitable individual' is invited to apply. Feminist researchers have taken up the complaint that the use of such an invitational system for filling professors' chairs, instead of the traditional system of open application, favours men over women. While an increasing number of chairs is filled by invitation, the number of women professors is decreasing – although it has never been particularly high when compared to the percentage of women among students or graduates (Husu 1998, 2000). In other words, women's under-representation in the highest university posts increases with the popularity of the invitational method. Similarly, nominating the high-ranking officials without declaring the jobs open for applications can be regarded as a kind of large-scale invitational process. All the 'important' people either at Engel or the SREA came there 'invited'. The head of the Engel concern used the expression 'manned with the best people' – manned, indeed.

Since there was no Engel or SREA, there could be no democratic or undemocratic organization to decide about the nominations. The head of the Engel concern was nominated in the spring of 1994, at which point he started planning and implementing its organization. The head of the SREA started at the beginning of 1995, more or less at the same time as the organization itself. The head of Engel named his top-ranking directors based on interviews. When they had been nominated they in turn nominated their closest subordinates. 'The posts were apparently open for applications, but I never heard of this' was a comment I heard from several of the interviewees. Some of those who got posts say they knew about the vacancies because somebody inside the house had pointed them out to them and advised them to apply! Obviously there are many ways of announcing places open for applications: a short time for handing in applications, a so-called noticeboard announcement, i.e. a single paper on a noticeboard which is seen by a limited circle of people, and so forth; all these narrow the selection of potential or actual applicants. A woman architect who did get a place at the SREA told that she had applied for dozens of places, but still believed that 'nobody could read those applications because there was no-one nominated for the selection job'.

Many ways of being invisible

Only a few employees got to bring about their nominations through a father or brother, whereas the ways of being invisible – out of the male clubs or their sight – are numerous. Making use of Mikhail Bakhtin's idea of polyphony (1987), one could say that since one and the same text can speak in different voices, it can also be silent or dumb in various ways. Since the organization I write about employed more than 3000 people in various places all over Finland, various actions resulted in different modes of visibility or invisibility.

When the NBB was closed down and people were 'nominated' to the SREA or Engel, visibility at the workplace was very important. If one's output was less than normal – due to sickness, maternity leave, taking care of relatives, etc. – the result was lesser visibility, the employee became 'unreliable' or worse than those who were present.

> I couldn't read the culture in the NBB before I'd already had the rug pulled from under me. The architect unit had all the status. They were talented, the artists of the NBB. I moved from the A office to the B voluntarily. In the A I would have been close to the head director. This other one had a bad physical location, besides which it had all the engineers and such. Only later I realised that symbolically this was a terrible devaluation. The whole transfer was seen as a displacement and I was too naïve to understand it. I just went along with this new thing and in the beginning, in the winter it was quite fun. But in the summer the future head of Engel came over with the recruitment and everything became a mess. The SREA's jobs were open, but I never realised when it happened.

This quote is from an interview with a young ambitious architect, Eeva, (the characterization is her own) who ended up working for Engel. Her story is concretely and symbolically quite enlightening for at least two reasons. First of all, the informant tells how being out of the directors' eyes meant falling into oblivion or being regarded as displaced. But there is a second plot in the story, which is tied up with the reason for moving from the centre to the periphery. That reason was a development programme which included research and a new kind of planning. One of the defining policies of the NBB during its last years too was 'research and development activity'. Thus those employees who took part in developing programmes were thought to be rewarded with a 'business card' which would help them with future employment outside the organizations built on the NBB's ruins. Eeva moved from Engel to a private agency by making use of her business card, 'specialising in office buildings'. She had to leave the office and she admitted that in the private sector the 'real estate business' became so tough that she just could not cope with it. Now she has short-term, semi-public employment. It looks very much as if 'knowing or doing well' would not be enough this time either (summer 2000), for she will probably be displaced by male architects who 'know the rhetoric among themselves', as Eeva put it.

A case similar to that of Eeva's is that of Marja, an unemployed architect aged around fifty. She also spent the 1990s learning a new way of working, learning how to use new tools, or what in project planning is known as 'problem seeking'. Only after having been unemployed for quite some time had she realized that the planning project itself was part of the close-down of the NBB. A few years later Marja described the situation thus:

> That's when they started talking about the end of the NBB, and people were moved from one room to another and rooms were rearranged. Already back then we said that those who were moved to the facade side, where you could see the street and the park, would be the ones to stay. Those who were given windows overlooking the backyard, like I was, would have to go – that's how it seemed.

Some move voluntarily out of sight, some are moved against their will to places less visible to the powerful. Invisibility grows also from duties of care taking like being a mother and a wife, together or separately. Tuija is a secretary employed in the SREA. She describes change and the recruitment in the following way:

> 'The first time I realised things were about to change, I reacted with fear and worry. There was the question of age, although I wasn't all that old then. I thought that it couldn't be all that horrible; I also saw it as a chance of moving forward. But I was also thinking about having children. When I realised that this change was really going to happen, I decided that this was the time to have the child'. Tuija had her child, which meant that she was on maternity leave during the time when transfers to the Engel or the SREA were negotiated. 'I went up to show my face even during the maternity leave, so that they wouldn't forget me. But I didn't get so stressed about it as to go to a doctor or something like that. But I was quite stressed.' [The statutory maternity leave is approximately a year.]

Moving away from the building of 'high command', moving to the backyard side of the building, going home on a maternity leave: all of these are real spatial descriptions, not merely symbolic or metaphoric expressions – although that also. In the next quote a cleaner called Maire describes her displacement:

> Now we'd heard from the employer that everyone was offered a job and all who were willing to continue could do so. But obviously this wasn't so; I was on a sick leave for the whole year and no-one contacted me or anything. Even the note of dismissal wasn't sent to me in time.

In addition to the sick leave, the woman in question was her department's chief shop stewardess and had been for almost twenty years. If the employer had not offered her a new job in the new organization, she would have been entitled to compensation for 'illegal dismissal'. Therefore the employer claimed to have offered her work, although this never happened. The cleaners' trade union was part of the Confederation of Finnish Trade Unions, but the employer did not like the white collar SAFA any better. And the chief shop steward representing the white collar union almost lost his job for the same reason as the cleaner: for being an active member of a trade union. Both were quite bitter towards their trade unions. The dismissed cleaner criticized the trade union for several reasons, although it had formerly played an important role in her life. Just before the interview (at the turn of 1998) she had lost her last connection to her branch of the union when it had been decided that unemployed members should not be engaged in its decision-making. 'They don't want us being critical in there anymore', she commented.

Getting out from an organization is also a spatial process. When talking about a long process of re-organizing, getting out is a step-by-step phenomenon or a long path with several standstills. The crucial steps out from the premises of the organization depend on the positions held. The cleaners got out of the organization in a different way than the architects. Mostly the cleaners refused to accept work with poor conditions. The common feature in the fate of both groups of female employees was that they had no possibility of negotiating their future; their fate would be decided somewhere else, in the clubs and meetings of the brothers.

There is quite a lot of violence embedded in the process which is difficult to convey. Kociatkiewicz and Kostera (1999) write about empty spaces, which are characterized as poetical and possessing the quality of feelings. The way out from NBB was poetical in the sense of feelings. These feelings were for example distress, depression, fear, stress, anger, even violence, and they were mostly expressed in terms of sleepless nights and nightmares as well as visits to (mental) health services.

Depressions, lacks and survivals

The uncertainty during the reform varied in length and degree, depending upon whether one knew for a fact that he or she was to become unemployed or whether there were some vague promises about the future. Eeva was one of those who did not know whether she would have a job with Engel or not:

> For half a year I didn't know whether I had been recruited or not and had to go to the deaconesses' institution, into a stress clinic, and then I paid a long visit to a friend in Asia. [The stress clinic in question is a private one, and Eeva paid for it herself.]

The other architect, Marja, also mentioned that she had gone to a mental health clinic (a free municipal service) because of her depression. In addition to losing her job, she also lost her husband who had been ill for several decades; becoming an unemployed widow was a hard blow for her. At the time of the interview her three-year unemployment had become a constant financial tightrope walk. She was worrying about the possibility of a large dentist's bill and was accumulating a specific 'dental fund' by collecting empty beer bottles (in Finland you get a 50-pence deposit for empty bottles) especially on Friday nights at the city centre. Marja told a bitter-sweet story of her experiences in bottle-collecting. Her story also presents her magnificent skills in observing:

> One weekend I was once again on a bus from the centre back home with bottles jingling in my bags. Two large plastic bags can take forty bottles, which makes twenty marks. In the same bus with me there was an ex-colleague from the NBB with his wife, probably coming from a party. I was so nervous that he would see me when I get off before him. But he didn't, or maybe he was discreet enough not to show it.

When I interviewed her, Marja was in the process of moving house. She had sold her apartment and was about to move into a smaller one. Her plan was to use the money from the apartment to assist her grown-up children and buy herself a computer with a CAD programme, a necessary tool in today's architecture. Marja had applied to enter a CAD course organized by the employment agency, but her application had been turned down because of her 'old' age. She had planned to buy the programme and practise using it at home, but she ran out of money. She also took part in an advanced course in community planning, which she paid for herself. She still had not given up hope of acquiring a job that would 'suit her training and be meaningful'. At the time of the interview she had just applied for a job and at first she had got an enthusiastic reception because of her wide experience, but after a discussion about her age someone had suggested a 'seniors' programme'; Marja did not get the job. Collecting empty bottles and moving into a smaller apartment are telling descriptions of a worsening standard of living and women's impoverishment.[1]

Martta is a retired cleaner, who at first was unemployed for a long time:

> At present there are many people worse off than I am. But back in '94 I made a lot of noise when I became unemployed while I had taken a loan and all. With just the dole money, I had to earn extra to keep me in bread. I did sewing, took care of young and even old people. Otherwise, I wouldn't have had the money to eat. It took some planning to have food every day. Now that I'm out of it and get the pension, my income has risen by over a thousand marks, and I'm still allowed to earn more than two grand on the side.

Maire, Martta and Marja are all mothers and grandmothers. All three have close ties with their children and grandchildren. During my interviews with each one there were phones ringing, children or relatives calling or visiting them. According to what I have seen and what they have said, loneliness is not their problem, but the lack of work and money is. While one is unemployed, it is possible to take care of relatives, grandchildren, or sick husbands. But the women's chances of giving financial assistance are little. The grown-up children of these women are in need of financial assistance, and these mothers feel it to be their responsibility, yet their resources are getting scarce. Among the consequences of the economic depression, the cuts directed at various 'family political' benefits have been considerable. The grandmothers saw getting to know their grandchildren and being able to look after them as positive aspects of their unemployment.[2]

Martta had gone into further training a few years before the organizational change in order to assure herself a job in the future as well. Four years after being dismissed she was still paying off her student loans. At the time of the interview she was a well-trained pensioner who had been trained as a seamstress, but had an institutional helper's qualifications besides.

Maire was not yet old enough for early retirement; she was on something of a 'waiting list'. Her long stretches of unemployment were disrupted by various courses organized by the employment agency. Maire had chosen courses on 'textile work' or 'creative handicraft' and bought a new sewing machine with the money received for the illegal dismissal. Thus the unemployed women still survive by further training or education and by taking care of the family – in other words, they go on doing what they did while they were employed, and probably had done even before that.

Out of sight, out of mind: an end to workers' solidarity

Martta, formerly an active trade union member, fell out with her branch when the trade union did not take a proper stand for the dismissed workers:

The others should have gone on strike instead of moving to Engel when some of their mates became unemployed. Like when the employer dismissed me without offering a place at Engel and still told the employment agency that I'd turned down the job. And the union didn't offer any help with it. . . . Besides, the trade union had agreed early on with the state, that they'd not make trouble, the worsened terms would be accepted. Then a private lawyer from Jyväskylä contacted the cleaners and asked if any of them wanted to take this case to court. He took the case free of charge. Then, when a certain group of cleaners had gone ahead with him, the trade union decided to act on the case. Couldn't do anything else.

Martta thinks that the trade union left her and the other dismissed cleaners on their own, and their case unattended. The union had 'tied its hands' by agreeing not to press the cleaners' case. The same view, that the trade union had tied its hands, was also presented in the newspapers right after the cleaners had won their case in court. However, the union representative denied this:[3]

The chairman of our union said right after the deal that lawyer X knows the labour law and has handled successfully a few similar cases. After the strike had ended we had a meeting and decided on the best way to handle the case. We decided to look for a place where we could present a clear case, and we found our spot in eastern Finland. There was no point in starting this on all frontiers at once, so we went for a precedent. We started the pilot project and let our people know. But people's anger, pain and uncertainty, all that happened, meant that we just didn't come across as all that trustworthy.

The same trade union representative also tells how they had tried to negotiate with the Ministry of Finance, to bring over their experts on labour law, etc. But the ministry was not interested in their views:

Late November 1994 Engel announced that they would start making contracts directly with people, based on the private sector's collective labour agreement. We sent letters to all our members, saying don't sign these papers, they are illegal. We expressed our disagreement about the contracts' legality and we threatened with industrial action. The strike started after Christmas and it held really well. Then the strike ended in a deal: the salaries were cut by 10 per cent instead of 30 per cent, as the employer had tried to, and we saved a few other benefits besides.

Maire felt that her twenty years with the trade union were a waste of time, actually even worse. Her attitude towards her former fellow employees was closer to 'murderous'. The cleaners who got jobs at Engel did not want to fight for those who became unemployed, and later became envious of the unemployment benefits, and the bitterness increased as the state paid compensation for the illegal dismissals. The cleaners who worked for Engel had salaries only slightly higher than the unemployment benefit, and yet their workload was manifold. When a member of parliament who happened to know Maire asked for her opinion about selling Engel to the stockmarket – i.e. the final stage of privatization – her comment was: 'Sell the lot! It's about time they got a Black Engel as we did back then. It was just before Christmas that we got to know about the dismissals. So now they'll get the Black Engel for Christmas'.

Perhaps there are some friendships left in the ruins of the NBB, although its closing down and the ensuing treatment seem to have wreaked havoc where solidarity between people is concerned. The architect who used to be in NBB as the chief shop steward of SAFA also stated that he had drawn the necessary conclusions for the future. He said that the negotiations had caused a conflict between himself and the employer, and this almost cost him his job. Therefore he had decided not to become a shop steward ever again.

Though unemployed, Marja has taken part in SAFA's training events at least once a year, but has considered resigning from her union. 'There is no point in belonging to the union. It's the same thing with us as it was with the cleaners – the dismissal was illegal but the union did nothing'. The result seems to be the same for everyone: out of the union, feeling angry or alienated. It seems that the trade unions have nothing to offer to the unemployed or those who inhabit a difficult slot in the labour market – except perhaps the exit sign.

Measurement takes over

In this chapter I have allowed a handful of people to represent a much larger group. They do not merely represent the former NBB, but other changed or changing public organizations as well. Since there are no large scale studies or follow-ups on the consequences that the privatization of state institutions have for women, I present my findings as well-grounded opinions. Closing down the NBB and turning it into the SREA is making 'real estate business and facility management' an increasingly male-dominated field. There are other causes too for this development. The uniformity of these activities gets further emphasized by the new dogma and the fashionable features of the new management. The keywords of the new dogma are 'facility management', 'managing the property mass', 'market-based rent', 'investment policy', etc. There is big money involved in the various building projects, while the former control mechanisms and/or democratic decision-making have been changed into new practices. As far as the end result, i.e. public buildings, is concerned, the situation seems to lead into more massive and efficiently planned buildings. Many of the female architects interviewed have internalized 'ambitious' architecture and planning. They keep on studying new and improved techniques and methods not yet employed. Presently there seems to be a 'decisive turning-point' between the old and new modes of doing things, one which many women find it hard to settle into and are not necessarily allowed to try out. The changes in labour culture concern the cleaners as well; they have to adapt to the changes in the quality of their work, the end of schooling and high professional standards, and deteriorating working conditions and hours.

The economic depression strongly affected the field of building, and throughout the 1990s architects' unemployment rates have been exceptionally high. The number of architects employed by the public authorities decreases everywhere: in addition to the state, the municipalities and counties are reducing the planners' role – and this makes women architects' employment an even more problematic issue.

The intensified competition for employment hits women from several directions. The highest posts are still divided amongst fathers and brothers, but the brothers are increasingly eager to settle even for middle management. Badly-paid jobs such as cleaning are done by 'outside agents' while the salaries are going down. When the state and the municipalities cease to employ cleaners, the others are practically left just to compete over how little they can pay. The state has been there to offer women in various organizational positions jobs with fixed working hours and without night or weekend shifts. This practice is disappearing. Jobs that are tied into office hours are getting fewer while the workload is getting greater even in the ones which, in principle, still keep to office hours.

In Finland the NBB has affected the whole country, since there are public buildings everywhere. For the planners this has meant constant travelling and being on the road. For example the most famous female architect employed by the NBB, Salme Setälä (1973), writes in her autobiography about constant travelling all around the country, especially during the Finnish reconstruction time after the Second World War. Architects travelled around a lot in any case, for various conferences and for study visits, to see places and buildings. Yet architects employed by the public authorities have had their 'official working hours' as a shield against unlimited travel requests. 'Long days, sudden trips and constant travelling doesn't suit the wife of a chronically ill husband', as an architect formerly employed by the NBB put it. She had also witnessed two of her colleagues in a similar situation, with chronically ill husbands. Salme Setälä also writes (1975) of her exceptionally heavy 'burden of care'; her duties included being a single mother and looking after a son handicapped from birth.

One could actually say that when the rationalization of the NBB took place, those women who needed the jobs most desperately were the last to get them. Heavy caring duties, being a single parent, sick husbands, as well as being an active member of a trade union, all became disadvantages as far as employment was concerned. The single parents and wives of chronically ill husbands are in need of money and jobs, but are in no position to compete with the childless and others who are free of heavy 'burdens of care'. Heather Höpfl (2001) writes that organizations have replaced the humane, reproduction, the feminine, the human body and the motherly by order, law and measurement. The 'sexual contract' discussed by Pateman explains the present-day development, in which a man constitutes the 'norm' for citizenship and professionalism, or more generally just the norm for an employee. When the employer has the chance to choose, he obviously chooses the individuals who suit his purposes. The ideal held dear by Finnish women – that of being able to have both a family and a career – seems, at least temporarily, to have become history with the company-ization of the state.

Salme Setälä ends her autobiography of the NBB in 1973 (covering five directors' time) with these words: 'Clearly times have changed during sixty years. I dare hope that the acceptance and respect due to women's work gets constantly greater. Now that those once mocked advocates for women's rights have become, should I say, bolder and more demanding, we might expect people to balance this world in the future, to give rise to impartial advocates of human rights!' Judging by the state's present-day actions, Setälä's prediction for the future, needing no advocates for women's rights, seems somewhat premature.

Although the state lost the lawsuit brought by its former employees, no-one has questioned the legitimacy of the change. Thus the same pattern re-emerges in other schemes for privatizing the public sector, the state as well as the municipalities. Right and wrong, black and white, all fall into new places. While the Ministry of Finance told that we are not dealing with a case of reforming a previous business, but rather bringing an end to the old one and starting a new one, the cleaners tell a completely different story: 'How could this Engel have been a new firm when the cleaners took up the brushes and buckets brought there by the NBB? They took them from where they'd left them the previous year'.

Coda: A bad black angel

It is time to reveal the genealogy of the name Engel, presented in my story as a synonym for the angel as well as a name for a company. One of the very first directors of the NBB (with a different name at the time) was a German architect, Carl Ludvig Engel, who came to Finland at the request of the Russian Tsar Alexander II. Finland had become part of Russia during the Napoleonic Wars; before that it had been part of Sweden. During Swedish rule the capital of Finland had been Turku, on the west coast. Now the Russian rulers wanted to have the capital nearer to the east and selected Helsinki for the purpose. The most famous monuments, or government and public buildings, in Helsinki were planned and constructed by C. L. Engel. He was quite skilled with the same styles that the tsars used in St Petersburg. Helsinki – or rather the governmental and monumental parts of it – is considered a miniature St Petersburg and this is mostly due to the work done by

C. L. Engel. Thus the name carries a lot of national history embedded in important buildings. But the contradictory message in black Engel is not discharged with the idea of combining this good guy with modern business. The figure of the angel is as such ambiguous, represents modern times or the terrors caused by capitalism. Walter Benjamin was one of the first to take up the idea of the angel, Angelus Novus, as the most powerful metaphor of modern times (Buci-Glucksmann 1994: 41–89).

Christine Buci-Glucksmann explains that 'the allegory of the angel meant to literary modernism something terrible, frightening and bizarre, that fundamental contretemps where humanity meets it own destruction by chance, where history as the storm of progress becomes one single catastrophe, where beauty is so terrible that it kills' (1994: 43). The figure of the angel refers to the very origins of otherness in organizations, to the uncanny, the feminine, the genitals and the womb. Thus the black angel, the angel of modern times, is sweeping away the old, the public institutions, the feminine and strange to make way for the new and less ambiguous world. The strangeness in front of the feminine can best be illustrated in the argumentation against cleaning: 'It is not the task of the state to do cleaning'. Why could the state not be clean?

The starting point of Benjamin's angel is *Angelus Novus*, a painting by Paul Klee that Benjamin owned and loved. The Angelus Novus, the modern angel, is a figure in Benjamin's manuscript of *Theses on the Philosophy of History* (1973) written before his suicide. Benjamin wrote the text while waiting to emigrate to America from France, which was no longer safe for Jews: 'The Angel of history melancholically shatters the temporal continuum, replacing it with a catastrophic, messianic instance that will release the future buried in the past and build it with the present'. This combining of past and present is called *Jetztseit* (time now), and means an intensive, qualitative time which 'becomes visible in "states of emergency", the moments when "culture engenders barbarism" and the infinitely repressed memory of those "without a name" (*Namenlosen*) finally re-appropriates a history dominated by the historicism of the rulers'. Benjamin's view of history is a pessimistic one, the only law or rule in history consisting of fighting and violence. Benjamin emphasizes that history is written from the viewpoint of the winners; history is the written history of rulers. The Angelus Novus is looking back into the ruins of history and sees people without a name in the ruins. In the *Thesis*, Benjamin states that the task of the historian is to save from the ruins of history the memory of the people without a name.

Thus it turns out that I have taken up for myself the messianic task of the historian, to save the memory of the marginalized women and give a name to some people who are buried in the ruins of history. That my story of the women from the ruins of the National Board of Buildings fits so beautifully with Benjamin's *Angelus Novus* and his thesis on history is a powerful proof of shared meanings. The figure of the angel seems to rise from the ruins during times of catastrophe and terror.

Figure 8.2 This photo was never taken. (Drawing by Jenny Eräsaari.)

Documents quoted

Hävitty juttu. (Lost case, red. Timo-Erkki Heino. TV1, Documentary 11.05.98, 8 pm)
Several reports in Finnish from a research project called 'Gender Structure in the Finnish Welfare State'.
Tuomari Nurmio: 'Musta enkeli' in Lasten mehuhetki, Johanna 1981.

Notes

1 No account of genderbound variation in income or property has been made in Finland. Generally speaking the differences have been relatively small, but after the depression in the 1990s, there have been greater differences of income and property; it is possible that in the future Finland will also know the European phenomenon called 'women's poverty'.
2 Here I do not refer just to the three former employees of the NBB in my interviews, but to a wider 'collection of letters', my collection of material on 'being a grandmother'.
3 The interview of the union representative was conducted by Riitta Hanifi and is quoted in an unpublished manuscript (1999).

9 The business case for diversity and the 'Iron Cage'[1]

Deborah R. Litvin

> Our workplace is changing and diversity is no longer the exception, it is the norm. Diversity is good for business and when we achieve unity in diversity, everyone wins.
>
> (McWilliams 1997: 7)

> Most diversity specialists will tell you they hear the same thing, in company after company. Women and minorities are sick of the status quo, and they're cynical about a lot of the programs out there.
>
> (Flynn 1998: 27)

This chapter explores the interplay among three elements: the *business case for diversity, diversity consultants*, and *diversity initiatives*. The business case for diversity provides the rationale and motivation for organizations and their members to pursue diversity initiatives. As an integral part of such initiatives, diversity consultants retell the business case. They do so in order to motivate organizational members to take on new behaviours and embrace the changes deemed necessary to create a 'diversity-friendly' organization, in which all differences are valued, individuals are empowered, and managers 'tap the potential of a diverse group of employees' in order to compete successfully in the global marketplace (Thomas 1992: 311).

'Making the business case' is widely advocated as the first step in securing organizational members' commitment to ambitious diversity initiatives. I argue that, ironically, 'making the business case' functions, instead, to reinvigorate the organizational *status quo*, while foreclosing possibilities for truly fundamental organizational change. The recounting of the business case fosters the reification of one particular social construction of reality as 'natural' and the legitimization of actions based upon that (socially constructed) reality as 'logical'. 'Buying' the business case, thus, creates blinders – a cognitive 'iron cage' – short-circuiting possibilities for alternative constructions of reality and the actions which might flow from these alternate worldviews. In the still relatively new and contested domain of diversity management, the business case for diversity can serve not as a catalyst for deep-rooted change, but as a defender of the organizational *status quo*, as it justifies and legitimates the enactment of ritual rather than substantive change.

In crafting this account of the business case for diversity, I follow Czarniawska, combining narrative and new institutionalist approaches to analysis. A narrative approach 'pays attention to the *forms* in which knowledge is cast and the effects that these have on an audience', while a new institutionalist approach adopts as its central concern the origin, development and homogenization of institutions, particularly through the processes of isomorphism (Czarniawska 1997a: 6). I demonstrate how the narrative of the business case for diversity functions as a cognitive 'iron cage' (Gerth and Mills 1946; DiMaggio and Powell 1991b) which orders organizational members' expectations, renders inconceivable alternative constructions of their organizational 'reality' and thus forecloses alternative plans of action. As DiMaggio and Powell explain,

> Institutional arrangements are reproduced, because individuals often cannot even conceive of appropriate alternatives . . . Institutions do not just constrain options: they establish the very criteria by which people discover their preferences.
>
> (1991a: 10, 11)

The 'iron cage' of the business case privileges a particular interpretation of 'facts' about changes in the demographic composition of the US workforce, and specifies particular reasons for organizations to 'do something' in response to these changes. It thereby rationalizes and legitimates – institutionalizes – a particular form of organizational response to what it has constructed as 'the problem.' The (only) legitimate response of an organization to the problem of its 'new' workforce is to pursue 'managing diversity' initiatives. Well-informed managers are thoroughly familiar with the business case and its rationale for diversity initiatives. When they invite independent diversity consultants in to 'pitch' their wares, these managers already know just what they want to buy. They select those consultants who propose to do for the organization that which best matches the 'product' naturalized, institutionalized and 'sold' by the business case. What is a consultant (with two kids to put through college) to do? And what of change?

This chapter forms part of a larger critical examination of the managerial discourse and practices of diversity management in the US (Litvin 2000), which brings to the fore concerns which are not typically part of the management *diversity* conversation: Why has *managing diversity* become so popular and acquired such wide advocacy in corporate America? Why have *diversity* and *diversity management* been defined as they have? How have their now taken-for-granted meanings achieved this status? What alternative definitions of 'reality' were and are available? And, last, what are the implications of these definitions for subjectivity within organizations?

The position from which I explore these questions is both critical and social constructionist. Mills and Simmons contrast 'critical' and 'main-stream' approaches to organizational analysis:

> We define a *critical approach* as one that takes as its starting point a *concern to understand and change the way that organizational arrangements impact on people*. In contrast to mainstream organizational analysis that concerns itself with the efficient use of people for formal organizational ends, a *critical approach sets out to uncover the ways in which organizational ends can be detrimental to people*.
>
> (1995: 9, emphasis added)

I combine this broadly critical approach with a social constructionist ontology, insisting that 'experience as well as all objects of experience are under all circumstances the result of *our* ways and means of experiencing' (Von Glasersfeld 1984: 29, 30). However, the meanings we make are necessarily structured and limited by the vocabularies and categories available to us within our culture, society and world. Meanings are continuously altered through personal interactions, which occur within a network of socially-produced and disseminated discourse. From this perspective, we see the world in which we live and the boundaries against which we strain as the products of our own limited vocabularies of thought and actions, individual and joint.

However, these limits can be revealed. The process through which 'objective reality' and 'common sense' come to be regarded as such can be explored. Through (at least partial) awareness of the conceptual limits we have allowed to contain our meaning-making and our complicity in the creation of our own 'iron cages,' we can increase our conceptual vocabulary and thereby make new meanings of our experiences. These new meanings will make it possible to consider previously inconceivable avenues of action.

The power of narrative

It is helpful to conceptualize the business case for diversity as a narrative in order to make sense of its connection with organizational change.[2] Narratives have been defined as 'thematic, sequenced accounts that convey meaning from implied author to implied reader' (Barry and Elmes 1997: 431). Alternatively, a narrative can be seen as 'the symbolic presentation of a sequence of events connected by subject matter and related by time' (Scholes 1981: 205) or, simply someone telling another that something occurred (Herrnstein Smith 1981; O'Connor 1997).

The power of the narrative lies in its role as a provider of (the appearance of) order in the midst of complex and ambiguous events. 'The narrative scheme serves as a lens through which the apparently independent and disconnected elements of existence are seen as related parts of a whole' (Polkinghorne 1988: 35). Narratives, thus, involve the *invention* of order and relationships, based on particular values (O'Connor 1996). A narrative is not simply an 'accurate report' of an 'objective reality.' It is, rather, an interpretation, based upon a particular set of assumptions, preferences and interests, of a sample of events selected out of a continuous stream. Further, a narrative is always told from a particular point of view, premised upon a particular constellation of interests. An organizational narrative, such as the business case for diversity, thus, 'can be conceived as more than simply a vehicle for diffusing information in an organization; it becomes a material social practice by means of which *ideological meaning formations are produced, maintained, and reproduced*' (Mumby 1987: 118, emphasis added).

The maintenance and reproduction of the 'ideological meaning formation' is achieved through the ongoing retelling of the narrative. Through repetition, the 'events in a story [and the linkages between them] become taken-for-granted by members of the culture ... The division between fiction and reality is blurred to the point where a narrative event becomes "real" if it is retold enough times' (Mumby 1987: 122). The humanly-constructed narrative becomes reified, 'perceived as "objective" and independent from those who created [it.] ... What is "real" becomes fixed and immutable, i.e., "the way things are"' (Mumby 1987: 119). Narratives thus serve as powerful, but usually invisible, legitimating devices. 'They often articulate an organizational reality that is accepted as "the natural order of things", thus constraining alternate interpretations of organizational events, which, if entertained, 'might be considered strange or lacking in sense' (Mumby 1987: 114).

Consequently, an organizational narrative also highlights and obscures possibilities for *action*. Individuals act in line with their understanding of their parts in the story. MacIntyre explains, 'I can only answer the question "What am I to do?" if I can answer the prior question, "Of what story or stories do I find myself a part?"' (1981: 216). Thus, through examining these stories, one can investigate the 'role of language as both opening and closing possibilities for social action' (O'Connor 1996: 6). The 'Business Case for Diversity' is one such story.

The business case for diversity

The business case for diversity appeared in the late 1980s, during a time of backlash against affirmative action policies, as advocates sought to obtain legitimacy for and commitment to their vision of organizational change.[3] These advocates insisted that managing diversity should (and could) be clearly differentiated from EEO and affirmative action programmes organizations had pursued for the preceding twenty years. Managing diversity was to be based on 'business' reasons, such as improved competitiveness, better customer service, and enhanced profitability.[4] These business reasons took on great (and sometimes strident) urgency after the publication of the 1987 *Workforce 2000* report, which predicted that native-born people of colour, women, and immigrants would continue to increase their presence in the labour force and their power as consumers (Johnston and Packer 1987).

Managing diversity, a 'business imperative', was differentiated from earlier programmes which had been pursued either because of legal requirements or moralistic values. This distancing of diversity from affirmative action was made clear in many early articles. The following excerpt provides an excellent example:

> The workforce-diversity issue has no relationship to the old affirmative-action and EEO programs. Affirmative action and EEO were equity issues . . . Now, the issue is not social justice; it's employer demand . . . New language is coming out of the presidents' and CEOs' offices . . . EEO language is out . . . Valuing diversity isn't concerned about fairness, filling quotas, or forcing things because they are moral, ethical or legal . . . Valuing diversity says that we have a diverse workforce, and diversity can be an advantage if it is managed well . . .
>
> (Jones *et al.* 1989: 13)

Along with the definition of managing diversity as 'not affirmative action' came the assertion that managing diversity did not single out 'minorities' or 'women' as its targets. Instead, managing diversity was intended to go 'beyond race and gender' to include all members of the workforce and embrace all differences. It would be future-oriented, looking toward emergent demographic shifts in the labour market and the globalization of markets. It would be a 'comprehensive managerial process for developing an environment that works for all employees' (Thomas, Jr. 1991: 10). To illustrate the development and institutionalization of the business case for diversity, it is useful to take a closer look at the work of R. Roosevelt Thomas, Jr.

R. Roosevelt Thomas, Jr. is one of the best-known advocates of 'managing diversity'. A former professor at the Harvard Business School and Dean of the Business School at Atlanta University, he founded the American Institute for Managing Diversity, Inc. in 1983. His ideas reached many through the 1990 publication in the *Harvard Business Review* of 'From Affirmative Action to Affirming Diversity', followed by his 1991 book, *Beyond Race and Gender: Unleashing the Power of Your Total Work Force by Managing Diversity*. While both of Thomas' publications advocate and explain his notion of managing diversity, in each one he adopts a different emphasis.

In *Beyond Race and Gender*, Thomas fully develops his ideas about managing diversity as a process of comprehensive organizational change:

> Managing diversity means approaching diversity at three levels simultaneously: individual, interpersonal, and organizational . . . seeing diversity as an issue for the entire organization . . .
>
> Managing diversity approaches diversity from a *management* perspective . . . [I]t deals with the way organizations are managed, the way managers do their jobs . . .

Managing diversity requires that line managers learn a new way. They are asked to spend less time 'doing' the work and more time enabling employees to do the work . . .

Managing diversity defines diversity broadly; it addresses the many ways employees are different *and* the many ways they are alike. Managing diversity goes beyond race and gender . . . it is about all managers empowering whoever is in their work force.

Managing diversity assumes that adaptation is a . . . mutual process beween the individual and the company . . .

Managing diversity is not a program . . . It calls for more than changing individual behaviors. It requires a fundamental change in the corporation's way of life . . .

(1991: 12)

These changes can only be achieved through a 'complex, multifaceted, and time-consuming process' of organizational culture change:

Examining an organization's corporate culture

Identifying those elements of the culture that are fundamental, the 'roots' from which corporate behaviors spring

Determining whether the roots support or hinder the aspirations for managing diversity

Changing the cultural roots that are hindrances

(Thomas 1991: 14)

The ambition of this *vision* is evident. Diversity initiatives are to be all-encompassing, on-going processes for changing a corporation's way of life. The *motivation* for organizations to undertake this change process is the self-interest of the company and its managers:

[Managing diversity is] something that is done for the benefit of the corporation in the interests of remaining competitive in an increasingly unfriendly environment. True, all groups will benefit, whether they are different in terms of age, lifestyle, gender, or race. But their benefit is not the driving motivation. Managing diversity presumes that the driving force is the manager's, and the company's self-interest.

(Thomas 1991: 168)

Clearly, the portrayal of corporate self-interest as the *motivation* for managing diversity is present in *Beyond Race and Gender*. However, the main thrust of the book is to detail Thomas' strategies for identifying and changing organizational structures and procedures, which disadvantage some while privileging others. It is, at bottom, concerned with fairness and equity. Managing diversity is a values-based vision and project in this book.

Thomas' emphasis is rather different in his 1990 *HBR* article, which focuses sharply on the 'good for business' theme. Thomas offers ten guidelines for managing diversity. The first is 'Clarify Your Motivation':

> A lot of executives are not sure why they should want to learn to manage diversity. Legal compliance seems like a good reason. So does community relations. Many executives believe they have a social and moral responsibility to employ minorities and women. Others want to placate an internal group or pacify an outside organization. None of these are bad reasons, but none of them are business reasons, and given the nature and scope of today's competitive challenges, I believe only business reasons will supply the necessary long-term motivation . . .
>
> (1990: 112–13)

The second guideline, 'Clarify Your Vision', asks: 'When managers think about a diverse workforce, what do they picture? Not publicly, but in the privacy of their minds?' (ibid). His response postulates an already-diverse workforce and avoids any taint of connection with affirmative action:

> The vision to hold in your own imagination and to try to communicate to all your managers and employees is an image of fully tapping the human resource potential of every member of the work force. This vision sidesteps the question of equality, ignores the tensions of coexistence, plays down the uncomfortable realities of difference, and focuses instead on individual enablement. It doesn't say, 'Let *us* give *them* a chance.' It assumes a diverse work force that includes us and them. It says, 'Let's create an environment where everyone will do their best work.'
>
> (1990: 113–14, emphasis in original)

Thomas does state that organizations should continue their affirmative action efforts, but he calls affirmative action 'an artificial, transitional, but necessary stage on the road to a truly diverse work force.' He claims that '[b]ecause of its artificial nature, affirmative action requires constant attention and drive to make it work' (1990: 117).

Thomas contrasts this with managing diversity: 'The point of learning once and for all how to manage diversity is that all that energy can be focused somewhere else' (ibid.: 117). This is a statement of a (usually unspoken) selling point of the business case. 'Doing' managing diversity *now* will result in getting *beyond* the need to attend to diversity in the future. This will allow the organization to get back to (its real) business. The executive reading this *HBR* article might well envision managing diversity as a finite programme, coming *after* affirmative action, geared toward enhancing corporate profitability and effectiveness by means of the nebulous 'focusing on individual enablement'.

Thomas's vision of managing diversity, *as detailed in his book*, is of fundamental structural and procedural change to remove barriers, creating an environment in which people of all descriptions will be unhindered in their ability to contribute. In his more widely circulated *HBR* article, however, this vision is subordinated to Thomas's marketing objective: to 'sell' managing diversity to executives by distancing it from affirmative action and positioning it as an exercise in enlightened self-interest. This is the 'vision' which develops into the narrative of the business case for diversity.

Lennie Copeland, another creator and disseminator of the foundations of the business case,[5] was also careful to separate managing diversity from EEO:

> Managing diversity is conceptually different from equal employment opportunity, which was primarily a battle against racism and prejudice. To *value* workforce diversity is to manage in a way designed to seize the benefits that differences bring.
>
> (Copeland 1988a: 51)

Copeland combines this 'business imperative' positioning with an apparent assumption that managing diversity *is* (simply) training *individuals* to alter their behaviours and/or attitudes. In her June, 1988 *Personnel* article, Copeland quotes a corporate Director of Personnel Relations: 'The issue is, how do I build a new *structure* to get people to accept people for what they bring –their race and their culture?' (emphasis added). Copeland adds another question: 'And how do multicultural organizations develop a new breed of managers and employees who are able to work well with people who are different from themselves?' She answers her own question only. She provides no response to the PR Director's concern with *structural change*:

> If you put people together, they won't necessarily learn to like each other; in fact, the interaction may be unsuccessful . . . But if *before* you bring them together, you give them some training – including briefing in different values and styles –and then give them a task that requires cooperation, and *manage* that interaction, results are much better.
>
> (Copeland 1988b: 58)

The following year, Copeland and her co-authors make much the same sense of managing diversity:

> By offering education, exposure, awareness, and behavior-modification techniques, we'll eventually see attitudes come around . . . [B]efore you throw people together, you should get them to move toward understanding and appreciating different ways of viewing the world, different kinds of values, and different ways of behaving . . . In that sense, diversity has to be managed . . .
>
> (Jones *et al.* 1989: 13)

In these writings, important elements of the business case for diversity emerge. Managing diversity is to be done for *business reasons*. Taking full advantage of the *newly-diverse* workforce will produce a *competitive advantage*. Managing diversity is positioned as *not affirmative action*. It is to come *after* and go *beyond* affirmative action. It will be a *future-oriented* response to *demographic changes* in both labour force and markets, not a backward-looking focus on legality or equity. It is to involve extensive *training and development* activities to increase employees' *exposure* to and *awareness* of the (pragmatic and instrumental) value of a diverse workforce.

Authors arranged selections from these defining statements into a chronological order, creating a cohesive story. They then used the story to motivate readers to 'buy into' the need for managing diversity. Consider the following examples:

> Multicultural workforces are becoming more prevalent in today's business environment. This trend is expected to continue into the next century. Businesses that will prosper under these conditions are those that will tap into the talents of the workforce and will value those differences. Those employers who realise that diversity relates directly to the bottom line will continue to be successful.
>
> (Hammond and Kleiner 1992: 6–9)

> The rapidly changing demographics of the US work force present a dramatic case for the need to manage diversity – especially between European American women and women of color in management. Today, these groups of women are working together in greater numbers and in a greater variety of formal relationships than ever before. For pioneers, there are no rules and no role models for understanding the complex differences that women bring to the workplace, or for handling the miscommunication and unproductive relationships that may result.
>
> (Betters-Reed and Moore 1992: 84)

Any narrative must have at least three elements: an original state of affairs, an action or event, and the consequent state of affairs. It must also have a plot, a way of connecting the elements into a meaningful whole. The establishment of a chronology is a common way to create a plot (Czarniawska 1998: 2). The elements of the business case for diversity, in their customary chronological order, are as follows:

Original state: The US workforce (and, therefore our organization's workforce) was *homogeneous.*

Event: Environmental changes happened, and will continue to happen. This has caused our organization's workforce to become *diverse.*

Consequent state: Unknown. Consequences of our workforce diversity are potentially good. However, they may be disastrous. *The outcome will depend on our ability to effectively manage this new workforce diversity.*

Diversity advocates attempted to place managing diversity on (top of) management's list of priorities by developing ever more complete and customized explanations of why and how managing diversity is a business imperative. To the basic narrative of the business case they attached a cluster of more specific business factors. Bernard Scales, manager of diversity at E. I. DuPont de Nemours, Inc., offered a list of areas that would be improved by well-managed diversity: 'workforce utilization, diverse customer marketbase, improved productivity, continuous quality improvement, recruitment and retention of skilled workers, avoidance of lawsuits' (Yarrow 1996: 8–9). Lente-Louise Louw, of Griggs Productions (a pioneer in the production of diversity training videos) added 'the globalizing market, increased creativity and innovation, and synergistic teamwork'. These enumerations of the ways managing diversity could impact the corporate bottom line depicted a further shift from values toward dollars and provided evidence of practitioner sophistication and increased 'savvy':

> Five years ago, the motivation for diversity work circled around issues of awareness and sensitivity . . . As the field evolved, the arguments for doing diversity have become more savvy. Both consultants and diversity managers have come to realize that, since the primary concern of business is profitability, the case for diversity has to be grounded in the business rationale.
>
> (Yarrow 1996: 8, 9)

The new and improved versions of the business case for diversity were replete with details germane to the particulars of each organization. Further, 'making the business case – linking diversity to the bottom line or profitability of an organization' (Michael Wheeler 1995: 11) was presented as the 'natural' and taken-for-granted starting point for *any* diversity effort:

> [W]hen confronted with a need to convince a reluctant management group about the need to manage diversity, you should start by referring to the business case and to an understanding of the value and benefits of a diverse work force . . .
>
> (Roger Wheeler 1997: 493)

Yarrow flatly states that '[f]or public and private organizations alike success [of the diversity initiative] hinges on communicating the business case effectively' (1996: 2). The business case is to be made to line managers, to boards of directors, to everyone in the organization. 'The City of Seattle . . . makes the case to everyone in the organization from department heads to field and support staff, according to Mayor Rice' (ibid). The details of the story vary for different target audiences, as 'different constituencies need different rationales. The marketing business case might be different from manufacturing; the R&D case differs from distribution and logistics. [DuPont] developed and tailored the argument to fit the specific functions' (ibid.: 2, 3).

Indeed, the business case for diversity became so familiar and accepted that it could be presented as a 'given', as 'common sense', as something that everybody already knows:

> The purpose of this article is not to establish the business case for diversity in the workplace. The need to value, to leverage, and to manage diversity has long been established. . . . It is well established that, over time, heterogeneous groups outperform homogeneous groups . . . A diverse organization . . . is more flexible and adaptable and, therefore, better able to . . . survive.
>
> (Roger Wheeler 1997: 493)

The details provided for a readership of tax executives might be different from those chosen for front-line manufacturing supervisors or public park maintainers, but *the narrative framework remains the same.*

As a narrative, the business case for diversity is a set of events, connected and made meaningful by the imposition of a plot (Czarniawska 1998: 2). It is thus a *fiction*, in the sense that it is made up, not that it is necessarily false (Barry and Elmes 1997). Yet, this *fiction* has attained the level of *common sense*, of that which 'everyone' knows to be true, and that upon which countless organizations base their *actions*. The business case for diversity has become an *institutional thought structure* (Warren *et al.* 1974).

An institutional thought structure is characterized by a set of basic assumptions that are taken to be 'axiomatic': It is accepted that they *exist*, that they are *shared* by the majority in the organizational field, and their existence is *evoked* in support of organizational action (Czarniawska 1997a: 68). Such a thought structure is based upon and reflects a *belief-value system*, which sets forth particular notions of what is good and bad, right and wrong, and true. Second, it enunciates a particular *strategy* for addressing problems, ignoring alternative possibilities. Third, it sets up an *organizational rationale* of *accepted* (and, by implication, *unaccepted*) structures and procedures to be used in implementing this strategy. The organizational rationale includes the *authority structure* deemed appropriate for addressing the problem: the place in the organizational hierarchy in which to locate responsibility for creation, adoption and implementation of that strategy. Fourth, the institutional thought structure provides *legitimacy*, as it sets out a *justification* for the organization to act in response to the defined problem(s) in the domain it claims.

The narrative of the business case for diversity and its underlying institutional thought structure were widely disseminated through practitioner-oriented books and journal articles. Thus, one might reasonably assume that any individual charged by his/her boss with the organization's 'diversity plan' would be, or would rapidly become, well acquainted with its general outline. Armed with this knowledge, he or she might contract for the services of a diversity consultant to assist in the planning and implementation process. We turn next to the accounts of three such diversity consultants.

Diversity consultants and the business case

Henry Corta, Herminia Cortez and Charles Jones[6] are 'front-line' diversity consultants and trainers, who compete for diversity consultation and facilitation contracts. They discuss their own involvement in 'diversity work' and describe their personal visions of what such work ought to be. They contrast those visions with the diversity work for which they have been engaged by US organizations. Henry, Herminia and Charles describe their commitment to doing 'this work' and their frustration with their inability to engage in the complex, long-term change processes which would be necessary to achieve workplaces supportive of human dignity and equitable treatment. Instead, they vie for the chance to provide diversity awareness training to all, as specified in corporate calls for proposals. These practitioners reveal the compromises they have had to make in order to supply the 'product' desired by their corporate customers. They also portray the omnipresent taken-for-grantedness of the business case for diversity and its power to foreclose possibilities of organizational transformation.

Henry Corta, independent organizational consultant

Henry Corta began his career as a psychologist and licensed clinical social worker. He then spent seven years as a human resource manager, human development specialist and diversity trainer at a leading US high technology corporation. His current work focuses on team building, leadership skills and diversity.

Henry sees the diversity 'problem' as the racist (sexist, etc.) assumptions that infuse our society:

> [I]t's not that people get up in the morning and say, 'I'm going to be a racist today!' The problem is that we live in a culture in which we integrate those racist behaviors, or racist patterns, or assumptions we don't know about . . .

So, diversity trainers tried an approach that was based on *confrontation* of these racist assumptions. This provoked participant anger: 'I didn't come here to be told I was a racist or I was sexist, or I was a male chauvinist.' In response, a non-threatening, non-confrontational, *awareness* approach became preferred. However, Henry finds it unsatisfactory, as it avoids dealing with the original problem – the racist/sexist assumptions of society:

> [T]hat's just bypassing the problem . . . sugar-coating the whole problem . . . now you're going to do a course where everybody's going to value each other's diversity . . . It's like putting a . . . layer of niceness on top of something that hasn't been dealt with . .

Consultant-trainers *know* that the more difficult issues must be confronted in order for any real change (in the trainees) to occur; however, they are constrained by a lack of time – and so they have compromised:

> [Consultants] *want* to confront those issues, but . . . you're limited in time. . . . There's not much you can do in one or two days . . . Most [consultants] . . . have probably chosen to go with 'Let's just go with the value of diversity, even though it may be in some cases superficial.'

What the consultants can do is also constrained by corporations' limited objectives. Executives are not interested in funding 'cultural transformation':

> I don't think the clients, meaning corporate America, want to pay money to be told that they're racist, or that they have racist employees or that racism lives in the minds of people . . . They don't want to pay money for cultural transformation. The guy will say 'OK! What we want to do is . . . create a diverse workforce . . . We're not here to deal with all the . . . evils of society!'

Companies engage diversity trainers to tell their employees they are now diverse, that diversity is good for business, and that they must learn to value diversity. Their task, in short, is to re-tell the business case for diversity:

> What most companies want is a quick awareness fix . . . Just tell us that diversity is a good thing. Tell us that we are diverse. Tell us what is diverse. Tell us how we're diverse and tell us that is a good thing . . . Some programs say the reason why it's a good thing is because it makes business sense, and they try to make a business case for it. Other ones say the reason it's a good thing is because we need to become better teams . . . So people usually get by the end of these programs . . . one, they have some assumptions that got in the way. Two, that it is a good thing to be diverse. And three, that there is some kind of business reason for it. . . . More and more programs try to make that business case.

The job of the diversity consultant is confined to business-enhancement:

> It's not designed to give people skills . . . It's not part of the package . . . We don't even give out bibliographies [about Hispanics, African Americans, gays, etc.] . . . They have other things to spend their money on. They

figure . . . our [the diversity consultants'] job is not necessarily to create better human beings. Our job is to create better workers.

Herminia Cortez, organization development consultant

Herminia Cortez became involved in organizational development through work at NTL, National Training Laboratories. She worked as a consultant in South America and Africa as well as in the US. In the 1980s she became involved in EEO and affirmative action training. In 1992, upon her return to the US after two years overseas, she discovered that 'diversity' had taken over:

> When I came in '92 . . . diversity was all over the place . . . There were all these consulting organizations doing diversity training . . . The Workforce [2000] thing had come out . . . and everybody was quoting it . . . All these books . . . There was nothing when I left [the US in 1990.] Nothing. I was a pioneer in this field. When I came back I was behind.

Herminia now finds that her potential US clients are very sure of what they want in a diversity initiative. They have already decided the nature of their problems, and they know that training is the solution:

> I see many organizations [that] . . . say, 'We want to do it.' And then, what they want to do is training . . . Or they don't want to collect data. They have all the data. They think they have figured out all the problems and they just want you to do what they want you to do.

In contrast to this closed mindset, Herminia's impression is that the consultants themselves maintain a 'systems perspective':

> [Diversity consultants] are trying to make organizations pay attention to performance systems, to recruiting, to structural pieces . . . their influence and discrimination . . . They're talking about cultural change . . . The organization . . . has embedded in it a lot of discriminatory processes . . . and you have to address those . . . I think that's the . . . most positive way of looking at what we're trying to do, people that call themselves diversity consultants . . .

Nevertheless, the interventions they contract to plan and implement turn out to depend on the delivery of diversity training as a first, 'awareness' step. A 'systems approach' would scare their clients:

> You really want to bring a systems perspective and it does get too complicated for people in the organization, and I think it's a bit scary . . . I think that's why many [large consulting groups] do a lot of training . . . A

lot of training has to do with helping people individually first to just be aware of the issues, so that they can move to a place where they are maybe able to make the whole a little bit less scary.

Why is Herminia sometimes willing to concentrate on training, leaving aside the deeper structural issues toward which her own systems perspective points as the proper focus of her efforts? She cites practical considerations: the need to balance principles and economic realities. She must meet the expectations of her client-customers, who know (from their familiarity with the business case for diversity) the 'product' they want to purchase:

> [I]t . . . depends if you have work. It's not just a matter of principle. I might need work very badly and I would do these three days [of awareness training] . . . not knowing what else is going on in the organization . . . They paid well, and somebody else is responsible, so I'll do it . . . I'm trying to follow some set of principles about organizational change and social justice, social differences at the level of the organization. But at another level I am also working on a business, and I think the two don't always jibe . . . Do we need to develop some 'products' . . . so that we have some stability around income . . . and so that we have a way of going to an organization and saying: 'Here, this is what you can get from us.' And that's very concrete.

To market anything different (such as 'a process for organizational change') is to risk alienating potential clients:

> When you go [to] an organization and say 'Well, I'll sell to you a process for collecting data and for feedbacking the data to you . . . and then you might learn, or you might not learn that you're having problems. We might do this or we might do that.' Who's going to buy that? It's hard . . . That's what I think I'm doing: balancing [trying to make a living] and be[ing] honest in what I think needs to be done.

Herminia points to a major flaw in much diversity work. This flaw stems from two improper assumptions: an organization's workforce *is already* diverse, and diversity will *always* be 'an issue'. These assumptions impede efforts to pursue more effective, but far more complicated, approaches toward helping managers with their everyday workplace experiences. Further, the assumption that 'race is all the time relevant' undercuts the credibility of the diversity initiative, as the participants themselves are fully aware of the complexity of their situations. Real problems require the ability to *differentiate*, a complex skill far beyond the scope of awareness training, and unspecified by the business case for diversity.

There's a limit to where diversity really is an issue in an organization. If you don't *have* diversity in a team, diversity is *not* an issue. . . . There's a big gap between that . . . and, for example, what [a large consulting group] is doing . . . training around race as if race was relevant *all* the time . . . But . . . if you're going to . . . say, 'Well, you have to differentiate between when is race an issue and when is it not,' then it gets very complicated. . . . Managers do know that it is *not* all the time relevant. . . . *When is diversity, when is race an issue here and when is it not?* . . . 'When is it that . . . I'm being sexist or the system is sexist, or when is it that this person is just not cutting it?' That's a very *real* struggle.

Charles Jones, professor and trainer

Charles is a professor in the management department of a New England college, where he also heads up the diversity initiative. He earns supplementary income as a diversity trainer, a subcontractor who co-facilitates two- to five-day workshops and retreats for one of the oldest, best-known diversity consulting groups in the US.

Charles cites the role of *Workforce 2000* in leading businesses to construct diversity management as the pragmatic thing, the new 'right thing to do':

[Workforce 2000 is] the rationale for why we're even going to talk about this. . . . We [corporate leaders] fixed this stuff in the sixties with the civil rights movement and the women's movement. . . . And then . . . during the 70s and early 80s, 'You're pissing me off here with this EEO stuff . . . affirmative action and so forth . . .'. And only a few [corporate leaders] would come out and say, 'We ought to do this, because we really *didn't* fix it in the 60s, and there's a *moral imperative* to deal with it.' But then, when Workforce 2000 comes out . . . 'There's another thing going on here besides just abiding by the laws we don't like related to affirmative action and EEO . . . We're doing the Right Thing.' Which is, 'It's in our self-interest to do this. And if we don't do this we're going to get caught short in the future, because of how the demographics are changing'. . . .

This notwithstanding, Charles insists that understanding the power dynamics between dominant and subordinate identity groups must be the foundation of real diversity work. He cites the views of the founder of his consulting group:

If you don't understand how . . . [people's memberships in] groups . . . affect their lives in organizations . . . then you're not going to 'get' diversity. Related to that is . . . the notion of dominant groups and subordinate groups. . . . If you don't include the kind of power dynamic in understanding diversity, you're missing a big piece of it. . . . It's not just that they're *different* from each other, but it's also that one group has more *power* than the other group does. . . .

Charles, as well as many of his consulting group colleagues (and Herminia Cortez), has a background in the 'NTL T-group tradition', which emphasizes systems and group dynamics. Despite this and the consulting group's power-focused conceptual framework, its approach to diversity work seems to 'fall into the trap of relying too much on [workshops]'. Charles, like Herminia, does believe that the workshops are necessary as a starting point:

> These issues of how race, gender, etc. operate in our society and in organ-
> izations are so misunderstood. . . . If you are a member of the dominant
> group . . . you are so unaware of your own dominance and the experience
> of people in the subordinate groups . . . that without that education you
> can't even begin to have conversations about . . . 'How do our systems
> need to be different here?'

Diversity awareness training *is* a necessary first step. But why do diversity initiatives get stalled in this supposedly preliminary phase? Why does 'changing the culture of the organization and so forth' not happen? Why are systemic changes not designed and implemented? Charles cites two complementary explanations, both related to the business case for diversity. First, the personal awarenesses that come out of diversity training lead to a feeling of having already accomplished enough:

> [The educational] piece has to be there, and it gets seductive . . . because
> the learnings that come out of it and the 'ahahs!' that people have . . .
> feels like: 'Oh, this is it! Now we've done it!'

Second, going any further – attempting systemic, structural changes – is just too difficult. Like Herminia, he sees that 'going further' is an exercise in complexity. Moving people beyond 'valuing diversity' to thinking and behaving differently and incorporating new systems into the organization seems just too difficult:

> That hard work of . . . saying, 'OK. How do we need to change our
> systems, and the way we operate, and our unwritten rules, and all that
> stuff?' . . . It feels too *hard.* . . .

> How do you get it into the daily thought process of people as they go
> about doing their everyday work? How do you get them to put on the
> diversity lens when they're reading a covering letter or considering a pol-
> icy, or interacting with an employee about some other, totally unrelated
> issue? *But diversity is there nonetheless, and they need to deal with it.*

The stories told by Herminia, Henry and Charles reveal the role played by the institutional thought structure of the business case for diversity. They reflect the overarching belief-value system of the business case, locating the beginnings of corporate interest in workforce diversity in the startling (and alarming) demographic changes predicted by *Workforce 2000* and the potential problems and opportunities posed by a (thus) newly-diversified organizational workforce. They chronicle the 'taken-for-grantedness' of a personal awareness/training approach as the expectation and norm for 'doing' diversity initiatives. Henry, Herminia and Charles all allude to organizations legitimating their investment in diversity work by deeming it a bottom line issue. This allows organizations to bypass other sources of legitimacy (e.g. the pursuit of fairness or equity), and leave out of the story (already resolved and 'fixed') persistent problems of equal employment opportunity and power relations among traditionally dominant and subordinate groups.

The business case's unitary emphasis on the 'good for business' rationale forecloses consideration of a more holistic conception of what is problematic. It thus eliminates any motivation to develop the long-term systemic strategies and complex action plans necessary to any effort at meaningful organizational transformation. Henry describes this gap between talk and action:

> The implementation phase ... that's still where the gap is. People can leave any [diversity] program and [feel] good, and that doesn't mean that they have changed ... You need a long-term sustained program ... a long-term strategy ... integrated into a holistic ... organizational transformation.

He contrasts this with his personal vision of an effective organizational transformation initiative:

> This is going to be a five-year intervention in which diversity happens to be one of the key ... strings in a tapestry of human transformation or organizational transformation. ... You could do a leadership strand. You could do a teamwork strand. ... The people may figure out how to do teamwork and then diversity spills into teamwork and teamwork spills into diversity, and leadership spills into this ... and [this] spills into that.

Herminia, Henry and Charles have described how they resolve the dissonance caused by the discrepancies between their beliefs about what ought to be done, and the desires of their (would-be) clients for restating the business case and awareness training. They have had to stake out positions somewhere between (an economically unviable) insistence on doing what they know is 'right' (proposing and implementing interventions aimed at systemic, structural change) and a (self-compromising) provision of the 'product' their clients wish to purchase (awareness training for everyone). In order to make a living, they sometimes set aside their 'systems orientation,' and their understanding of the role of organizational structures and procedures in preserving the *status quo*. They swallow hard, and propose Diversity 101 for all, as expected by their (always-already indoctrinated by the business case) clients.

How did the work of diversity management come to be defined so widely by the business case for diversity? To theorize an answer to this question, a second 'lens', that of the 'New Institutionalism', proves useful. When combined with the narrative approach, New Institutionalist concepts help to explain the wide acceptance of the business case for diversity as 'natural' and 'common-sensical', and the role it plays in organizational (non)change.

The new institutionalists' 'iron cage'

A new institutionalist approach focuses on the processes through which organizations' structures and practices become more and more similar over time. It can explain how the interactions among the business case for diversity, professional diversity consultants, and managers 'tasked' with implementing diversity programmes have resulted in greater homogeneity, rather than diversity, among diversity initiatives.

DiMaggio and Powell, central figures of the new institutionalism, contend that most organizational theorists assume a world of varied organizational structures and behaviours. Traditional theorists, then, propose explanations for those variations. DiMaggio and Powell, however, posit a different starting point. They observe homogeneity rather than diversity among organizations, and ask 'why there is such startling homogeneity of organizational forms and practices?' They seek, thus, to 'explain homogeneity, not variation' (1991b: 64).

DiMaggio and Powell revisit Max Weber's metaphor of the 'iron cage' to advance their explanation. The forces of bureaucratization and rationalization in the service of capitalism create Weber's 'iron cage.' Bureaucracy is such an efficient and powerful means of controlling people that, once established, its path is irreversible. For Weber, the relentless power of bureaucracy creates and sustains structures of domination, foreclosing options for individual action (DiMaggio and Powell 1991b; Morgan 1997). Weber notes that domination can be achieved through the use of direct threat or force. However, he points out that domination can also be achieved more subtly. Domination also occurs through a process of legitimation, whereby the dominated come to believe that the dominator has the right to 'rule over' them. The driving force for this process is the quest for ever greater (bureaucratized and rationalized) efficiency (Morgan 1997).

New institutionalists contend, however, that sufficient rationalization and bureaucratization already having been achieved, modern organizational change does not necessarily have anything to do with increasing efficiency or improving organizational performance. Instead, change is directed toward the achievement of *legitimacy*:

> [The new institutionalism] is a theoretical perspective that focuses on
> organizational conformity with social rules and rituals rather than with

efficient processing of inputs and outputs. It is a perspective concerned more with legitimacy than efficiency.

(Orrù *et al.* 1991: 361)

The process through which organizations become increasingly similar to one another in their pursuit of legitimacy is called 'institutional isomorphism,' which DiMaggio and Powell declare to be the new 'engine of organizational rationalization' (1991b: 63).

Institutional isomorphism is driven by competition among organizations not only for resources and customers, but also for political power, legitimacy and social fitness. Isomorphism occurs through three mechanisms: coercive, mimetic and normative (DiMaggio and Powell 1991b: 66). *Coercive isomorphism* occurs in response to formal and/or informal *pressures* exerted by the government or other organizations, or by prevailing cultural/societal expectations. Organizations change because they feel *compelled* to do so: to maintain their legitimacy they must live up to legal mandates as well as to society's expectations. Changing a company's recruitment and selection procedures to 'deemphasize race' (in response to new anti-affirmative action court decisions) and converting the organization's former Affirmative Action Director into its new Director of Workforce Diversity (in response to a 'sea change' in societal attitudes) are examples of coercive isomorphism. Adding the organization's 'commitment to diversity' to its mission statement and 'making the business case for diversity' to all its employees can be interpreted as additional examples.

Mimetic isomorphism is a response not to outside pressure, but to *uncertainty*. In response to ambiguous situations or vaguely-defined problems with unclear solutions, individuals and the organizations they manage copy the choices made by others in similar situations. They adopt the structural and procedural choices of other organizations, similar to themselves, but which they perceive as more successful. Models may be spread unintentionally, through employee transfer or turnover, or intentionally by consultants, trade journals and other publications. For example, the Conference Board's 1995 report, *Diversity: Business Rationale and Strategies*, which reports on the diversity activities of American Express, Bank of America, Bechtel, General Electric, IBM, Wisconsin Bell and Philip Morris (Michael Wheeler 1995), provides legitimated models of 'best practices' for use in the design of new diversity programmes. The manager newly tasked with creating her organization's diversity initiative – and *uncertain* of how to go about it properly – can comfortably (and legitimately) model her proposal on the 'best practices' about which she has read. She can attend a workshop on 'How to Make the Business Case for Diversity for Your Organization', where she will be provided with ways to resolve her uncertainty in the form of models and assistance in conforming to them.

Normative isomorphism proceeds from a process of professionalization, 'the collective struggle of members of an occupation to define the conditions and methods of their work . . . and to establish a cognitive base and legitimation for their occupational autonomy' (DiMaggio and Powell 1991b: 70). In order to become and remain 'professionals,' members of occupations such as 'diversity consultant' or 'manager of workforce diversity' experience occupational socialization in the forms of trade associations, workshops, in-service educational programmes, consulting arrangements, employer-professional school networks, and trade publications. For example, the Conference Board holds annual diversity conferences and publishes reports based on those conferences (e.g. Conference Board Reports No. 1013 [1992], 1083–94–RR [1994], 1130–95–RR, 1995). The invitation to their '1999 Diversity Conference, Strategic Diversity for Business Performance Enhancement', illustrates the normative isomorphic pressures upon diversity 'professionals' to keep current with the latest trends in their field:

> Join us at our annual diversity conference to hear from business leaders who are working to translate diversity into performance enhancement . . . You will hear about some new solutions to familiar issues. It will help provide you with the knowledge and insights to move forward and to think of corporate diversity in new, strategic, and innovative ways . . .
>
> Come be a part of this national forum for business leaders and learn leading-edge company practices, exchange information on how better to respond to dynamic work place realities, and how to build competitiveness through people.
>
> (Conference Board 1999)

While mimetic isomorphism is a response to *uncertainty*, normative isomorphism occurs in pursuit of *professionalism*, of being 'in-the-know,' *au courant* of the latest 'professional' knowledge and practices. The already-savvy and experienced diversity professional brings his up-dated knowledge back from the conference. He can then (attempt to) re-configure his organization's diversity initiative according to his reinvigorated expertise. The result will be an organization 'on the cutting edge' of 'best diversity practices,' (and ripe for being copied by other organizations, as the mimetic and normative processes reinforce one another.)

Clearly, all three isomorphic mechanisms operate together to institutionalize the business case for diversity. Responses to external pressures, quests for ways to deal with ambiguity and uncertainty, and needs to maintain and reinforce the appearance of professionalism all further the diffusion of the business case for diversity, the homogenized ritualization of organizational responses, and thus, the solidification of the 'iron cage' inhibiting alternative avenues of thought and action.

Beyond the business case

To be sure, it is not the iron cage of the business case *alone* which is responsible for the absence of 'results' in the form of structural, systemic changes in organizations. The *status quo* has been quite rewarding to powerful individuals. The redistribution of power, realignment of structures, and revision of systems all threaten the comfort, continued earning power and professional advancement of those who are dominant in organizations. There is, thus, a genuine *conflict of interest*, which would motivate the powerful to withhold support for the comprehensive changes outlined by Thomas in *Beyond Race and Gender*. Henry Corta portrays their efforts as directed elsewhere:

> Most CEOs are not necessarily looking for an organizational . . . transformation. They're not. They're usually buying the non-intervention deal. . . . And their goals are more to keep the machine producing whatever they're supposed to produce. If it's supposed to produce more cars, let's produce more cars. . . . Very few companies take on major [transformations.] They make piecemeal efforts.

Furthermore, the deep-rooted systemic changes envisioned both by Thomas and by Henry, Herminia and Charles would require years of effort and the expenditure of considerable funds: far more than could probably be justified by *quantifiable* jumps in organizational productivity and profitability *directly* attributable to having become a diversity-friendly organization.[7] To go *this* far – to transform the organization – *might not make quantifiable business sense*. So, there is a coldly *logical* conclusion to be drawn by those operating within the iron cage of the business case for diversity and its endorsement of bottom-line enhancement as the 'right thing.' That conclusion is that funding the 'talk' but not the 'walk' is a business imperative. In the larger context, then, the business case for diversity serves as a powerful weapon in the hands of the defenders of the *status quo*. It legitimates their implementation of *ritualistic* practices such as mission statements and universal awareness training along with their failure to implement holistic, systemic attempts at organizational transformation. Both are rendered justifiable by reference to, and by retelling, the business case for diversity.

The iron cage

As we have seen, the narrative of the business case for diversity has been retold and embellished countless times in publications and diversity training sessions. Through isomorphic processes its basic plot has become naturalized into an institutional thought structure. This institutional thought structure functions as an 'iron cage', which legitimates as 'common knowledge' particular, narrow constructions of diversity and managing diversity while foreclosing alternative conceptions and strategies. The adoption and dissemination of the business case reifies a fiction constructed from an interpretation of selected statistics about US demographics, assumptions about the nature of managing, and a particular conception of the problematic of 'workforce diversity'. Other interpretations of what is problematic and what to do about it simply do not fit into the story. The thought structure disseminated by the retelling of the business case legitimates non-consideration of issues of equity, along with the adoption of symbolic, ritualistic practices, such as the drafting of mission statements and the institution of one-day diversity awareness workshops. The picture is of executives who have come to believe that 'making the business case' for diversity together with publishing it through mission statements and awareness training for all employees *is* 'doing diversity'. This picture is reflected in the description of a symposium entitled 'Competitiveness and the Role of Diversity' which took place during the 1998 conference of the American Society for Competitiveness. It illustrates how the thought structure of the business case for diversity functions as an 'iron cage' foreclosing lines of thought (and, thus, of action) while legitimating the avoidance of difficult (but only too relevant) concerns:

> This panel will focus on the role of diversity in business organizations in relation to competitiveness. The impact of diversity, generally defined in a business context as the active inclusion as employees of those members of society meeting certain classifications under federal law, will be addressed in a neutral, non-judgmental manner with an eye toward drawing conclusions that may be helpful to organizations seeking to maintain and extend existing competitive advantage. It is intended that topics such as affirmative action, discrimination, racism, sexism, and sexual harassment *not* be discussed, except, perhaps, as issues ancillary to competitiveness.
>
> (American Society for Competitiveness 1998: 10, 11, emphasis in original)

This insistence on the separation of the 'competitiveness' aspects of diversity from any discussion of power relations, privilege or equal employment opportunity clearly displays the overarching presence of the institutional thought-structure of the business case. This description also illustrates Mumby's thesis regarding the political function of narrative in organizations:

> Narratives provide members [of organizations] with accounts. . . . Such accounts potentially legitimate dominant forms of organizational reality, and lead to discursive closure in the sense of restricting the interpretations and meanings that can be attached to organizational activity.
>
> (Mumby 1987: 113)

Mumby's argument goes further, pointing toward the power of narratives not only to communicate to members of organizations the nature of their organizational reality, but also to *create* that reality and thereby legitimate only particular courses of action as *logical* and *rational.*

> [N]arratives do not simply *inform* organization members about the values, practices and traditions to which their organization is committed. Rather, they help to *constitute* the organizational consciousness of social actors by articulating and embodying a particular reality, and subordinating or devaluing other modes of 'organization rationality.'
>
> (Mumby 1987: 125, emphasis in original)

The narrative of the business case for diversity constitutes a version of reality which has become naturalized and taken-for-granted as an institutional thought structure. The institutionalization of this thought structure continues through the processes of isomorphism, now on a global basis. Witness 'Migration media release 64/98' published via the Internet by Australia's Minister for Immigration and Multicultural Affairs:

> The Minister for Immigration and Multicultural Affairs, Philip Ruddock, today called on New South Wales businesses to make better use of their culturally-diverse workforces in order to generate economic benefits and improve business efficiency. 'Australia is at its best when it taps the skills and knowledge of our diverse workforce. To dismiss this resource is to lose a competitive advantage in a tough business environment,' Mr. Ruddock said.
>
> (Migration Media Release 1998)

This (seemingly inexorable) isomorphic process continues, even in the face of mounting dissatisfaction with US diversity programmes, especially among the 'diverse' constituencies toward which out-dated, unfashionable equity-oriented efforts had been previously targeted:

> 'I don't know of anybody who's satisfied,' says Harris Sussman, director of the human-relations firm Workways Consulting in Cambridge, Massachusetts. 'Almost everybody's angry. To me, that indicates that the diversity initiatives of most companies have been badly mishandled. It's no wonder it's hard to find any fans of employer-sponsored diversity programs. People of color and women feel kind of mislead about what changes were going to occur, when in fact almost no changes have occurred in all these years.'
>
> (Flynn 1998: 28)

The business case for diversity is an 'iron cage' as it creates homogeneity without effectiveness. It provides legitimacy for the enactment of ritual while foreclosing paths of thought and action that might lead to systemic and structural organizational transformation.

Notes

1 I thank Linda Smircich for her guidance, and Robin Ely, Jill Woodilla, Erica Foldy, and Joel Litvin for their comments and suggestions.
2 Alternative accounts might have been built, however, upon other conceptualizations, such as rhetorical formation, schema, template, etc.
3 For one view of 'How Affirmative Action Became Diversity Management,' see Kelly and Dobbin 1998. Lynch (1997a,b) offers another account of the origins of diversity management.
4 It is interesting to note that this 'good business' positioning was, in fact, not new to managing diversity. Affirmative action had already been described as 'an essential management tool which reinforces accountability and maximizes the utilization of the talents of [the firm's] entire work force' (Kelly and Dobbin 1998: 969). Also, a brief filed by the National Association of Manufacturers in 1986 described affirmative action as a 'business policy which has allowed industry to benefit from new ideas, opinions and perspectives generated by greater workforce diversity' (*Harvard Law Review* 1989: 669). Kelly and Dobbin suggest that these descriptions 'prefigured the diversity management discourse of the late 1980s and early 1990s' (1998: 969).
5 Copeland wrote (or co-authored) a number of articles which appeared in *Training*, *Personnel Administrator*, *Training and Development Journal* and *Personnel* between May, 1988 and February, 1989. She was one of the producers of the *Valuing Diversity* video series (which subsequently became a best-seller for use in diversity training).
6 All names have been changed.
7 Much attention is currently being given to quantifying and measuring the impact of diversity initiatives. A session at the 1999 Diversity Conference (held by the Conference Board) is entitled 'Diversity Measurement: A Framework and Methodologies for Performance and Accountability'. Nevertheless, empirical support for the 'bottom line' value of having a diverse work force has proven elusive and conflicting (Nkomo 1998).

10 Casting the native subject

Ethnographic practice and the (re)production of difference[1]

Pushkala Prasad and Anshuman Prasad

Ethnography, a hybrid activity . . . appears as writing, as collecting, as modernist collage, as imperial power, as subversive critique.

(James Clifford 1988)

In the 1980s, the recognition that organizations are cultural entities requiring cultural analysis transformed the study of management and organizations.[2] Relying on the lens of culture meant eschewing large-scale surveys and laboratory experiments in favour of in-depth researcher immersion in local fieldsites conducted under the label of ethnography. Ethnography's main epistemological claim is an endogenic or 'insider' one – that it offers an understanding of 'natives' in their own cultures. Within the wider anthropological tradition in which ethnography is rooted, the term itself denotes the practice of writing (*graphy*) about cultures (*ethno*), typically about 'other' and 'native' cultures (Axtell 1981; Vidich and Lyman 1994). Within the Anglo-American and French traditions, ethnography is often used to refer to the actual fieldwork that yields 'ethnological' insights, though both terms (ethnography and ethnology) are sometimes used interchangeably. Often referred to as an *emic* (as opposed to *etic*) tradition, conventional ethnography does not merely imply intense researcher involvement in the field, but is committed to understanding and presenting the natives from an 'inside' point of view (Gregory 1983; Schwartzman 1993).

Ethnography's *emic* claim, we would argue, raises some interesting, sometimes troubling questions about the meaning of terms such as 'insider' and 'native', and their implications for ethnographic knowledge. Ethnography has systematically placed natives at the heart of all scholarly inquiry, setting up a complex set of interconnections between ethnographers themselves, the natives they study, and the knowledge that is produced out of these encounters. By frequently claiming to offer native interpretations of reality, ethnography implicitly raises troubling questions about the possibilities of doing so, the right to speak of others' experiences, and the consequences of such actions. Terms such as 'native', 'emic' and 'insider', are therefore, we would argue, in need of some unpacking. It is our further contention that concerns around these issues have been growing increasingly urgent as conventional conceptions of 'natives' are dramatically altered in an increasingly globalized world where natives simultaneously inhabit multiple organizational and cultural worlds, and resist ethnographic attempts to fix them within specific cultural spaces (Behar 1993).

In importing the methodology of ethnography, organization studies have inherited many of the predicaments raised by these native questions, although the discipline does not always display a conscious reflexivity about them. Further, by tailoring ethnography to suit its own substantive focus, organization studies transforms the dynamics around these native questions recasting them in a somewhat different mould. The goal of this chapter is twofold. First, it seeks to historically trace the complex relationship between ethnography, ethnographers and natives. And second, it tries to understand how this triadic relationship is embedded in, and influenced by, the wider socio-political and institutional contexts of both cultural anthropology and organization studies, resulting in specific intended and unintended effects. Our premise here is that epistemological questions around knowledge production of the natives are not decided in academic isolation, but are shaped by the economic and cultural milieux in which they are located.

Within organization studies, prior reflections on the nature of interpretive dilemmas (Van Maanen 1995; Yanow 2000), while offering interesting insights, have neglected the network of knowledge interests and expectations that undergird such issues. This chapter hopes to remedy this by looking at *emic* debates through a historical and contemporary examination of the native subject within scholarly ethnography. We begin with a historical analysis of ethnography and its depiction of natives, and move on to an analysis of contemporary native questions in anthropology and organization studies. We conclude with some reflections on continuing challenges posed by these issues.

Getting to know the natives: the genesis of the ethnographic tradition

The native as primitive stranger

Within the anthropological tradition, the practice of ethnography emerged out of the intense *strangeness* and uncertainty provoked by the first European encounters with the natives of the so-called 'New World' (Asad 1973; Axtell 1981). Confronted with a set of bewilderingly unfamiliar cultures that were in the process of being colonized, Europeans needed quite urgently to 'know' or understand these natives from a European standpoint. Accordingly, the earliest ethnographies can be found in detailed accounts of native customs and cultures in the logs and diaries maintained by European travellers, adventurers, missionaries and traders, as well as in reports written by colonial administrators (Asad 1973; Tedlock 1991).

In time, the writing of such accounts (or ethnographies) came to be formally sponsored and *organized* by a number of state and educational institutions in Europe and North America. Contrary to a widespread feeling that ethnography has always occupied a marginal position in the Academy, historians of anthropology emphasize that it also has to be understood as an institutional by-product of colonization and conquest. It is not entirely accidental that the ethnographic movement was strongest in Great Britain, France and the USA, three major imperial powers whose recurrent and troubling encounters with *difference* required a body of 'scientific' knowledge that rendered these different groups more understandable and therefore more amenable to governance (Stocking 1983; Clifford 1988). Ethnographers in the latter part of the nineteenth and in the first half of the twentieth century were invariably sponsored by powerful organizations in their home countries. These included universities, government agencies, learned ethnological societies and specific reputed institutions such as the *Institut d'Ethnologie* in France, and the Smithsonian Institution and the Bureau of Indian Affairs in the USA (Stocking 1983; Vidich and Lyman 1994). In fact, colonial administrators who were to be despatched to various French colonies, were often required to do a course on ethnography at the *Institut* as part of their training. While French and British ethnographers were mainly engaged in studying 'exotic' cultures in different outposts of the empire (Malinowski 1922; Griaule 1938), American ethnographers were working closer to home, examining native American cultures under the aegis of the Bureau of Indian Affairs (Cushing 1920; Curtis 1924).[3]

The institutional organization of ethnography created expectations that it would deliver a portrait of the native subject (Caribbean, Pacific Islander or Iroquois) that was intelligible to European and North American governing bodies, and that would legitimate the colonial domination of 'native' cultures. Not surprisingly, early ethnographies vividly highlighted the strangeness of the native as 'other', represented as embodying an abhorrent (Youngs 1992) or exotic (Curtis 1924) form of primitivism and savagery. Either way, native cultures were constituted as 'backward', and consequently in need of European or western governance.

The collectible native

Ethnography in the nineteenth and early twentieth centuries did more than provide useful information on the native subjects of colonial governance. Prominent anthropologists such as Malinowski and Marcel Griaule were often cast (by themselves or an admiring professional audience) as heroes on a mission of ethnographic adventure resulting in the appropriation of countless native objects and cultural artifacts destined for museums and private collections back home. Some ethnographic expeditions such as the famous

French Mission Dakar–Djibouti were merely part of a much larger museum collection venture, intended to collect African artifacts for the Musée de l'Homme in Paris (Clifford 1988). This emphasis on *collecting* in the ethnographic tradition sometimes even extended to native subjects themselves. Natives were occasionally imported by ethnographers to both Europe and North America and placed on display in museums, scientific exhibitions and anthropology departments (Gidley 1992).

The importation of natives for the purpose of public display in the cause of furthering scientific knowledge about natives became more prevalent in the late nineteenth and early twentieth centuries. Perhaps the best known incident is the case of Ota Benga, the African 'pygmy' who was brought to the USA by missionary ethnologist Samuel Phillips Vermeer, to be displayed as a native 'exhibit' in the St Louis World Fair of 1904 (Bradford and Blume 1992). After being subject to the public gaze in St Louis, Ota Benga was placed in the Monkey House in the Bronx zoo to demonstrate the closeness between 'primitive' peoples and primates until his eventual release a few years later. Nearly thirty years earlier, the Centennial Exposition in Philadelphia celebrating one hundred years of US national independence, had displays of 'wild children' from Borneo organized by ethnographers (Slotkin 1985). Then, in 1911, one of the so-called last surviving members of the Yahi tribe spent several years living in the anthropological museum at the University of California at Berkeley, where he demonstrated several aspects of traditional Yahi culture (Kroeber 1976). In all these cases, the incarceration and exhibition of 'natives' was socially acceptable since such displays were seen as being part and parcel of the process of gaining knowledge about other cultures (Gidley 1994). Early ethnography quite frequently turned its subjects into objects and *collectibles* that were necessary in order to advance western knowledge about 'savage' cultures (Bradford and Blume 1992; Robinson 1994).

The rise of the professional ethnographer

In constituting the native as primitive other and collectible object, ethnography implicitly delineated certain rules to be followed by ethnographers. In essence, the 'native subject' was brought under the scientific gaze of ethnographers who were required to demonstrate a close familiarity with native cultures while simultaneously standing apart from them. At the same time, the wide institutional support received by ethnography resulted in growing pressures for it to turn into a more professional 'academic' and legitimate enterprise. The professionalization of ethnography was primarily characterized by a rigorous theoretical training and the emergence of shared norms regarding its conduct. This theoretical emphasis was reflected in the constant deployment of the conceptual lens of *culture*, used to enter and understand different native societies. While the concept of culture itself has been used in a wide variety of ways, ranging from the early structural functionalism of

Radcliffe-Browne (1922) to its more Marxian use in the 1960s and 1970s (Ortner 1984), it has remained a constant theoretical backdrop for professional ethnography, offering it the academic framework not found in earlier amateur accounts.

To understand native cultures, professional ethnography relied predominantly on the method of participant observation, simultaneously demanding an intimate closeness to and distance from natives being studied. Since the native was so clearly marked by his/her otherness, the ethnographer needed to get really close to her/him for a meaningful understanding. But since the native was also a scientific object and collectible, it was necessary to study him/her with some degree of detachment and distance. In sum, the constitution of the native as an objectified other posed an interesting paradox for professional ethnography, setting up a series of unresolved tensions around closeness to and distance from native subjects. Ethnographers aimed for a close and intimate relationship with their subjects, but eventually masked this closeness in their writings through the adoption of a dispassionate researcher voice signalling distance from them (Tedlock 1991; Prasad 1998).

More important, early ethnography's claims of intimacy with the natives needs to be approached with some caution. Ethnography's systematic portrayals of native cultures as subordinate and inferior, raises questions about how any closeness or intimacy might have been possible under these conditions. Further, such a relationship seriously jeopardized the production of what natives might recognize as 'authentic' accounts about themselves. Despite the promise of *emic* knowledge, what was repeatedly produced were accounts that mirrored the colonial fantasies and worldviews of the nineteenth and early twentieth centuries (Axtell 1981; Gidley 1992), leaving the native with little to say about his or her own culture.

We are the natives: ethnography in management and organization studies

Ethnography entered organization studies because of the growing popularity of *organizational culture* as a concept. While traditional ethnographic methods such as participant observation had already been popularized by organizational sociologists working out of the Chicago School (Whyte 1955; Dalton 1959) and Tavistock (Turner 1971) traditions, 'full-blown ethnography' (Schwartzman 1993) located within the theoretical matrix of culture appeared in organization studies with the so-called 'culture-rage' that gripped the western management world in the 1980s. The recognition that businesses and other contemporary administrative institutions also 'had' cultures and were therefore inhabited by organizational natives was, in part, triggered by the Japanese economic miracle which was widely attributed to unique facets of Japanese culture (Vogel 1979; Ouchi 1981). Cultural explanations for Japan's industrial and economic success resulted in an overall focus on cultural dimensions such as ceremonies, rituals and taboos found in organizations. These notions were further amplified in Peters and Waterman's (1982) bestseller *In Search of Excellence*, which transferred the culture metaphor into North American organizations, arguing that not only national, but organizational cultures also contained special ingredients for economic success. Once organizations were established as cultural entities, ethnography seemed the obvious method of choice for understanding them.

Organizational ethnographers treat industries and organizations as cultural wholes with customs and conventions that are regularly followed by natives (managers and employees). Studies of Disneyworld (Van Maanen and Kunda 1988), Silicon Valley professionals (Gregory 1983), an advertising agency (Rosen 2000), etc. all focus on cultural patterns of behaviour from an insider viewpoint. In essence, these ethnographies 'turn the anthropological lens inwards' (Rabinow 1977), employing a methodology used to come to grips with intense otherness for the purpose of understanding contemporary organizations. On the surface it might seem that organizational ethnography would now be in a position of producing *emic* knowledge about organizational natives. In actual practice, however, the project of understanding the native remains as complex as ever before. As Jeffcutt (1994) acutely observes, organizational ethnographers have imported and re-described techniques of working and writing that were originally developed over sixty years ago in anthropology. In doing so, ethnographers of the workplace can unwittingly continue to reproduce imperialist assumptions and agendas, while simultaneously initiating new problematics around the production of *emic* knowledge about organizational natives.

The professional stranger

While organizational natives no longer occupy the stark role of *primitive* Other assigned by early ethnographers to their subjects, they continue (for the most part) to be approached with the same desire for closeness and distance characterizing earlier studies. To Czarniawska (1998: 21), the field remains a place where 'the Other' lives, and 'fieldwork is an expression of curiosity of the Other . . .'. No matter what kind of organizational culture is being looked at, organizational ethnographies tend to conform to the norms of the professional ethnographic tradition. Studies are marked by long periods of researcher immersion in native cultures, followed by withdrawal and detachment in the production of the ethnographic account (Prasad 1993, 1995). Even when the more personal 'I' form is used in writing, the studies are characterized by a certain professional distance between the researcher and his/her subjects. In other words, the researcher role is one of a '*professional stranger*' (Agar 1980), an outsider who has a sharper vision of a culture than the natives, even though this vision is achieved only through the help of the natives themselves.

The elusive natives

Even when focusing on one's 'own' culture (i.e. contemporary organizations), the 'authentic' native can remain as elusive as before. One might even argue that organizational ethnographers encounter a series of problems that were not part of the world of traditional anthropological inquiry. For instance, in contemporary organizations, ethnographers enter into very different relationships with native subjects, some of whom occupy positions of power and privilege which protect them from the ethnographic gaze. As Rosen (2000) points out, observing managers and corporate elites implies studying a significantly powerful group who can exert considerable influence over the conduct and presentation of an ethnography. Organizational natives at higher ends of the hierarchy can also impose several constraints on ethnographers, committing them to confidentiality, not permitting the scrutiny of files and records on grounds of organizational security, etc. (Rosen 2000). In sum, organizational cultures can be quite closed as a result of bureaucratic conventions and privileges, and the self-interested practices of managerial elites.

Entire segments of native organizational life are therefore systematically closed to ethnographers who cannot take the same liberties with organizational leaders that were often taken by their anthropological predecessors with native leaders. Not surprisingly, perhaps, organizational ethnographers show a marked tendency to focus on natives at the lower rungs of the organizational hierarchy. Countless studies examine the inside worlds of blue-collar workers (Thompson 1983; Collinson 1992), service workers (Leidner 1993; Van Maanen and Kunda 1988) and middle managers (Jackall 1988). Very few explore the sub-cultures of the corporate boardroom or the world of the administrative elites, for the simple reason that these more powerful natives are shielded from ethnographic observations. Organizational leaders are glimpsed in ethnographies only in public and ceremonial situations, as in Rosen's (2000) study of a celebratory breakfast in an advertising agency. For the most part, an important slice of organizational culture is kept firmly hidden from view.

Falling short of professional standards

To some observers, organizational ethnographers fail to provide authentic insights into native worlds because their methodological commitments are less stringent than those of their counterparts in anthropology. Barry Turner (1986), for instance, deplored the tendency of organizational scholars to turn themselves into 'pop-culture magicians' offering simplistic and superficial readings of native organizational cultures. For Turner, what is needed are 'honest grapplers', who follow in the footsteps of anthropologists, making serious and committed attempts to grasp an organization's cultural nuances from a native standpoint.

A similar and even harsher critique was levelled by Bate (1997) who charged organizational ethnographers with falling short of the standards of professional anthropological research. Disparaging organizational ethnographers for being 'quasi-anthropological', Bate took them to task for not being sufficiently faithful to the rigorous anthropological tradition:

> On closer examination 'thick description' invariably turns out to be 'quick description', yet another business case study or company history, a pale reflection of the experientially rich social science envisaged by early writers like Agar. 'Prolonged contact with the field' means a series of flying visits rather than a long-term stay (jet plane ethnography). Organizational anthropologists rarely take a toothbrush with them these days. A journey into the organizational bush is often little more than a safe and closely chaperoned form of anthropological tourism.
>
> (ibid.: 1150)

Bate's critique is infused with a strong sense of nostalgia for the heroic ethnography of Malinowski and Marcel Griaule, where the fieldworker accesses the native worlds of subjects through prolonged periods of immersion in the field. What he ignores is the highly contested nature of knowledge that was and continues to be produced from these ethnographic contacts.

More to the point perhaps, is Rosen's (2000) observation that these so-called quasi-anthropological ethnographies are not merely matters of convenience. They are also compatible with the publishing requirements within organization science, favouring journal articles over full-length books and monographs. Yet ethnographies do not lend themselves to neat intellectual distillations, losing much of their texture in the process. Journal articles, however well-crafted, give us at most an *ethnographic slice* rather than an ethnographic picture of a particular situation. To complicate matters, organizational ethnographies are invariably judged in the review process according to the criteria of conventional positivism calling for reliability, falsification, etc. (Kleppesto 1998). Such criteria cripple the presentation of ethnographic work, turning it into something quite unrelated to the anthropological tradition.

The problem of cultural blindness

Organizational ethnographers are also confronted with the unique problem of studying places inhabited by people very much like themselves (Rosen 2000). When ethnographers share many aspects of a culture with the 'natives' they are studying, they are often unable to notice the more taken-for-granted aspects of the culture itself. Alvesson (1993), for instance, points out that organizational ethnographers often take central features of contemporary organizations completely for granted, failing to see them as unique historically produced cultural practices. This 'cultural blindness' as he calls it, is reflected in the failure of organizational ethnographers to note that 'the preoccupation with "managing", "organizing" and making things as "efficient" as possible is a key feature of Western culture and of business organizations in particular' (ibid.: 47). Unlike anthropologists who are starkly confronted with 'otherness', organizational ethnographers have to worry about 'staying at home and claiming sufficient bravado to transform that which is culturally familiar into a subject upon which to interpret under-standings' (Rosen 2000: 58).

Turning native: experimental moments in the ethnographic tradition

Professional ethnographers in both cultural anthropology and organization studies have thus been equally troubled by the question of 'authentic' repre-sentation. In practice, even while claiming to offer native standpoints and interpretations, professional ethnography has always been presented with an academic detachment that, paradoxically, questions the very authenticity it claims to offer. Can 'professional strangers' actually 'know' the natives espe-cially when the natives inhabit strikingly unfamiliar worlds? While this nag-ging question has provided few easy answers, one of the more controversial responses to it has taken the form of 'gone-native' ethnography.

'Gone-native' ethnographers take immersion in the field to something of an extreme (Tedlock 1991). They do not merely spend extended periods of time in the native cultures they are studying, but aim to 'become' one of the natives themselves in order to *experience* at the most authentic level possible, the everyday dimensions of a particular culture (Vidich and Lyman 1994). Some noteworthy examples of 'gone-native' ethnography include Cushing's (1882, 1901) celebrated work with the Zuni during which period he became a Zuni shaman and war priest (Vidich and Lyman 1994; Evans 1999). More contemporary 'gone-native' ethnographers include Lisa Dalby who 'became' a Japanese geisha (Dalby 1983) and Hunter Thompson (1985) who joined the infamous 'Hell's Angels' in order to conduct a study of their local cultures.

A variant of 'gone-native' ethnographies can be found in a genre combin-ing personal experiences and reflections, referred to as either self-ethnography (Alvesson 1998) or auto-ethnography (Hayano 1979). In these works, the writer's *personal* experiences and interpretations are the focus of the entire ethnography. Rather than turning native in order to enter the lifeworlds of another culture, the ethnographer's own detailed experiences and com-mentaries become the source and target of the entire study. In our minds, the classic controversial self-ethnography *par excellence* remains Carlos Castaneda's (1968) amazing story of his own spiritual learning with the help of Don Juan, a native Shaman. Though Castaneda does not characterize his work as ethnographic, his completely personal narrative nevertheless suc-ceeds in providing the reader with a close view of the peyote sub-culture of the American south-west. A similar and more outrageous self-ethnography is

Hunter Thompson's (1974) classic, *Fear and Loathing in Las Vegas* describing the Republican Convention entirely from Thompson's somewhat psychedelic experiences of the time.

'Gone-native' and self-ethnographies are not very common in organization science even though turning native in many work situations is much more easily accomplished. Ethnographies based on the kind of *total membership* demanded by these traditions are most common in blue-collar contexts where researchers have become factory workers in order to understand the dynamics of the local culture (Roy 1961; Burawoy 1976). Typically however, the native experiences of the researcher are later explained and analyzed from a distinctly academic lens. Burawoy (1979) for instance uses neo-Marxism to explain the process of 'making out' on the shop floor, while Thompson (1983) offers a cultural critique of worker identity in a meat factory. These ethnographies differ from Cushing's (1882) work which was both experienced and written from a Zuni standpoint. Even when turning native, organizational ethnographers are eventually likely to return to a more professional platform from which to analyze their native experiences.

An interesting paradox mediates the legitimacy of turning native. While researchers of culture have often been castigated for their distance from native subjects triggered by their excessive professionalism, once researchers turn native, they confront a new set of accusations regarding the cultural myopia they develop as a result of their attempts at complete cultural immersion. While accounts based on turning native often hold wide popular appeal, the most serious opposition to this tradition is to be found within academia itself, which appears more unwilling to be convinced of the legitimacy of such accounts.

First, sceptics of this tradition point out that total membership in a culture does not necessarily guarantee insider knowledge and insights. Can an ethnographer ever become one of the natives? And will natives really trust a researcher who tries to become one of them? To some critics, an emic analysis based on turning native is neither easily accomplished nor always possible. Wax (1983) argues that 'natives' themselves are more likely to trust ethnographers who clearly recognize the limits of their own acculturation. To be effective, 'going-native' needs to be treated as *performance* by the ethnographer who consciously takes on the 'native' role rather than trying to genuinely transform him/herself. 'Perhaps good fieldwork is more like play-acting than most of us are willing to admit. Respondents rarely resent a fieldworker's "acting like them" or "learning their ways" as long as the fieldworker makes it clear that he knows he is only playing a part and that his newly acquired skills do not entitle him to any privileges which they are not willing to offer him' (Wax 1983: 197). For Wax, therefore, the most effective form of going native takes place when it is performed as a *masquerade*, played out within clearly delineated rules and limits.

To others engaged in understanding cultures, the attempt to completely identify oneself in the culture one is studying is not only impossible, but questionable in terms of what it can offer scholarly inquiry. In his incisive essay on 'thick description', Geertz (1975) dismisses the practice of going native as being of value only to romantics and spies. On closer examination however, Geertz's dismissal may not be entirely warranted. Spies, for instance, do not attempt native conversions for the purpose of gaining authentic insider insights into cultures. Rather, they consciously enter a culture as native impersonators solely to gather information for the cultures they serve and represent, though in the process of doing so, some may well decide to either join the natives (thereby betraying their country), or to turn into double agents.

On further reflection, Geertz's equation of 'gone-native' ethnography with professional espionage may well be so powerful in its dismissal of such attempts because it hints at some disquieting moments in the history of American anthropology. In 1919, Franz Boas, the leading anthropologist, charged several of his colleagues with spying for the US government under the guise of conducting ethnographies in Central America. Interestingly enough, the American Anthropological Association (AAA) voted to censure Boas for bringing these accusations, instead of investigating them. Decades later, revelations by the US government itself indicate that Boas's charges were closer to the mark (Price 2000). Similar scandals linking ethnographers to espionage recurred during the Korean and Vietnamese wars as well, while more recently charges have been levelled against ethnographers engaged in documenting specific blue-collar cultures for the explicit consumption of segments of corporate America (Price 2000). The point that is worth noting here is that genuine espionage was to be found more among professional ethnographers than among those who had turned native despite Geertz's ironic castigation of going native as being of interest only to spies.

Of even greater interest are the issues lying behind such a strong antipathy to the practice of turning native. At the heart of this opposition is the continuing implicit conviction that the 'expert' has a better access to native knowledge than natives themselves, and therefore those who try to turn native. As Tedlock (1991: 71) points out,

> what seems to lie behind the belief that 'going native' poses a serious danger to the fieldworker is the logical construction of the relationship between objectivity and subjectivity, between scientist and native, between self and other, as an unbridgeable opposition. The implication is that a subject's way of knowing is incompatible with the scientist's way of knowing and that the domain of objectivity is the sole property of the outsider.

From this perspective, researchers who have turned native are suspect precisely because of their closeness to natives, because familiarity and intimacy belong to the realm of the subjective, and cause a loss of the objective. The more skilfully an ethnographer turns native, the more likely that his/her interpretations will be greeted with suspicion. Ultimately, this debate around complete ethnographic identification remains locked in an impasse since it is caught between two incommensurable paradigms. On the one hand, ethnographers rooted in the subjectivist position can see the value of researcher immersion and identification. On the other hand, the overwhelming logic of positivist science sees knowledge about the natives as being possible only through maintaining an objectivity implied by professional distance.

There may be even more to this antagonism toward going native than meets the eye. The notion of turning native was an unspoken fear haunting early amateur ethnographers, European missionaries, colonial administrators and other culturally dislocated individuals. The fear that 'experts' from the 'civilized' world might lose themselves in the cultures they were temporarily inhabiting or studying was one that held sway over colonial adventurers and scholars of all kinds (Clifford 1988). In the USA, such fears were encoded in draconian laws punishing European settlers who turned native in the mid-nineteenth century (Axtell 1981). The spirit of such fears is captured evocatively in Kevin Costner's popular Hollywood film, *Dances with Wolves* where the movie's white protagonist is severely punished for embracing the Sioux way of life. The same intense fears are reflected in the writings of Marcel Griaule, the celebrated French ethnologist who warns ethnographers of the dangers of going native as one becomes more closely involved in the culture one is studying (Griaule 1938). To avoid such a catastrophe, Griaule himself increasingly reverted to the use of aerial photographs and the examination of artifacts in his study of the Dogon of Niger (Clifford 1988).

Ethnography's colonial legacy is thus still felt in the widespread suspicion of turning native among its adherents. Rooted in the same logic, turning native also continues to be feared on grounds of cultural contamination that will result in a loss of identity (both professional and personal) that is possibly irrecoverable. Given such strong anxieties, it is not surprising that researcher efforts to metamorphose themselves into natives is not likely to acquire legitimacy in the wider scholarly community.

Native fictions: ethnography in a pluralistic world

For all the effort spent on providing native accounts of specific cultures, both organizational and other professional ethnographers have succeeded only in emphasizing the distance between the native and the expert researcher, with the ethnographer's voice dominating and speaking for the natives. The colonial worldviews undergirding ethnography, and the demands of science have jointly also allocated a passive position to native subjects whose role is to be represented rather than to represent their own cultures. In the last two to three decades, however, changes in geo-political and cultural hierarchies have resulted in the conventional 'native' subjects of ethnography taking on far more active roles. As 'natives' become participants in the drama of the research process, fundamental new questions are raised about the goals and practices of ethnography.

Not just anthropology, but the entire social sciences and humanities have taken what is sometimes referred to as a narrative turn (Czarniawska 1998). The narrative turn is a highly creative direction in western scholarship that reflects (a) the changing configurations of global interrelationships (Said 1989; Chow 1993), and (b) an increasing disenchantment with conventional and reductionist scientific knowledge, often characterized as nothing more than another language game (Lyotard 1984). Linked to strands of postcolonial and post-structural theory, the first trend sees ethnography as a distinctive variant of the *western narrative genre* that has grown out of a sustained neoimperial 'gaze' directed towards 'natives'. The second trend, which is more driven by literary theory, asserts that ethnographic texts are primarily literary productions, telling readers more about how the texts are fashioned than about the native practices they depict (Clifford and Marcus 1986). Earlier debates about the authenticity of a text have, as a result, increasingly given way to critical questions regarding *rhetoric* and *representation* in ethnography (Clifford and Marcus 1986; Golden-Biddle and Locke 1993; Atkinson and Hammersley 1994).

These compelling intellectual directions have forced an acknowledgement of ethnographies as convincing 'fictions' about natives. The term 'fiction' here is not to be equated with falsehood. Rather, the term underscores the constructed nature of ethnographic narratives, and serves to highlight the role of personal and institutional interests in shaping the final document (Marcus and Cushman 1982). As Van Maanen (1995) astutely remarks, this recognition of the not-so-innocent character of ethnographic writing has made its practitioners more self-conscious, embarrassed and ironic about their own roles in representing native cultures: 'If anything, the moral ambiguity and political complicity associated with ethnography has grown ever more obvious and problematic in the shrinking and increasingly interconnected post-colonial world' (Van Maanen 1995: 8).

Simultaneously, ethnographers have had to grapple with the disappearance of the native. Globalization, with all its multidirectional cultural influences, has severely compromised the notion of the 'pure' native inhabiting 'pristine' cultures. The dominant metaphors used to designate cultures in anthropology today are *hybridity, creolization* and *syncretism* (Clifford 1988; Friedman 1995), all of which imply that natives inhabit diverse cultures and simultaneously influence many other cultures as well. 'Natives' have also become increasingly resistant to being represented by outside experts, and have begun to appropriate new roles for themselves as legitimate storytellers within ethnographic descriptions (Tedlock 1991). Natives of erstwhile 'primitive' cultures have also begun to conduct counter-ethnographies of the west, blurring conventional boundaries between ethnographers and natives themselves. In a world that is so determinedly plural, ethnography has had to refashion some of its own contours. Two of these traditions are discussed below.

Ethnographic memoir

The widespread acknowledgement of the 'fictitious' nature of ethnography
has encouraged many researchers to place themselves within ethnographic
texts as active and 'human' participants, frequently committing foolish
'mistakes' in the course of writing about the natives. This tradition, best
characterized as 'ethnographic memoir' (Tedlock 1991), reveals a sense of
researcher fraility and displays considerable literary influences from the genre
of the *autobiography*: 'In the ethnographic memoir, an author takes us back
to a corner of his or her own life in the field that was unusually vivid, full of
affect, or framed by unique events' (Tedlock 1991: 77). An early forerunner
of contemporary ethnographic memoirs is Gerald Berreman's (1962) intri-
cate account of his sojourn in a Himalayan village. Berreman presents his
ethnography as a form of impression management performed by both the
ethnographer and the native subjects of a study. More prominent contemporary ethnographic memoirs include the work of Paul Rabinow (1977)
and Nigel Barley (1983). The first piece, written in a distinctively literary
style, provides a vivid portrait of an ethnographic research project in
Morocco, while the second presents an image of the ethnographer as a sadly
incompetent but likeable novice in Africa.

The ethnographic memoir, also referred to as 'the confessional tale' (Van
Maanen 1988) has fleetingly touched organizational ethnographers, who on
rare occasions have provided their readers with some glimpses of their fieldwork experiences and day-to-day dilemmas. These include discussions of
gaining and losing insider status in different organizational contexts (Van
Maanen and Kolb 1985) and the role of personal cultural histories in shaping
an ethnographer's research focus (Kunda 1992).

Ethnographic memoirs hold considerable implications for the constitution
of natives and their cultures. First, by reinserting the ethnographer into the
text, they give the researcher a constant visible presence which is somewhat
different from the conventional role of researcher as an expert, but invisible
outsider. Memoirs like those of Nigel Barley (1986) portray ethnographers
alternately as incompetent intruders, pathetic figures and likeable dupes in
alien cultures (Czarniawska 1998). This open admission of ethnographic
inadequacy serves to diminish the ethnographer's infallibility by demystifying
his/her expertise. Their autobiographical flavour also disrupts the typically
smooth presentation of ethnographic texts, underlining their capricious and
constructed nature.

In many ways, the ethnographic memoir is a conscious attempt to publicize
the personal component of the ethnographic experience which hitherto had a
place only in the private realm of the ethnographer's diary. Everyday tales of
tedium and tribulation can be found in the diaries of Marcel Griaule (1934)
and Malinowski (1967) alongside instances of 'blatant racial bigotry' and
even physical violence directed against native informants (Young 1984;
Clifford 1988; Stocking 1991). Such frank personal accounts could often be

deeply troubling. Malinowski's diaries, published several years after his death, were regarded as nothing short of scandalous in anthropology, given their subversion of the professional practice of ethnography and the heroic reputation of Malinowski himself.

In short, ethnographic memoirs make it very difficult to maintain the 'fiction' of the non-fictitious text. The very focus and subject matter of any ethnography is, as Kunda (1992) points out, largely shaped by a researcher's own cultural affinities. Speaking of some of the cultural anxieties confronting an Israeli in America, he shows how they influenced his own preoccupation with corporate culture and ideological control. Ethnographic memoirs pose greater challenges to positivist conventions than even 'gone-native' ethnographies because they never pretend to offer any kind of textual authenticity or 'true story'. Rather, they make one uncomfortably aware of the discontinuities and contradictions present in the crafting of an ethnography, allowing us to read it as only one fiction in a world of several possible ones. Above all, they transform the subject positions of natives, turning them from exotic collectibles into active individuals, capable of outwitting the ethnographer and even disrupting the research project. Once this happens, the question of authority over culture reverts to the natives.

Narrative ethnography

Literary considerations and questions of plural participation are even more vividly reflected in a contemporary tradition designated as narrative ethnography (Tedlock 1991; Prasad 1998). Like ethnographic memoirs, narrative ethnographies are based on the notion of ethnographies as 'fictions'. These fictions, however, are seen as being produced not only by the authors who script them, but also *indirectly* by institutional structures such as conventions of ethnographic writing, common unquestioned conceptual categories such as class and identity which are used to analyze native actions, and deeply-sedimented dichotomies between researchers and subjects, theory and data etc. (Crapanzano 1977; Clifford 1988; Kondo 1990). The objective of narrative ethnography is to both resist these influences and simultaneously communicate an awareness of them in the actual writing of the ethnography itself.

Narrative ethnographies are also committed to portraying the processual nature of an ethnography and its emergence out of negotiations between researcher and multiple native actors 'within shifting fields of power and meaning' (Kondo 1990: 8). To Tedlock (1991), the primary distinction between ethnographic memoir and narrative ethnography can be found in the changing focus from the ethnographer to the character and process of the ethnographic encounters. Kondo's (1990) work in a Japanese confectionery factory is a vivid example of portraying this process through multiple vignettes of encounters between the ethnographer and the natives.

Narrative ethnographers are also committed to destroying the monologic nature of their texts. Having recognized ethnographies as 'fictions', the central task becomes the inclusion of native voices as *co-producers* of these fictions (Behar 1993). Influenced by Bakhtin's (1981) notions of textual dialogue, narrative ethnographies are often designed to permit the participation of natives in the text itself. Needless to say, this practice can turn quite disruptive when native voices 'take over' ethnographic texts. However, it is this *disruption* that signals the beginning of genuine plurality in the text.

Above all, ethnographers like Behar (1993) and Kondo (1990) convey an awareness of their own textual embeddedness in globalized discourses of power and hegemony. As Kondo asserts, diverse institutional dimensions such as race, gender, academic training and political-historical agendas underlying America's scholarly interest in Japan, all constitute the 'matrices of power' within which her own study was conducted. For narrative ethnographers, the trick is to work as subversively as possible within these constraints while simultaneously weaving an awareness of them in the crafting of an ethnography.

Re(casting) the native subject: the ethnographic imagination in contemporary organizational worlds

Throughout its emergence and institutionalization, ethnography's primary mandate has been the preparation of legible accounts of 'different' cultures in order to facilitate governance, trade, religious conversions and colonial conquest. In the course of fulfilling this mandate, ethnography has also produced a distinct category – that of the *native*, typically referring to individuals from non-European cultures and races. Ethnographic practice also implied that knowledge about natives and native cultures was the sole prerogative of the outside expert, even while this outsider or 'professional stranger' (Agar 1980) often made a considerable effort to be with the natives and learn their customs.

Ethnography's legacy however, has been even more lasting than the production of knowledge about native cultures. Rather, it has left us with what Brad Evans (1997, 1999) calls an 'ethnographic imagination' – a powerful and vivid mindscape of images and tropes casting natives and their observers in specific sets of social roles. By the late nineteenth century, ethnography and several prominent ethnographers played vital roles in the cultural imagination of western societies. Ethnographers such as Cushing, Griaule and later, Margaret Mead, were cast as heroic, adventurous and glamorous figures in popular magazines such as *Harper's* and the *Century Illustrated Monthly Magazine* where both ethnographers and their subjects were equally romanticized. With the increased professionalization of the practice, the ethnographic imagination took a more scholarly twist, though it remained fixated on the generation of knowledge about native cultures. In essence, the ethnographic imagination has left us with (a) the notion of the native as an established social category, and (b) different and increasingly contested approaches for producing knowledge about natives.

The importation of ethnography into organization studies has certainly shaken this imagination since many organizational natives are privileged and powerful individuals who refuse to fit into traditional notions of the native. However, as we have shown, many organizational ethnographers continue to be enmeshed within the same old set of assumptions about boundaries between the researcher and the native. Recent movements in anthropology have ruptured the expert status of the ethnographer, and have attempted to create spaces for the articulation of native voices within discourses of native cultures. Above all, newer ethnographic genres such as memoirs and narrative ethnographies have forced us to grapple with the problematic relationship between ethnographers and their native subjects. Today's ethnographic imagination is therefore a much more contested mindscape, with less clarity about the positions of either natives or their researchers, therefore carrying more complex implications for the intellectual projects of understanding so-called native cultures. We explore some implications of understanding contemporary organizations from this more complex new ethnographic imagination.

The institutionalization of nostalgia and the constitution of the new natives

Within the conventional ethnographic imagination, the notion of culture (including organizational culture) has been predicated on relatively stable and enduring images of nativity and belonging. However, major recent trends within both popular and academic discourses have shattered the ideas of 'pure' or 'pristine' cultures inhabited by relatively fixed populations of natives. This is a particularly striking feature of organizational worlds that are increasingly constituted by restless rather than stable natives. Contemporary pressures of globalization imply, among other things, the persistent *flow* of ideas, capital and bodies (Appadurai 1990) from one geographical location to another. These flows problematize existing boundaries, reconstituting natives and others in contexts that are not entirely devoid of power and domination. For organizational ethnography to remain relevant, it needs to focus on these institutional reconfigurations of native spaces and identities within organizational locations.

At one level, it is tempting to infer that the native as a significant social category is a mere remnant of a bygone colonial imagination. However, a closer look at current social institutions indicates that new native categories are constantly being produced and reproduced within organizational sites such as tourism and museum industries for the appeasement of the contemporary ethnographic imagination. Recent discussions of these two industries have highlighted their tendencies to commodify and institutionalize the western nostalgia for a romanticized and pre-industrialized past (Clifford 1988; Lowenthal 1997). Ethnographic and folk museums, for instance, collect and display artifacts from non-western cultures in ways that convey a sense of innocence and simplicity that is lost with the onset of modernity in these cultures (Stewart 1984). For Root (1996), most museums reproduce an associative belief that natives from such cultures rightfully belong only to the past and have little relevance in the globalized world of today. Museums are 'large edifices containing ... the paraphernalia of cultures believed to be dead or dying, all organized according to a current scientific theory' (Root 1996: 108). Ethnographic museums in particular become organizational sites confining natives to pre-industrial pasts and limiting their roles in the present.

Remnants of an imperial ethnographic imagination are also at work in the discourse of tourism which sells many destinations by commodifying their cultures through the construction of images of nostalgic pasts and exotic differences (Laxson 1991). Natives of third world countries and indigenous peoples from first world ones are both represented as different, exotic and available (in different forms) for tourist consumption (Laxson 1991; Root 1996). The province of British Columbia in Canada, for instance, markets its native aboriginal cultures as one of its principal attractions. Traditional arts and crafts, native ceremonial events and totem poles are all marketed to tourists in romaticized and culturally de-contextualized forms (Crosby 1991). Root (1996) and others contend that such representations are pernicious because they convert native cultures into tourist playgrounds where natives are represented as playthings, and where natives are once again constituted as the exotic collectibles found in the discourse of early ethnography. In sum, as Chow (1996: 36) observes, 'the problem of the native is also the problem of modernity and modernity's relation to "endangered authenticities".'

Widening the sights of organizational ethnography

To most of us, the task of organizational ethnography has always centred around the description and depiction of native organizational cultures. This chapter however, calls for an expanded ethnographic project that systematically scrutinizes the ethnographic imagination that is produced in and by different organizations, and that is simultaneously catered to by many of them. In other words, it is our contention that the organizational sites of native productions should engage the attention of organizational ethnography. Hitherto, organizational ethnographers have almost entirely focused on single-sited observation and participation, analysing the cultural and sub-cultural meaning systems of local native subjects (Collinson 1992; Kunda 1992; Watson 1994). In all these efforts, the focus of inquiry is bounded by notions of cultural walls around specific organizational populations. Moreover, at their most reflective moments, organizational ethnographers are prepared, at best, to being in a few biographical episodes or to reflect on some institutional influences on their own fieldwork and storytelling practices. However, many of the issues raised in this chapter demand that organizational ethnographers convert their awareness/self-consciousness of their own and organizations' embeddedness in a world system (Marcus 1995) into objects of inquiry. One way of doing this is to examine organizational processes that constitute native subjects within institutional fields of power and meaning. This, in turn, demands a movement out of 'the single sites and local situations of conventional ethnographic research designs to examine the *circulation of cultural meanings, objects and identities* in diffuse time-space' (Marcus 1995: 96, emphasis added).

This becomes another way of turning the anthropological lens inward – by using the insights of narrative ethnography to examine the institutional processes whereby conventional ethnographic imaginations regarding natives, cultures etc. continue to be reproduced in today's organizational worlds with significant consequences. While we have dwelt considerably on the construction of native spaces in the institutional fields of tourism and museums, they are far from being the only organizational sites producing native images and native roles. In many workplaces, the new discourse of diversity casts managers, employees and prospective organizational hires into distinct ethnic moulds that vividly recall the native roles of early colonialist anthropology. These new ethnic organizational natives are often *exoticized* in diversity workshops and training materials in ways that call into question their own fitness for organizational work (Prasad 2000). In other instances, managerial training programmes conducted by western companies and consultants in the erstwhile Soviet Bloc countries systematically cast eastern European managers as economically and culturally backward individuals resembling the natives of the colonial era, who could only be 'saved' by Christian missionaries (Kostera 1995). To Kostera, the entire institutional package of western management training in eastern Europe is dangerously similar to earlier missionary tendencies in its attempts to 'convert' and 'rescue' the native manager from his/her own cultural inadequacies. What is highlighted in all these cases is that a powerful ethnographic imagination is at work in a multitude of organizational settings – constituting a variety of native subjects and stimulating a demand for their consumption, either as objects of the tourist gaze or as backward populations eternally in need of western assistance. In this process, natives of different kinds are cast once again into moulds that emphasize their otherness and their unequal status in organizations and society. Since our complex ethnographic traditions have partly influenced these ethnographic imaginations, it is only fitting that we transform contemporary ethnographic practice in ways that enable it to interrogate these institutional imaginations.

Notes

1 The authors would like to thank Dvora Yanow and Richard Sotto for their encouraging and helpful comments on earlier versions of this chapter.
2 While a number of sociologists and anthropologists at the fringes of organization studies (Whyte 1955; Roy 1960; Turner 1971) had already adopted some form of

cultural analysis to understand organizations and workplaces, the notion of organizations as predominantly cultural entities entered mainstream management science only in the 1980s.
3 While personal circumstances may well have determined the choice of certain 'exotic' sites for ethnographic study, the point to be remembered is that these studies were enormously influential partly because of the current *Zeitgeist* that found resonances in these portrayals of romanticized primitive natives.

References

Abma, Tineke (1998) 'Babylonische spraakverwarring in een organisatie.' *MandO. Tijdschrift voor organisatiekunde en sociaal beleid*: 41–59.

Acker, Joan (1990) 'Hierarchies, Jobs, Bodies: A Theory of Gendered Organizations.' *Gender and Society*, 4(1): 139–58.

Acker, Joan (1992) 'Gendering Organizational Theory.' In Albert J. Mills and Peta Tancred (eds) *Gendering Organizational Analysis*. Newbury Park: Sage, 248–60.

Agar, Michael (1980) *The Professional Stranger*. New York: Academic Press.

Agarwal, Bina (1992) 'The Gender and Environment Debate: Lessons from India.' *Feminist Studies*, 18 (1): 119–58.

Ahl, Helene Jonson (2001) *A Rhetorical Analysis of Research Articles on Women's Entrepreneurship:The 'Hows', the 'Whys' and the 'Whats'*. Paper presented at the 16th Scandinavian Academy of Management Research Conference, Uppsala, Sweden.

Ahl, Helene Jonson, and Samuelsson, Emilia Florin (2000) *Networking Through Empowerment and Empowerment Through Networking* (Research report 2000–1). Jönköping: Jönköping International Business School.

Aldrich, Howard, Reese, Pat Ray, Dubini, Paola, Rosen, B., and Woodward, B. (1989) *Women on the Verge of a Breakthrough? Networking Among Entrepreneurs* in the United States and Italy. *Entrepreneurship and Regional Development, 1*, 339–56.

Alvesson, Mats (1993) *Cultural Perspectives on Organizations*. Cambridge: Cambridge University Press.

Alvesson, Mats and Billing, Yvonne Due (1992) 'Gender and Organization. Towards a Differentiated Understanding.' *Organization Studies*, 1: 13/12: 73–102.

Alvesson, Mats and Billing, Yvonne Due (1997) *Understanding Gender and Organizations*. London: Sage.

Alvesson, Mats, and Billing, Yvonne Due (1999) *Kön och organisation*. Lund: Studentlitteratur.

Alvesson, Mats and Sköldberg, Kaj (1994) *Tolkning och reflektion*. Lund: Studentlitteratur.

American Society for Competitiveness (1998) *Competitiveness in the Global Marketplace*, 1998 Conference Program, October 22–24. Symposium. Competitiveness and the Role of Diversity.

Anderson, Fiona, Grey, Chris, and Robinson, Keith (1998) ' "Work Hard, Play Hard": An Analysis of Cliché in Two Accountancy Practices.' *Organization*, 5(4): 565–92.

Antaki, Charles, and Widdicombe, Sue (eds) (1998) *Identities in Talk*. London: Sage.

Appadurai, Arjun (1990) 'Disjuncture and Difference in the Global Cultural Economy.' *Public Culture*, 2: 15–24.

Asad, Talal (ed.) (1973) *Anthropology and the Colonial Encounter*. London: Ithaca Press.

Atkinson, Paul, and Hammersley, Marilyn (1994) 'Ethnography and Participant Observation.' In Norman K. Denzin and Yvonna Lincoln (eds), *Handbook of Qualitative Research*. Thousand Oaks, CA: Sage Publications, 248–61.

Avery, Robert W. (1968) 'Enculturation in Industrial Research'. In Barney G. Glaser, (ed.) *Organizational Careers. A Sourcebook for Theory*. Chicago: Aldine Publishing Company.

Axtell, James (1981) *The European and the Indian: Essays in the Ethnohistory of Colonial America*. Oxford: Oxford University Press.

Bailey, F.G. (1996) *The Civility of Indifference. On Domesticating Ethnicity*. New York: Cornell University Press.

Bakhtin, Mikhail (1987) *Problems of Dostoevsky's Poetics*. Minneapolis: University of Minnesota Press.

Barberis, Corrado (1985) *Sociologia Rurale*. Bologna: Edagricole.

Barley, Nigel (1983) *Adventures in a Mud Hut: An Innocent Anthropologist Abroad*. New York: Vanguard Press.

Barnard, Chester (1938) *The Functions of the Executive*. Cambridge, MA: Harvard University Press.

Barry, David and Elmes, Michael (1997) 'Strategy Retold: Toward a Narrative View of Strategic Discourse.' *Academy of Management Review*, 22(2): 429–52.

Bate, S. Paul (1997) 'Whatever Happened to Organizational Anthropology? A Review of Organizational Ethnography and Anthropological Studies.' *Human Relations*, 50: 1147–75.

Bauman, Zygmunt (1995) *Life in Fragments. Essays in Postmodern Morality*. Oxford: Blackwell.

Bauman, Zygmunt (1998) *Globalization. The Human Consequences*. Cambridge: Polity Press.

Behar, Ruth (1993) *Translated Woman: Crossing the Border with Esperanza's Story*. Boston: Beacon Press.

Benjamin, Walter (1973) 'Thesis on the Philosophy of History.' In *Illuminations*. London: Fontana.

Benschop, Yvonne and Doorewaard, Hans (1998a) 'Six of One and Half a Dozen of the Other: The Gender Subtext of Taylorism and Team-based Work.' *Gender, Work and Organization* 5(1): 5–18.

Benschop, Yvonne and Doorewaard, Hans (1998b) 'Covered by Equality: The Gender Subtext of Organizations.' *Organization Studies*, 19(5): 787–806.

Berger, Peter and Luckmann, Thomas (1966) *The Social Construction of Reality: A Treatise in the Sociology of Knowledge*. London: Penguin Books.

Bergh, Cecilia, and Per Södersten (1996a) 'Anorexia Nervosa, Self-starvation and the Reward of Stress. *Nature Medicine*, 2(1): 21–22.

Bergh, Cecilia, and Per Södersten (1996b) 'Anorexia Nervosa – More than an Eating Disorder – Reply.' *Nature Medicine*, 2(4): 367.

Bergh, Cecilia, Ekelund, Ståle, Eriksson, Mats, Lindberg, Greger and Södersten, Per (1996a) 'A New Treatment of Anorexia Nervosa.' *Lancet*, 348 (9027): 611–12.

Bergh, Cecilia, Eriksson, Mats, Lindberg, Greger and Södersten, Per (1996b) 'Selective Serotonin Reuptake Inhibitors in Anorexia.' *Lancet*, 348 (9039): 1459–60.

Berreman, Gerald D. (1962) *Behind Many Masks: Ethnography and Impression Management in a Himalayan Village.* Society for Applied Anthropology, Monograph 4. Ithaca, NY: Cornell University Press.

Betters-Reed, Bonita and Moore, Lynda (1992) *The Technicolor Workplace. MS,* Nov/Dec.

Beyer, Ann (1996) *Den kvinnliga företagarprofilen.* Stockholm: Företagarnas Riksorganisation.

Billing, Yvonne Due (1999) 'Gender and Bureaucracies. A Critique of Ferguson's *The Feminist Case Against Bureaucracy.*' In *Tagungsbeiträge: Rationalisation Organisation Gender.* Dortmund: Sozialforschungsstelle. (http://www.sfs-dortmund.de/transfer/beitrageausderforschung/beitrage_111/beitrage_111.html.)

Billing, Yvonne Due and Alvesson, Mats (1989) 'Four Ways of Looking at Women and Leadership.' *Scandinavian Journal of Management,* 5(1): 63–80.

Birch, David (1979) *The Job Generation Process.* Cambridge, MA: MIT Press.

Bloor, David (1976) *Knowledge and Social Imagery.* Chicago: University of Chicago Press.

Boomen, Marianne van den (1995) *Internet ABC voor vrouwen. Een inleiding voor d@t@dames en modemmeiden.* Amsterdam: Instituut voor Puliek en Politiek.

Bordo, Susan (1993) *Unbearable Weight: Feminism, Western Culture, and the Body.* London: University of California Press.

Borgström, Eva (1998) 'Queerstudier i USA – och i Sverige?' *Kvinnovetenskaplig tidskrift,* 98(1): 8–22.

Bowker, Geoffrey C. and Star, Susan Leigh (1999) *Sorting Things Out. Classification and its Consequences.* Cambridge, MA: The MIT Press.

Bradford, P.V. and Blume, H. (1992) *Ota Benga: The Pygmy in the Zoo.* New York: St Martin's Press.

Broom, Leonard, Siegel, Bernard J., Vogt, Egon Z., and Watson, James B. (1954/1967) 'Acculturation: An Exploratory Formulation.' In Paul Bohannan and Fred Plog (eds) *Beyond the Frontier. Social Process and Cultural Change.* New York: Natural History Process, 255–86.

Brush, Candida G. (1992) 'Research on Women Business Owners: Past Trends, a New Perspective and Future Directions.' *Entrepreneurship, Theory and Practice,* 16(4): 5–30.

Brush, Candida G. (1997) 'Women-owned Businesses: Obstacles and Opportunities.' *Journal of Developmental Entrepreneurship,* 2(1): 1–24.

Buci-Glucksmann, Christine (1994) *Baroque Reason. The Aesthetics of Modernity.* London: Sage.

Burawoy, Michael (1979) *Manufacturing Consent.* Chicago: University of Chicago Press.

Butler, Judith (1990) *Gender Trouble: Feminism and the Subversion of Identity.* London: Routledge.

Buttner, E. Holly (2001) 'Examining Female Entrepreneurs' Management Style: An Application of a Relational Frame.' *Journal of Business Ethics,* 29(3): 253–69.

Calás, Marta B. and Smircich, Linda (1991) 'Voicing Seduction to Silence Leadership.' *Organization Studies,* 12(4): 567–602.

Calás, Marta B. and Smircich, Linda (1992) 'Using the "F" Word: Feminist Theories and the Social Consequences of Organizational Research.' In Albert J. Mills and Peta Tancred (eds) *Gendering Organizational Analysis.* London: Sage.

Calás, Marta B. and Smircich, Linda (1993) 'Dangerous Liaisons: The "feminine-in-management" meets "globalization".' *Business Horizons,* March-April: 73–83.

Callon, Michel (1986) 'Some Elements of a Sociology of Translation: Domestication of the Scallops and the Fishermen of St-Brieuc Bay." In John Law (ed.) *Power, Action and Belief : A New Sociology of Knowledge?* London: Routledge and Kegan Paul, 196–233.

Campbell, Donald T. (1972) Introduction. In Melville J. Herskovits, *Cultural Relativism. Perspectives in Cultural Pluralism*. New York: Vintage Books.

Carter, Richard B., Van Auken, Howard E. and Harms, Mary B. (1992) 'Home-Based Businesses in the Rural United States Economy, Differences in Gender and Financing.' *Entrepreneurship and Regional Development*, 4(3): 245–57.

Case, John (1992) *From the Ground Up: The Resurgence of American Entrepreneurship*. New York: Simon & Schuster.

Cassell, Catherine (2000) 'The Business Case and the Management of Diversity.' In Marilyn Davidson and Ronald Burke (eds) *Women in Management, Current Research Issues, Volume II*. London: Sage, 250–62.

Castaneda, Carlos (1968) *The Teachings of Don Juan: A Yaqui Way of Knowing*. Berkeley, CA: University of California Press.

Caudron, Shari and Hayes, Cassandra (1997) 'Are Diversity Programs Benefiting African Americans?' *Black Enterprise*, February: 121–32.

Charles, Nickie and Davies, Charlotte (1997) 'Contested Communities: The Refuge Movement and Cultural Identities in Wales. *The Sociological Review*, 45(3): 416–36.

Chernin, Kim (1986) *The Hungry Self: Daughters and Mothers. Eating and Identity*. London: Virago Press.

Chia, Robert (1996) *Organisational Analysis as Deconstructive Practice*. Berlin: de Gruyter.

Chodorow, Nancy (1978) *Femininum-Maskulinum*. Stockholm: Bokförlaget Natur och Kultur.

Chow, Rey (1993) *Writing Diaspora: Tactics of Intervention in Contemporary Cultural Studies*. Bloomington: Indiana University Press.

Clifford, James (1988) *The Predicament of Culture: Twentieth-Century Ethnography, Literature and Art*. Cambridge, MA: Harvard University Press.

Clifford, James and Marcus, George E. (1986) *Writing Culture: The Poetics and Politics of Ethnography*. Berkeley, CA: University of California Press.

Cockburn, Cynthia (1991) *In the Way of Women. Men's Resistance to Sex Equality in Organizations*. London: Macmillan.

Cohen, Anthony (1985) *The Symbolic Construction of Community*. London: Routledge.

Collinson, David L. (1992) *Managing the Shop Floor*. Berlin: de Gruyter.

Collinson, David L. and Hearn, Jeff (1996) *Men as Managers, Managers as Men*. London: Sage.

Copeland Griggs Productions (1987) *Valuing Diversity Part I: Managing Differences, Part II: Diversity at Work, Part III: Communicating Across Cultures*. San Francisco, CA: Copeland Griggs Productions.

Copeland, Lennie (1988a) 'Learning to Manage a Multicultural Workforce.' *Training*, 25(5): 48–56.

Copeland, Lennie (1988b) 'Ten Steps to Making the Most of Cultural Differences at the Workplace.' *Personnel*, 63: 58–60.

Copeland, Lennie (1988c) 'Valuing Diversity, Part 2: Pioneers and Champions of Change.' *Personnel*, 65: 44–49.

Copeland, Lennie (1988d) 'Valuing Workplace Diversity: Ten Reasons Employers

Recognize the Benefits of a Mixed Work Force.' *Personnel Administrator*, 33(11): 38–39.

Coser, Lewis A. (1974) *Greedy Institutions. Patterns of Undivided Commitment*. New York: The Free Press.

Crapanzano, Vincent (1977) 'On the Writing of Ethnography.' *Dialectical Anthropology*, 2: 69–73.

Crompton, Rosemary and Harris, Fiona (1997) 'Women's Employment and Gender Attitudes: A Comparative Analysis of Britain, Norway and the Czech Republic.' *Acta Sociologica*, 40: 183–202.

Crompton, Rosemary and Le Feuvre, Nicole (1992) 'Gender and Bureaucracy: Women in Finance in Britain and France.' In Mike Savage and Anne Witz (eds) *Gender and Bureaucracy*. Oxford: Blackwell.

Crosby, Marcia (1991) 'Constructions of the Imaginary Indian.' In S. Douglas (ed.), *Vancouver Anthology: The Institutional Politics of Art*. Vancouver: Talon Books, 267–94.

Curtis, Edward S. (1924) *The North American Indian*. Cambridge, MA: Harvard University Press.

Cushing, Frank Hamilton (1882) 'My Adventures in Zuni.' *Century Illustrated Monthly Magazine*, 25: 191–207.

Cushing, Frank Hamilton (1920) *Zuni Breadstuff*. New York: Museum of the American Indian.

Czarniawska-Joerges, Barbara (1994) 'Editorial: Modern Organizations and Pandora's Box.' *Scandinavian Journal of Management*, 19(2): 95–98.

Czarniawska, Barbara (1997a) *Narrating the Organization. Dramas of Institutional Identity*. Chicago: The University of Chicago Press.

Czarniawska, Barbara (1997b) 'Diskrimineras vi likadant? Om det sociala könet, lokala kulturer och förändringar i den offentliga sektorn.' In Elisabeth Sundin (ed.). *Om makt och kön. I sparen av offentliga organisationers omvandling*. SOU 1997: 83. Stockholm: Arbetsmarknadsdepartement, 366–84.

Czarniawska, Barbara (1998) *A Narrative Approach to Organization Studies*. Thousand Oaks, CA: Sage.

Czarniawska, Barbara (2001) 'Anthropology and Organizational Learning.' In Meinholf Dierkes, Arianne Berthoin Antal, John Child and Ikujiro Nonaka (eds) *Handbook of Organizational Learning and Knowledge*. Oxford: Oxford University Press, 118–36.

Dalby, Lisa C. (1983) *Geisha*. Berkeley, CA: University of California Press.

Dale, Karen (1997) 'Identity in a Culture of Dissection: Body, Self and Knowledge.' In Kevin Hetherington and Rolland Munro (eds) *Ideas of Difference*. Oxford: Blackwell, 94–113.

Dallmayr, Fred (1997) 'The Politics of Nonidentity.' *Political Theory*, 25 (1): 33–57.

Dalton, Melville (1959) *Men Who Manage*. New York: John Wiley & Sons.

David, Miriam and Woodward, Diana (1998) 'Introduction.' In Miriam David and Diana Woodward (eds) *Negotiating the Glass Ceiling: Careers of Senior Women in the Academic World*. London: The Falmer Press, 14–21.

Davidsson, Per (1989) *Continued Entrepreneurship and Small Firm Growth*. Stockholm: Stockholm School of Economics.

Davidsson, Per, Lindmark, Leif and Olofsson, Christer (1994) *Dynamiken i svenskt näringsliv*. Lund: Studentlitteratur.

Davies, Bronwyn (1988) *Frogs and Snails and Feminist Tales. Preschool Children and Gender*. Sydney: Allen & Unwin.

de Beauvoir, Simone (1949/1986) *Det andra könet* (4th edn). Stockholm: Norstedts.

De Ruijter, Arie (1998) 'Problematische privacy'. In Rathenau Instituut, *Privacy geregistreerd*. Amsterdam: Otto Cramwinkel, 281–304.

Derrida, Jacques (1978) *Writing and Difference*. London: Routledge.

DiMaggio, Paul J. and Powell, Walter W. (1991a) 'Introduction.' In Paul J. DiMaggio and Walter W. Powell (eds), *The New Institutionalism in Organizational Analysis*. Chicago: University of Chicago Press, 1–38.

DiMaggio, Paul J. and Powell, Walter W. (1991b) 'The Iron Cage Revisited: Institutional Isomorphism and Collective Rationality in Organizational Fields.' In Paul J. DiMaggio and Walter W. Powell (eds), *The New Institutionalism in Organizational Analysis*. Chicago: University of Chicago Press, 63–82.

Douglas, Mary (1986/1987) *How Institutions Think*. London: Routledge and Kegan Paul.

Douglas, Mary (1992) *Risk and Blame. Essays in Cultural Theory*. London: Routledge.

Du Gay, Paul, Hall, Stuart, Janes, Linda, Mackay, Hugh, and Negus, Keith (1997) *Production of Culture. Cultures of Production*. London: Sage.

Duncan, Simon (1998) 'Theorising Gender Systems in Europe.' In Birgit Geisler, Friederike Maier, and Birgit Pfau-Effinger (eds) *FrauenArbeitsMarkt*. Berlin: edition-sigma, 195–227.

Durkheim, Emile and Mauss, Marcel (1903/1963) *Primitive Classifications*. Chicago: University of Chicago Press.

Edding, Cornelia (1983) *Einbruch in den Herrenclub*. Reinbek beim Hamburg: rororo.

Elias, Norbert (1987) *Die Gesellschaft der Individuen*. Frankfurt am Main: Suhrkamp.

Elshtain, Jean Bethke (1995) *Democracy on Trial*. New York: Basic Books.

Ely, Robin J. (1995) 'The Power of Demography: Women's Social Constructions of Gender Identity at Work.' *Academy of Management Journal*, 38(3): 589–634.

Engelin perintö (Engel's Legacy) (1995) Valtion rakentaminen käännekohdassa. Rakennushallitus.

Eräsaari, Leena (1999) 'Musta engeli – naisia rakennushallituksen raunioista.' In Vesa Keskinen (ed.) *Lama.nousu@hel.fi*. Helsinki: Helsingin kaupungin tietokeskus, 95–105.

Ericson, Richard V. and Kevin D. Haggerty (1997) *Policing the Risk Society*. Oxford: Clarendon Press.

Ericsson, Daniel and Nilsson, Pernilla (1997) *Recognizing "the Other" – An Inquiry into the Entrepreneurial Identity*. Working Paper, Jönköping International Business School.

Esping-Andersen, Gösta (1990) *The Three Worlds of Welfare Capitalism*. Princeton, NJ: Princeton University Press.

Evans, Brad (1997) 'Cushing's Zuni Sketchbooks: Literature, Anthropology and American Notions of Culture.' *American Anthropology Quarterly*, 49: 717–45.

Evans, Brad (1999) *The Ethnographic Imagination in American Literature: A Genealogy of Cultures, 1865–1930*. Unpublished PhD Dissertation, University of Chicago.

Fagan, Colette and O'Reilly, Jacqueline (1998) 'Conceptualizing Part-Time Work: The Value of an Integrated Comparative Perspective.' In Jacqueline O'Reilly and Colette Fagan (eds) *Part-time Prospects: An International Comparison of Part-time Work in Europe, North America and the Pacific Rim*. London: Routledge.

Fanfani, Roberto (1998) *L'agricultura in Italia*. Bologna: Il Mulino.

Feldberg, Roslyn L. and Glenn, Evelyn Nakano (1979) 'Male and Female – Job Versus Gender Models in the Sociology of Work.' *Social Problems*, 26(5): 524–38.

Ferguson, Kathy (1984) *The Feminist Case Against Bureaucracy*. Philadelphia: Temple University Press.

Fernler, Karin and Helgesson, Claes-Fredrik (2001) 'Constructing a Curing Commodity: The Case of a Curing Plate.' In Hans Glimmel, and Oscar Juhlin (eds) *The Social Production of Technology*. Gothenburg: BAS.

Fischer, Eileen M., Reuber, A. Rebecca and Dyke, Lorraine S. (1993) 'A Theoretical Overview and Extension of Research on Sex, Gender and Entrepreneurship.' *Journal of Business Venturing*, 8(2): 151–68.

Fletcher, Joyce (1999) *Disappearing Acts: Gender, Power and Relational Practice at Work*. Cambridge, MA: The MIT Press.

Flynn, Gillian (1998) 'The Harsh Reality of Diversity Programs.' *Workforce*, 77(12): 26–35.

FolkhälsoinstitutetochSocialstyrelsen (1993) *Ett liv av vikt*. Stockholm.

Foucault, Michel (1970) *The Order of Things: An Archeology of the Human Sciences*. London: Tavistock.

Foucault, Michel (1972) *The Archeology of Knowledge*. London: Tavistock.

Foucault, Michel (1977) *Discipline and Punish: The Birth of the Prison*. Harmondsworth: Penguin.

Foxall, Gordon (1984) 'Evidence for Attitudinal-Behavioral Consistency: Implications for Consumer Research Paradigms.' *Journal of Economic Psychology*, 5(1): 71–92.

Friedel-Howe, Heidrun (1990) 'Zusammenarbeit von weiblichen und männlichen Fach- und Führungskräften.' In Michael Domsch and Erika Regnet (eds) *Weibliche Fach- und Führungskräfte. Wege zur Chancengleichheit*. Stuttgart: Schäffer, 16–34.

Friedman, Jonathan (1995) 'Global System, Globalization and the Parameters of Modernity.' In Michael Featherstone, Scott Lash and Roland Robertson (eds) *Global Modernities*. London: Sage, 69–90.

Gastelaars, Marja (1985) *Een geregeld leven. Sociologie en sociale politiek in Nederland 1925–1968*. Amsterdam: SUA.

Gastelaars, Marja (ed.) (2000) *On Location. The Relevance of the 'Here' and 'Now' in Organisations*. Maastricht: Shaker.

Gastelaars, Marja (in print) 'About Individual Autonomy and the Relational Self: The Performance of Privacy in Contemporary Organisations.' In Ad van Iterson, Willem Mastenbroek, Tim Newton and Dennis Smith (eds) *The Civilized Organisation. Norbert Elias and the Future of Organisation Studies*. Amsterdam: Benjamins.

Geertz, Clifford (1973) *The Interpretation of Cultures*. New York: Basic Books.

Geertz, Clifford (1980) 'Blurred Genres: The Refiguration of Social Thought.' *The American Scholar*, 49: 165–79.

Gergen, Kenneth J. (1991) *The Saturated Self. Dilemmas of Identity in Contemporary Life*. New York: Basic Books.

Gerth, Hans H. and Mills, C. Wright (eds) (1946) *From Max Weber*. New York: Oxford University Press.

Gherardi, Silvia (1994) 'The Gender We Do, the Gender We Think in Our Everyday Organizational Lives.' *Human Relations*, 47(6): 591–610.

Gherardi, Silvia (1995) *Gender, Symbolism and Organizational Cultures*. London: Sage.

Gidley, Mike (ed.) (1992) *Representing Others: White Views of Indigenous Peoples.* Exeter: University of Exeter Press.

Gilligan, Carol (1982) *In a Different Voice.* Cambridge, MA: Harvard University Press.

Goffman, Erving (1961) *Asylums.* New York: Anchor Press Doubleday.

Goffman, Erving (1997/1983) 'The Interaction Order.' In Charles Lemert and Ann Braman (eds) *The Goffman Reader.* Oxford: Blackwell, 233–61.

Golden-Biddle, Karen and Locke, Karen (1993) 'Appealing Work: An Investigation of How Ethnographic Texts Convince.' *Organization Science*, 4: 595–616.

Gottschall, Karin (1999) 'Doing Gender While Doing Work'. In *Tagungsbeiträge: Rationalisation Organisation Gender.* Dortmund: Sozialforschungsstelle. (http://www.sfs-dortmund.de/transfer/beitrageausderforschung/beitrage_111/beitrage_111.html).

Grace, Margaret and Lennie, June (1998) 'Constructing and Reconstructing Rural Women in Australia: The Politics of Change, Diversity and Identity.' *Sociologia Ruralis*, Special Issue on 'The Empowerment of Farm Women', 38 (3): 351–70.

Gregory, Kathleen (1983) 'Native-View Paradigms: Multiple Cultures and Culture Conflicts in Organizations.' *Administrative Science Quarterly*, 28: 359–76.

Griaule, Marcel (1938) *Masques Dogons.* Paris: Institut d'Ethnologie.

Grossberg, Lawrence (1997) *Bringing It All Back Home.* Durham, NC: Duke University Press.

Gutek, Barbara A. (1989) 'Sexuality in the Workplace: Key Issues in Social Research and Organizational Practice.' In Jeff Hearn, Deborah L. Sheppard, Peta Tancred-Sheriff and Gibson Burell (eds) *The Sexuality of Organization.* London: Sage.

Haavio-Mannila, Elina (1986) 'Nainen "miesten töissä": Naisinsinöörinä Suomessa.' In Hannele Varsa (ed.) *Naiset, tekniikka ja luonnontieteet.* Helsinki: Tasa-arvo-asiain neuvottelukunnan raportteja 8/1986 (Reports of the Council of Equality), 14–22.

Hacking, Ian (1990) *The Taming of Chance.* Cambridge: Cambridge University Press.

Hall, Edward T. and Mildred Reed Hall (1990) *Understanding Cultural Differences. Germans, French and Americans.* Yarmouth Maine: Intercultural Press.

Hallier, Jerry and James, Philip (1999) 'Group Rites and Trainer Wrongs in Employee Experiences of Job Change.' *Journal of Management Studies*, 36(1): 45–67.

Hammond, Teresa R. and Kleiner, Brian H. (1992) 'Managing Multicultural Work Environments.' *Equal Opportunities International*, 11(2): 6–9.

Hanifi, Riitta (1999) *Uhmattaret kunnian kentillä.* Unpublished MS.

Hanmer, Jalna and Hearn, Jeff (1999) 'Gender and Welfare Research.' In Fiona Williams, Jennie Popay and Ann Oakley (eds) *Welfare Research: A Critical Review.* London: UCL Press, 106–30.

Hannerz, Ulf (1991) 'Scenarios for Peripheral Cultures.' In Anthony King (ed.) *Culture, Globalization and the World System.* Binghampton, NY: SUNY Press, 107–28.

Hayano, Dennis (1979) 'Auto-Ethnography: Paradigms, Problems and Prospects.' *Human Organization*, 38: 99–104.

Hearn, Jeff and Parkin, Wendy (1995) *'Sex' at 'Work'. The Power and Paradox of Organisation Sexuality.* Hemel Hempstead: Prentice Hall/Harvester Wheatsheaf.

Hebdige, Dick (1992/1989) 'After the Masses.' In David Mercer (ed.) *Managing the External Environment. A Strategic Perspective.* London: Sage, 166–74.

Hekman, Susan (1999) *The Future of Differences: Truth and Method in Feminist Theory.* Cambridge: Polity Press.

Helgesson, Claes-Fredrik (1999) *Making a Natural Monopoly. The Configuration of a Techno-Economic Order in Swedish Telecommunication*. Stockholm: Stockholm School of Economics.

Hepworth, Julie (1999) *The Social Construction of Anorexia Nervosa*. London: Sage.

Herrnstein Smith, Barbara (1981) 'Narrative Versions, Narrative Theories.' In Ira Konigsberg (ed.) *American Criticism in the Poststructuralist Age*. Ann Arbor: University of Michigan, 162–86.

Herskovits, Melville J. (1972) *Cultural Relativism. Perspectives in Cultural Pluralism*. New York: Vintage Books.

Herzfeld, Michael (1992) *The Social Production of Indifference. Exploring the Symbolic Roots of Western Bureaucracy*. Chicago: The University of Chicago Press.

Herzfeld, Michael (1997) *Cultural Intimacy. Social Poetics in the Nation State*. New York: Routledge.

Hetherington, Kevin (1999) *Entangling the Not: Visual Impairment, Spectatorship and the Elgin Marbles*. Paper presented at the ESRC seminar series on 'Complexity and the Social Sciences', 29 September, Milton Keynes, Open University.

Hetherington, Kevin and Law, John (2000) 'Guest Editorial.' *Environment and Planning D: Society and Space*, 18: 127–32.

Hetherington, Kevin and Lee, Nick (2000) 'Social Order and the Blank Figure.' *Environment and Planning D: Society and Space*, 18: 169–84.

Hill, Alvin C. J. and Scott, James (1992) 'Ten Strategies for Managers in a Multicultural Workforce.' *HR Focus*, (69)8: 6.

Hirdman, Yvonne (1990) Genussystemet. In SOU. *Demokrati och Makt i Sverige*. Stockholm: Allmänna-Förlag, 73–116.

Hirdman, Yvonne (1992) *Den socialistiska hemmafrun och andra kvinnohistorier*. Stockholm: Carlssons.

Hirschman, Albert O. (1992) *The Rhetoric of Reaction. Perversity, Futility, Jeopardy*. Cambridge, MA: The Belknap Press of Harvard University Press.

Hochschild, Arlie Russell (1997) *The Time Bind. When Work Becomes Home and Home Becomes Work*. New York: Metropolitan Books.

Höök, Pia (1999) 'Ledarskap som okontrollerbar sexualitet.' In Sven-Erik Sjöstrand, Jörgen Sandberg and Mats Tyrstrup (eds) *Osynlig företagsledning*. Lund: Studentlitteratur.

Höpfl, Heather (1997) 'The Melancholy of the Black Widow.' In Kevin Hetherington and Rolland Munro (eds) *Ideas of Difference*. Oxford: Blackwell, 228–42.

Höpfl, Heather (2000a) 'The Aesthetics of Reticence: Collections and Recollections.' In Steve Linstead and Heather Höpfl (eds) *The Aesthetics of Organization*. London: Sage, 93–110.

Höpfl, Heather (2000b) 'On Being Moved.' *Studies in Cultures, Organizations and Societies*, 6(1): 15–34.

Höpfl, Heather (2000c) 'The Suffering Mother and the Miserable Son, Organising Women and Organising Women's Writing'. *Gender, Work and Organisations*, 7(2): 98–105.

Höpfl, Heather (2001) 'The Mystery of the Assumption: Mothers and Measures'. In Nick Lee and Rolland Munro (eds) *The Consumption of Mass*. Oxford: Blackwell, 60–72.

Hornaday, Robert W. (1990) 'Dropping the E-words from Small Business Research: An Alternative Typology.' *Journal of Small Business Management*, October: 22–33.

Husu, Liisa (1998) 'Mustan aukon mysteeri. Naiset ja tutkijanura Suomessa 1990-luvulla.' *Naistutkimus-Kvinnoforskning*, 11(1): 37–42.

Husu, Liisa (2000) 'Gender Discrimination in the Promised Land of Gender Equality.' *Higher Education in Europe*, 25(2): 221–8.

Inhetveen, Heide (1998) 'Women Pioneers in Farming: A Gendered History of Agricultural Progress.' *Sociologia Ruralis*, Special Issue on 'The Empowerment of Farm Women', 38 (3): 265–84.

INIPA (1999) *Agricoltura e sviluppo rurale*. Rome: INIPA.

ISTAT (1992) *Struttura e produzione delle aziende agricole*. Rome: ISTAT.

Itzin, Catherine and Newman, Janet (eds) (1995) *Gender, Culture and Organizational Change*. London: Routledge.

Jagose, Annamarie (1994) *Lesbian Utopics*. New York: Routledge.

Jamieson, David and O'Mara, Julie (1991) *Managing Workforce 2000: Gaining the Diversity Advantage*. San Francisco: Jossey-Bass.

Jeffcutt, Paul (1994) 'From Interpretation to Representation in Organizational Analysis: Postmodernism, Ethnography and Organizational Symbolism.' *Organization Studies*, 15: 241–74.

Johnston, William B. and Packer, Arnold H. (1987) *Workforce 2000: Work and Workers for the 21st Century*. Indianapolis: Hudson Institute.

Jones, Robert T., Jerich, Barbara, Copeland, Lennie and Boyles, Monica (1989) 'How Do You Manage a Diverse Workforce?' *Training and Development Journal*, 43(2): 13–22.

Julkunen, Raija (1994) 'Suomalainen sukupuolisota?' In Sara Heinämaa and Sari Näre (eds) *Pahan tyttäret. Sukupuolitettu pelko, viha ja valta*. Helsinki: Gaudeamus, 17–33.

Kanter, Rosabeth Moss (1977) *Men and Women of the Corporation*. New York: Basic Books.

Kappeler, Susan (1997) *The Will to Violence: The Politics of Personal Behaviour*. Cambridge: Polity Press.

Kelly, Erin and Dobbin, Frank (1998) 'How affirmative Action Became Diversity Management: Employer Response to Antidiscrimination Law. 1961 to 1996.' *American Behavioral Scientist*, 41(7): 960–84.

Keränen, Marja (1993) *Modern Political Science and Gender: A Debate Between the Deaf and the Mute*. Jyväskylä: Jyväskylä Studies in Education, Psychology and Social Research, 103.

Kirchhoff, Bruce A. (1994) *Entrepreneurship and Dynamic Capitalism: The Economics of Business Firm Formation and Growth*. Westport, CT: Praeger.

Kirsch-Auwärter, Edith (1996a) 'Anerkennung durch Dissidenz. Anmerkungen zu einer Kultur der Marginalität.' In Ilse Modelmog (ed.) *Kultur in Bewegung*. Freiburg: Kore, 25–47.

Kirsch-Auwärter, Edith (1996b) 'Emanzipatorische Strategien an den Hochschulen im Spannungsverhältnis von Organisationsstrukturen und Zielvorstellungen.' *VBWW Rundbrief* 12: 51–5.

Kleppesto, Stein (1998) 'On the Literary Qualities of Qualitative Research.' Working Paper. Lund: Lund University, Economic Research Institute.

Knorr Cetina, Karin (1994) 'Primitive Classifications and Postmodernity: Towards a Sociological Notion of Fiction.' *Theory, Culture and Society*, 11(3): 1–22.

Kociatkiewicz, Jerzy and Kostera, Monika (1999) 'The Anthropology of Empty Spaces.' *Qualitative Sociology*, 22(1): 37–50.

Kolehmainen, Sirpa (1999) *Naisten ja miesten työt. Työmarkkinoiden segregoituminen Suomessa 1970–1990*. Research Report 227. Helsinki: Statistics Finland.

Kolvereid, Lars, Shane, Scott and Westhead, Paul (1993) 'Is It Equally Difficult for Female Entrepreneurs to Start Businesses in All Countries?' *Journal of Small Business Management*, 31(4): 43–51.

Kondo, Dorinne (1990) *Crafting Selves: Power, Gender and Discourses of Identity in a Japanese Workplace*. Chicago: University of Chicago Press.

Konecki, Krzysztof (1990) 'Dependency and Worker Flirting.' In Barry A. Turner (ed.) *Organizational Symbolism*. Berlin: de Gruyter, 55–66.

Korvajärvi, Päivi (1998) *Gendering Dynamics in White-Collar Work Organizations*. Acta Universitatis Tamperensis 600. Tampere: University of Tampere.

Kostera, Monika (1995) 'The Modern Crusade: The Missionaries of Management Come to Eastern Europe.' *Management Learning*, 3: 331–52.

Kostera, Monika and Wicha, Maciej (1995) 'The Symbolism of the Communist Managers Roles: A Study of Scenarios.' *Scandinavian Journal of Management*, 11(2): 139–58.

Kroeber, Theodora (1976) *Ishi in Two Worlds: A Biography of the Last Wild Indian in America*. Berkeley, CA: University of California Press.

Kuijlaars, Anne-Marie (1999) *Het huis der getallen. De institutionele geschiedenis van het Centrale Bureau voor de Statistiek (CBS) en de Centrale Commissie voor de Statistiek (CCS), 1899–1996*. Amsterdam, Stichting beheer IISG.

Kuitenbrouwer, Frank (1991) *Het recht om met rust gelaten te worden*. Amsterdam: Balans.

Kunda, Gideon (1992) *Engineering Culture: Control and Commitment in a High-Tech Corporation*. Philadelphia: Temple University Press.

Kymlicka, Will (1998) *Finding Our Way. Rethinking Ethnocultural Relations in Canada*. Toronto: Oxford University Press.

Lagrave, Rose-Marie (1987) 'L'agricultrice inclassable: les fonctions sociales du flou statistique.' In Christiane Albert. Martine Berlan, Juliette Caniou and Martyne Perrot (eds) *Celles de la terre: Agricultrice, l'invention politique d'un metier*. Paris: Editions de l'Ecole des Hautes Etudes en Sciences Sociales, 89–110.

Lane, Christel (1995) 'Gender and the Labour Market in Europe: Britain, Germany and France Compared.' *International Journal of Sociology*, 25: 8–38.

Latour, Bruno (1987) *Science in Action: How to Follow Scientists and Engineers Through Society*. Cambridge, MA: Harvard University Press.

Latour, Bruno (1993) *We Have Never Been Modern*. Cambridge, MA: Harvard University Press.

Latour, Bruno (1999) *Pandora's Hope – Essays on the Reality of Science Studies*. Cambridge, MA: Harvard University Press.

Laxson, J.D. (1991) 'How "We" See "Them": Tourism and the Native Americans.' *Annals of Tourism Research*, 18: 365–91.

Lee, Nick and Brown, Steve (1994) 'Otherness and the Actor-Network: The Undiscovered Continent.' *American Behavioral Scientist*, 37: 772–90.

Leidner, Robin (1991) 'Serving Hamburgers and Selling Insurance: Gender, Work, and Identity in Interactive Service Jobs.' *Gender and Society*, 5(2): 154–77.

Leidner, Robin (1993) *Fast Food, Fast Talk. Service Work and the Routinization of Everyday Life*. Berkeley: University of California Press.

Lewis, Jane (1992) 'Gender and the Development of Welfare Regimes.' *Journal of European Social Policy*, 2(3): 159–73.

Lewis, Jane and Ostner, Ilona (1994) *Gender and the Evolution of European Social Policies*. Arbeitspapier 4/94. Bremen. Zentrum für Sozialpolitik.

Lindgren, Gerd (1985) *Kamrater, kollegor och kvirnor*. Research Report. Umea: Department of Sociology, University of Umea.

Litvin, Deborah R. (2000) *Defamiliarizing Diversity*. Unpublished PhD dissertation. University of Massachusetts, Amherst.

Loden, Marilyn and Rosener, Judy (1991) *Workforce America*. Homewood, IL: Business One Irwin.

Lowenthal, David (1997) *The Heritage Crusade and the Spoils of History*. Cambridge: Cambridge University Press.

Lynch, Frederick R. (1997a) *The Diversity Machine*. New York: Free Press.

Lynch, Frederick R. (1997b) 'The Diversity Machine.' *Society*, 34(5): 32–45.

Lyotard, François (1984) *The Postmodern Condition: A Report on Knowledge*. Manchester: Manchester University Press.

McClelland, David C. (1961) *The Achieving Society*. New York: Van Nostrand.

MacIntyre, Alasdair (1981) *After Virtue*. Notre Dame, IN: University of Notre Dame Press.

McWilliams, Nancy J. (1997) 'Diversity: How Do You Define It?' *Professional Safety*, 42(4): 7.

Malinowski, Bronislaw (1922) *Argonauts of the Western Pacific*. London: Routledge.

Malinowski, Bronislaw (1967) *A Diary in the Strict Sense of the Term*. Stanford, CA: Stanford University Press.

March, James G., and Olsen, Johan P. (1989) *Rediscovering Institutions*. New York: Free Press.

Marcson, Simon (1968) 'Career Development of Scientists.' In Barney G. Glaser (ed.) *Organizational Careers. A Sourcebook for Theory*. Chicago: Aldine.

Marcus, George E. (1995) 'Ethnography in/of the World System: The Emergence of Multi-Sited Ethnography.' *Annual Review of Anthropology*, 24: 95–117.

Marcus, George E., and Cushman, D. (1982) 'Ethnographies as Text.' *Annual Review of Anthropology*, 11: 25–69.

Marshall, Judy (1984) *Women Managers: Travellers in a Male World*. Chichester/New York: John Wiley & Sons.

Martin, Emily (1994) *Flexible Bodies: Tracking Immunity in American Culture from the Days of Polio to the Age of AIDS*. Boston: Beacon.

Medicinska Forskningsrådet (1993) *Konsensusuttalande: Behandling av anorexia nervosa (självsvält)*. Stockholm: Medicinska forskningsrådet/SPRI.

Merchant, Carolyn (1980) *The Death of Nature: Women, Ecology and the Scientific Revolution*. San Francisco: Harper and Row.

Metz-Göckel, Sigrid (1993) 'Frauen in akademischen Berufen: Wie sie kooperieren, konkurrieren und sich aus dem Weg gehen.' In Claudia Koppert (ed.) *Glück, Alltag und Desaster. Über die Zusammenarbeit zwischen Frauen*. Berlin: Orlanda, 128–46.

Meyer, John W., and Rowan, Brian (1977/1991) 'Institutionalized Organizations: Formal Structure as Myth and Ceremony'. In Walter W. Powell and Paul J. DiMaggio (eds) *The New Institutionalism in Organizational Analysis*. Chicago: University of Chicago Press, 41–62.

Migration media release 64/98 (1998) *Businesses Profit from Culturally-diverse Workforces*. Release from Minister for Immigration and Multicultural Affairs, Philip Ruddock, M.P. (http://www.minister.immi.gov.au/media98/r98064.htm).

Mills, Albert J. and Simmons, Tony (1995) *Reading Organization Theory*. Toronto: Garamond.

Minson, Jeffrey (1993) *Questions of Conduct. Sexual Harassment, Citizenship, Government*. Basingstoke: Macmillan.

Möller, Lotte (1979) *Självsvält*. Helsingborg: Wahlström & Widstrand.

Morgan, Gareth (1997) *Images of Organization* (2nd edn). Thousand Oaks, CA: Sage.

Müller, Ursula (1998) 'Asymmetrische Geschlechterkultur in Organisationen und Frauenförderung als Prozeß – mit Beispielen aus Betrieben und der Universität.' In Daniela Rastetter, Schwerpunktheft 'Geschlechterdifferenzen und Personalmanagement', *Zeitschrift für Personalforschung*, 12(2): 123–42.

Mumby, Dennis K. (1987) 'The Political Function of Narrative in Organizations.' *Communication Monographs*, 54 (June): 113–27.

Munro, Rolland (1997) 'Ideas of Difference: Stability, Social Spaces and the Labour of Division.' In Kevin Hetherington and Rolland Munro (eds) *Ideas of Difference*. Oxford: Blackwell, 3–24.

Nelkin, Dorothy (1987/1995) *Selling Science. How the Press Covers Science and Technology*. New York: W.H. Freeman and Company.

Nicholson, Linda (ed.) (1990) *Feminism Postmodernism*. London: Routledge.

Nilsson, Pernilla (1997) 'Business Counselling Services Directed Towards Female Entrepreneurs – Some Legitimacy Dilemmas.' *Entrepreneurship and Regional Development*, 9(3): 239–58.

Nkomo, Stella, M. (1998) 'Competitiveness and the Role of Diversity.' *Competitiveness in the Global Marketplace*, 1998 Conference of the American Society for Competitiveness, October 23.

Nyberg, Anita and Sundin, Elisabeth (1997) 'Inledning.' In *Ledare, makt och kön*. Stockholm: SOU 1997, 135.

O'Connor, Ellen S. (1996) *Contributions of the Language-Based Disciplines to Organizational Studies*. Unpublished MS.

O'Connor, Ellen S. (1997) 'Compelling Stories: Narrative and the Production of the Organizational Self.' In Oliver F. Williams (ed.) *The Moral Imagination: How Literature and Films Can Stimulate Ethical Reflection in the Business World*. Notre Dame, IN: University of Notre Dame Press, 185–202.

O'Connor, Julia (1996) 'From Women in the Welfare State To Gendering Welfare State Regimes.' *Current Sociology*, 44 (2).

Orbach, Susie (1978) *Fat Is a Feminist Issue*. London: Hamlyn.

Orbach, Susie (1986) *Hunger Strike: The Anorectic's Struggle as a Metaphor for Our Age*. London: Faber and Faber.

Orrù, Marco, Biggart, Nicole W. and Hamilton, Gary G. (1991) 'Organizational Isomorphism in East Asia.' In Paul J. DiMaggio and Walter W. Powell (eds), *The New Institutionalism in Organizational Analysis*. Chicago: University of Chicago Press, 361–89.

Ortner, Sherry (1984) 'Theory in Anthropology Since the Sixties.' *Society for Comparative Study of Society and History*, 26: 126–66.

Ouchi, William G. (1981) *Theory Z: How American Business Can Meet the Japanese Challenge*. New York: Avon.

Palazzoli, Mara Selvini (1963/1979) *Anorexi. Boken om självsvält*. Stockholm: Natur och Kultur.

Parker, Martin (1997) 'Dividing Organizations and Multiplying Identities.' In Kevin Hetherington and Rolland Munro (eds) *Ideas of Difference*. Oxford: Blackwell, 114–38.

Pateman, Carole (1988) *The Sexual Contract*. Cambridge: Polity Press.

Payne, John W., Bettman, James R. and Johnson, Eric J. (1992) 'Behavioral Decision Research: A Constructive Processing Perspective.' *Annual Review of Psychology*, 43: 87–131.

Penrose, Edith (1995) *The Theory of the Growth cf the Firm* (2nd edn). Oxford: Oxford University Press.

Peters, Tom and Waterman, Robert H. (1982) *In Search of Excellence*. New York: HarperCollins.

Pfau-Effinger, Birgit (1994) 'Analyse internationaler Differenzen in der Erwerbsbeteiligung von Frauen.' *Kölner Zeitschrift für Soziologie und Sozialpsychologie*, 48(3): 462–92.

Pfau-Effinger, Birgit (1998a) 'Arbeitsmarkt- und Familiendynamik in Europa – Theoretische Grundlagen der vergleichenden Analyse.' In Birgit Geisler, Friederike Maier and Birgit Pfau-Effinger (eds) *FrauenArbeitsMarkt*. Berlin: edition-sigma, 177–94.

Pfau-Effinger, Birgit (1998b) 'Culture or Structure as Explanations for Differences in Part-time Work in Germany, Finland and the Netherlands?' In Jacqueline O'Reilly and Colette Fagan (eds) *Part-time Prospects: An International Comparison of Part-time Work in Europe, North America and the Pacific Rim*. London: Routledge, 177–98.

Pile, Stephen (1990) *The Private Farmer: Transformation and Legitimation in Advanced Capitalist Agriculture*. Aldershot: Gower.

Plant, Judith (ed.) (1989) *Healing the Wounds: The Promise of Ecofeminism*. Philadelphia: New Soc Publishers.

Polkinghorne, Donald E. (1988) *Narrative Knowing and the Human Sciences*. Albany, NY: State University of New York Press.

Prasad, Pushkala (1993) 'Symbolic Processes in the Implementation of Technological Change: A Symbolic Interactionist Study of Work Computerization.' *Academy of Management Journal*, 36: 1400–29.

Prasad, Pushkala (1995) 'Working with the "Smart" Machine: Computerization and the Discourse of Anthropomorphism in Organizations.' *Studies in Cultures, Organizations and Societies*, 1: 253–65.

Prasad, Pushkala (1997) 'Systems of Meaning: Ethnography as a Methodology for the Study of Information Technologies.' In A. Lee, J. Liebenau and J. DeGross (eds), *Information Systems and Qualitative Research*. London: Chapman and Hall, 101–18.

Prasad, Pushkala (1998) 'When the Ethnographic Subject Speaks Back.' *Journal of Management Inquiry*, 7: 31–36.

Prasad, Pushkala (2000) *Promising Rainbows: An Institutional Analysis of Diversity Management in North America*. Paper presented at the Annual Meeting of the Academy of Management, Toronto, August.

Preuss, Eva (1987) *Die Frau als Manager*. Bern, Stuttgart: Haupt-Verlag.

Price, David (2000) 'Anthropologists as Spies.' *The Nation*, November 20: 24–27.

Pringle, Rosemary (1988) *Secretaries Talk*. London: Verso.

Profiles (1983) *Pioneering Women Architects from Finland*. Helsinki: Museum of Finnish Architecture.

PRV (1996) Patentskrift # 502 873.

Puxty, Anthony G. (1993) *The Social and Organizational Context of Management Accounting*. London: Academic Press.

Rabinow, Paul (1977) *Reflections on Fieldwork in Morocco*. Berkeley, CA: University of California Press.

Radcliffe-Brown, Alfred (1922) *The Andaman Islanders*. Cambridge: Cambridge University Press.

Radin, Paul (1927) *The Story of the American Indian*. New York: Boni & Liveright.

Rantalaiho, Liisa (1997) 'Contextualising Gender.' In Lisa Rantalaiho and Tuula Heiskanen (eds), *Gendered Practices in Working Life*. London: Macmillan, 16–30.

Rasmussen, Bente (1999) *Dehierarchization – Reorganizing Gender?* Trondheim: Norges teknisk-naturvitenskapelige universitet.

Redfield, Robert, Linton, Ralph and Herskovits, Melville J. (1936/1967) 'Memorandum for the Study of Acculturation.' In Paul Bohannan and Fred Plog (eds) *Beyond the Frontier. Social Process and Cultural Change*. New York: Natural History Process, 181–86.

Ressner, Ulla (1987) *Den dolda hierarkin*. Stockholm: Raben und Sjögren.

Riley, Denise (1988) *Am I That Name? Feminism and the Category of 'Women' in History*. Minneapolis: University of Minnesota Press.

Robinson, Charles (1994) 'Ota Benga's Flight through Geronimo's Eyes: Tales of Science And Multiculturalism.' In D. Goldberg (ed.) *Multiculturalism: A Critical Reader*. London: Basil Blackwell, 385–405.

Roggenkamp, Viola (1993) 'Begehren statt entbehren. Frauen im Konkurrenzkampf.' In Claudia Koppert (ed.) *Glück, Alltag und Desaster. Über die Zusammenarbeit zwischen Frauen*. Berlin: Orlanda, 115–27.

Root, Deborah (1996) *Cannibal Culture: Art, Appropriation and the Commodification of Difference*. Boulder, CO: Westview Press.

Rosa, Peter, Carter, Sara and Hamilton, Daphne (1994) *Gender as a Determinant of Small Business Performance: Insights from a British Study* (Working Paper). Stirling: Department of Management and Organization, University of Stirling.

Rosen, Michael (2000) *Turning Words, Spinning Worlds: Chapters in Organizational Ethnography*. Reading: Harwood

Roy, Donald (1960) 'Banana Time: Job Satisfaction and Informal Interaction.' *Human Organization*, 18: 156–68.

Rule, James B. (1974) *Private Lives and Public Surveillance*. New York: Schocken Books.

Russell, Gerald (1979) 'Bulimia Nervosa: An Ominous Variant of Anorexia Nervosa. *Psychological Medicine*, 9: 429–48

Sachs, Carolyn (1996) *Gendered Fields*. Boulder, CO: West View Press.

Said, Edward (1989) 'Representing the Colonized: Anthropology's Interlocutors.' *Critical Inquiry*, 15: 205–25.

Sainsbury, Diane (ed.) (1994) *Gendering Welfare States*. London: Sage.

Sargisson, Lucy (1996) *Contemporary Feminist Utopianism*. London: Routledge.

Schein, Edgar H. (1978) *Career Dynamics: Matching Individual and Organizational Needs*. Reading, MA: Addison-Wesley.

Schirinzi, Gina (1998) *La presenza delle donne nell'agricultura*. Rome: Instituto Nazionale di Statistica.

Scholes, Robert (1981) 'Language, Narrative and Anti-narrative.' In W. J. Thomas Mitchell (ed.), *On Narrative*. Chicago : University of Chicago Press, 200–08.

Scott, James C. (1998) *Seeing Like a State. How Certain Schemes to Improve the Human Condition Have Failed*. New Haven: Yale University Press.

Sennett, Richard (1991) *The Conscience of the Eye. The Design and Social Life of Cities*. New York: Knopf.

Sennett, Richard (1994) *Flesh and Stone. The Body and City in Western Civilization.* London: Faber and Faber.

Serres, Michel (1991) *Rome: The Book of Foundations.* Stanford, CA: Stanford University Press.

Setälä, Salme (1973) *Epäasiallinen kronikka viiden pääjohtajan ajalta.* Porvoo-Helsinki: WSOY.

Setälä, Salme (1975) *Kirjeitä pojalleni.* Porvoo-Helsinki: WSOY.

Shiva, Vandana (1988) *Staying Alive: Women, Ecology and Development.* New Jersey: Zed Books.

Showalter, Elaine (1997) *Hystories. Hysterical Epidemics and Modern Culture.* London: Picador.

Silius, Harriet (1992) *Den kringgärdande kvinnligheten. Att vara kvinnlig jurist i Finland.* Åbo: Åbo Akademins Förlag.

Silius, Harriet (1995) 'Sukupuolitetun ammatillisuuden julkisuus ja yksityisyys.' In Leena Eräsaari, Raija Julkunen and Harriet Silius (eds) *Naiset yksityisen ja julkisen rajalla.* Tampere: Vastapaino, 49–63.

Slotkin, Richard (1985) *The Fatal Environment: The Myth of the Frontier in the Age of Industrialization, 1800–1890.* New York: Atheneum.

Solomon, Charlene M. (1989) 'The Corporate Response to Work Force Diversity.' *Personnel Journal,* August: 43–53.

Sotirin, Patty and Gottfried, Heidi (1999) 'The Ambivalent Dynamics of Secretarial "Bitching": Control, Resistance, and The Construction of Identity.' *Organization,* 6(1): 57–80.

SOU (1994) *Mäns föreställningar om kvinnor och chefskap.* Stockholm: Fritzes, 3.

Starr, Jennifer and Yudkin, Marcia (1996) *Women Entrepreneurs: A Review of Current Research* (CRW 15) Wellesley: Center for Research on Women, Wellesley College.

Stevenson, Lois A. (1990) 'Some Methodological Problems Associated with Researching Women Entrepreneurs.' *Journal of Business Ethics,* 9(4–5): 439–46.

Stewart, Susan (1984) *On Longing: Narratives of the Miniature, the Gigantic, the Souvenir, The Collection.* Baltimore: Johns Hopkins Press.

Stocking, George (1983) *Observers Observed: Essays on Ethnographic Fieldwork.* Madison: University of Wisconsin Press.

Stocking, George (1991) 'Maclay, Kubary, Malinowski: Archetypes from the Dream-time of Anthropology.' In George Stocking (ed.), *Colonial Situations: Essays on the Contextualization of Ethnographic Knowledge.* Madison, WI: University of Wisconsin Press, 9–74.

Stone, Deborah A. (1988) *Policy Paradox and Political Reason.* New York: HarperCollins.

Strathern, Marilyn (1996) 'Gender: Division or Comparison?' In Nickie Charles and Felicia Hughes-Freeland (eds) *Practising Feminism: Identity, Difference, Power.* London: Routledge.

Sundin, Elisabeth (1998) *Män passar alltid?* SOU, Stockholm: Fritzes, 4.

Sundin, Elisabeth and Holmquist, Carin (1989) *Kvinnor som företagare.* Malmö: Liber.

Tancred-Sheriff, Peta (1989) 'Gender, Sexuality and the Labour Process.' In Jeff Hearn, Deborah Sheppard, Peta Tancred-Sheriff and Gibson Burrell (eds) *The Sexuality of Organization.* London: Sage, 45–55.

Tarkastuskertomus (1998) 'Yhtiöittäminen – valtion virastojen, laitosten ja liikelaitosten tai niiden osien muuttaminen valtioenemmistöiseksi osakeyhtiöksi.' *Valtiotalouden tarkastusvirasto,* 16.

Taylor, Charles (1992) 'The Politics of Recognition.' In Charles Taylor and Amy Gutmann (eds) *Multiculturalism: Examining the Politics of Recognition*. Princeton, NJ: Princeton University Press, 25–74.

Taylor, Mark (1993) *Nots*. Chicago: Chicago University Press.

Tazza, Alessandra (1997) 'Un'imprenditività velata.' *Quaderni di Azione Sociale*, 3: 61–69.

Tedlock, Barbara (1991) 'From Participant Observation to the Observation of Participation: The Emergence of Narrative Ethnography.' *Journal of Anthropological Research*, 47: 69–74.

The Conference Board (1999) *1999 Diversity Conference, Strategic Diversity for Business Performance Enhancement*. Invitation to conference. New York: The Conference Board.

Theobald, Hildegard (1999) *Geschlecht, Qualifikation und Wohlfahrtsstaat. Deutschland und Schweden im Vergleich*. Berlin: edition-sigma.

Thomas, Roosevelt R., Jr. (1990) 'From Affirmative Action to Affirming Diversity.' *Harvard Business Review*, March-April: 107–17.

Thomas, Roosevelt R., Jr. (1991) *Beyond Race and Gender. Unleashing the Power of Your Total Work Force by Managing Diversity*. New York: AMACOM.

Thomas, Roosevelt R. Jr. (1992) 'Managing Diversity: A Conceptual Framework.' In Susan E. Jackson (ed.) *Diversity in the Workplace: Human Resources Initiatives*. New York: Guilford, 13–35.

Thompson, William E. (1983) 'Hanging Tongues: A Sociological Encounter with the Assembly Line.' *Qualitative Sociology*, 6: 215–37.

Tienari, Janne (1999) 'The First Wave Washed Up On Shore: Reform, Feminization and Gender Resegregation.' *Gender, Work and Organization*, 6: 1–19.

Tienari, Janne, Quack, Sigrid and Theobald, Hildegard (1998) *Organizational Reforms and Gender: Feminization of Middle Management in Finnish and German Banking*. Discussion Paper FS I 98–105, Social Science Research Center Berlin.

Trice, Harrison M. and Beyer Janice M. (1993) *The Cultures of Work Organizations*. New Jersey: Prentice-Hall.

Turner, Barry A. (1971) *Exploring the Industrial Subculture*. London: Macmillan.

Turner, Barry A. (1986) 'Sociological Aspects of Organizational Symbolism.' *Organization Studies*, 7: 101–15.

Turner, Victor (1969) *The Ritual Process*. New York: Cornell University Press.

Turner, Victor (1982) *From Ritual to Theatre*. New York: PAJ Publications.

Van Gennep, Arnold (1908/1960) *The Rites of Passage*. London: Routledge and Kegan Paul.

Van Maanen, John (1973) 'Observations on the Making of Policemen.' *Human Organization*, 32: 407–18.

Van Maanen, John (1976) 'Breaking In: Socialization to Work.' In Robert Dubin (ed.) *Handbook of Work, Organization and Society*. Chicago: Rand McNally, 67–130.

Van Maanen, John (1982) 'Fieldwork on the Beat.' In John Van Maanen, John M. Dobbs and Robert Faulkner (eds), *Varieties of Qualitative Research*: Beverly Hills, CA: Sage, 103–51.

Van Maanen, John (1988) *Tales of the Field: On Writing Ethnography*. Chicago: University of Chicago Press.

Van Maanen, John (1995) 'An End of Innocence: The Ethnography of Ethnography. In John Van Maanen (ed.) *Representation in Ethnography*. Thousand Oaks, CA: Sage, 1–35.

Van Maanen, John and Kolb, Deborah (1985) 'The Professional Apprentice: Observations on Fieldwork Roles in Two Organizational Settings.' *Research in the Sociology of Organizations*, 4: 1–33.

Van Maanen, John and Schein, Edgar (1979) 'Toward a Theory of Organizational Socialization.' *Research in Organizational Behavior*, 1: 209–64.

Van Maarseveen, J.G.S.J. and Gircour, M.B.G. (eds) (1999) *A Century of Statistics. Counting, Accounting and Recounting in the Netherlands*. Amsterdam: Stichting beheer IISG.

Ventura, Flaminia (1994) 'Women in Italian Agriculture: New Roles and Arising Problems.' In Margreet van der Burg and Marina Endeveld (eds) *Women on Family Farms: Gender Research, EC Policies and New Perspectives*. Wageningen: CERES.

Vidich, Arthur J. and Lyman, Scott M. (1994) 'Qualitative Methods: Their History in Sociology and Anthropology.' In Norman K. Denzin and Yvonne Lincoln (eds) *Handbook of Qualitative Methods*. Thousand Oaks, CA: Sage, 23–59.

Vogel, Ezra F. (1979) *Japan as Number One: Lessons for America*. Cambridge, MA: Harvard University Press.

Von Glasersfeld, Ernst (1984) 'An Introduction to Radical Constructivism.' In Paul Watzlawick (ed.) *The Invented Reality: How Do We Know What We Believe We Know?* New York: Norton.

Wahl, Anna (1992) *Könsstrukturer i organisationer. Kvinnliga civilekonomers och civilingenjörers karriärutveckling*. Handelshögskolan i Stockholm: Ekonomiska forskningsinstitutet.

Wahl, Anna, Holgersson, Charlotte and Höök, Pia (1998) *Ironi och sexualitet. Om kön och ledarskap*. Stockholm: Carlssons.

Wajcman, Judy (1998) *Managing Like a Man – Women and Men in Corporate Management*. Cambridge: Polity Press.

Ward, Anne, Jane Tiller, Janet Treasure and Gerald Russell (2000) 'Eating Disorders: Psyche or Soma?' *International Journal of Eating Disorders*, 27: 279–87.

Warren, Roland L., Rose, Stephen M. and Bergunder, Ann F. (1974) *The Structure of Urban Reform: Community Decision Organizations in Stability and Change*. Lexington, MA: D.C. Heath.

Watson, Tony (1994) *In Search of Management*. London: Routledge.

Wax, Rosalie H. (1983) 'The Ambiguities of Fieldwork.' In R.E. Emerson (ed.) *Contemporary Field Research*. Boston: Little and Brown, 191–202.

Wedbjer, Susanne (1998) *Projekt Mandometern. Delrapport 1: Informationsinsamling och analys*. Stockholm: Konstfack.

Weedon, Chris (1987) *Feminist Practice and Poststructuralist Theory*. Cambridge, MA: Blackwell.

Weedon, Chris (1999) *Feminism, Theory and The Politics of Difference*. Oxford: Blackwell.

Weick, Karl E. (1995) *Sensemaking in Organizations*. Thousand Oaks, CA: Sage.

Wells, Betty (1998) 'Creating a Public Space for Women in US Agriculture: Empowerment, Organisation and Social Change.' *Sociologia Ruralis*, Special Issue on 'The Empowerment of Farm Women', 38 (3): 371–90.

Westin, Alan F. (1970) *Privacy and Freedom*. New York: Atheneum.

Whatmore, Sarah (1991) *Farming Women: Gender, Work and Family Enterprise*. Basingstoke: Macmillan.

Whatmore, Sarah (1994) 'Theoretical Achievements and Challenges in European

Rural Gender Studies,' In Margreet van der Burg and Marina Endeveld (eds), *Women on Family Farms: Gender Research, EC Policies and New Perspectives*. Wageningen: CERES, 107–20.

Wheeler, Michael L. (1994) *Diversity Training*. (Research Report #1083–94–RR). New York: The Conference Board.

Wheeler, Michael L. (1995) *Diversity: Business Rationale and Strategies* (Research Report #1130–95RR). New York: The Conference Board.

Wheeler, Roger D. (1997) 'Managing Workforce Diversity.' *Tax Executive*, 49(6): 493–95.

Whyte, William Foote (1955) *Street Corner Society*. Chicago: University of Chicago Press.

Wicker, A. W. (1969) 'Attitudes v. Actions: The Relationship of Verbal and Overt Responses to Attitude Objects.' *Journal of Social Issues*, 25: 41–78.

Widdicombe, Sue (1998) '"But You Don't Class Yourself": The Interaction Management of Category Membership and Non-Membership.' In Charles Antaki and Sue Widdicombe (eds) *Identities in Talk*. London: Sage, 52–70.

Williams, Fiona (1996) 'Postmodernism, Feminism and the Question of Difference.' In Nigel Parton (ed.) *Social Theory, Social Change and Social Work*. London: Routledge, 61–76.

Wilson, Fiona (2000) *Managing Equality in the Profession of Architecture Where the Woman Architect Is an Oxymoron*. Paper presented at EGOS Colloquim, Helsinki.

Winterle, Mary J. (1992) *Workforce Diversity: Corporate Challenges, Corporate Responses* (Research Report # 1013–92RR). New York: The Conference Board.

Witz, Anne and Savage, Mike (1992) 'The Gender of Organization.' In Mike Savage and Anne Witz (eds) *Gender and Bureaucracy*. Oxford: Blackwell, 3–62.

Yanow, Dvora (2000) 'Doing Organizational Ethnographies.' Introduction to Michael Rosen, *Turning Words, Spinning Worlds*. Reading: Harwood, 1–19.

Yarrow, Judith (1996) 'The Evolving Case for Diversity.' *Cultural Diversity At Work*, 8(4): 8–9.

Young, M. W. (1984) 'The Intensive Study of a Restricted Area, or Why Did Malinowski go to the Trobriand Islands.' *Oceania*, 55: 1–26.

Youngs, Tim (1992) 'The Medical Officer's Diary: Travel and Travail with the Self in Africa.' In M. Gidley (ed.) *Representing Others: White Views of Indigenous Peoples*. Exeter: Exeter University Press, 25–36.

Index